EDITOR'S PREFACE.

The first German edition of this work was published in 1904 and met with such signal success that its author Herr Alexander Speltz was called upon to bring out a second edition two years later. In this edition the number of plates was increased from three to four hundred which enabled the author to give a more complete representation of ornament as developed in England and America than had been at first contemplated.

The original work was undertaken with the object of representing the entire range of ornament in all its different styles from pre-historic times till the middle of the 19th century and to illustrate the different uses to which it had been applied. The whole of the illustrations which were taken from the best authorities on each subject and period were drawn specially for the work and evince the remarkable industry and knowledge of the author and his artistic power in representing ornament. In fact it is only necessary to glance through the several plates to see how closely the author has caught the style and character of each period. Acknowledgments of the sources are made throughout the work and in addition a special list of books of reference, including those which have been drawn upon for illustrations, has been inserted at the end of the volume.

An English edition was published in America in 1906 for sale in that country only, but the historical accounts were not in accordance with the latest research and many of the descriptions to the plates had suffered so much in translation that very considerable revision was necessary in preparing the present issue. Three new plates of English Ornament have been added to this edition taking the place of others which it was found necessary to delete, various changes have also been made in the headings to some of the chapters and in the terms employed, more particularly in the section devoted to the Renaissance period; for instance the term "Barocco", which although well-known and recognised throughout Germany is but seldom used here, has been replaced by "Later Renaissance" which is more familiar to the English student and includes that which used to be known as the pure Italian style introduced by Inigo Jones.

The term Rococo has been retained as it would have been difficult to find any other to suggest the vagaries of the Louis XV. style which spread through Italy, France, Spain, Germany and Flanders and here in England led to Chippendale's work; the terms adopted to distinguish the later periods are adhered to as in the original edition.

The plates and their accompanying descriptions being arranged throughout in chronological sequence renders an index a very important adjunct and special care has been taken in preparing that given in the work. The examples are entered according to both subject and material and the periods to which they relate are indicated, thus enabling any particular object in any style to be immediately referred-to.

The 400 plates in which the several styles of ornament are illustrated contain a larger and much more varied series than in any work hitherto published, indeed the volume forms a veritable encyclopaedia of the evolution development and application of ornament in architecture and the decorative arts throughout the ages, and it should prove of great value to the architect, craftsman, designer and student.

LONDON, January 1910.

R. PHENE SPIERS.

THE
STYLES OF
ORNAMENT

Published in Canada by General Publishing Company, Ltd., 30 Lesmill Road, Don Mills, Toronto, Ontario.
Published in the United Kingdom by Constable and Company, Ltd., 10 Orange Street, London WC 2.

This Dover edition, first published in 1959, is an unabridged and unaltered republication of David O'Connor's translation from the second German edition.

Standard Book Number: 486-20557-6
Library of Congress Catalog Card Number: 59-65147

Manufactured in the United States of America
Dover Publications, Inc.
180 Varick Street
New York, N. Y. 10014

CONTENTS.

INTRODUCTION.

**Initial from a German manu-
script. 12th century** (Dolmetsch).

ightly understood, the conformation of an ornament should be in keeping with the form and structure of the object which it adorns, should be in complete subordination to it, and should never stifle or conceal it. As varied and as many-sided as it may be, still, the Art of ornamentation is never an arbitrary one; besides depending on the form of the object, it is influenced also by the nature of the material of which the same is made, as well as by the style or manner in which natural objects are reproduced in ornamentation by different peoples at different times. The art of ornamentation, therefore, stands in intimate relationship with material, purpose, form, and style. The oldest forms of ornamentation consisted of geometric figures, small circles, bands, straight and curved lines, &c, all of which were drawn with categorical regularity and according to a certain rhythm. With the advance in the intellectual development of mankind, artists acquired more technical skill, and ventured even to make use of animals, plants, and, finally, of the human figure itself, for ornamental purposes. A plant or a living being can be employed in ornamentation in two ways, firstly, just as it is formed by nature—which is naturalistic Ornament, and secondly, in a form which reflects the spirit of the times, the political or religious ideas of the peoples, or the effects of foreign influence—where by was formed the stylistic Ornament. Each style exhibits one and the same plant and one and the same animal in a different fashion. Each country sought the models for its own ornamentation in its own Fauna and Flora, and each style had certain plants and animals which it preferred to all others. Style is really more the product of one epoch of time rather than of a single people, and it is according to this chronological standpoint that the present work has been arranged. In keeping with the tendency of the work, it may be remarked that the illustrations, are all reproductions of such objects only as were really produced at the period for which the style is characteristic.

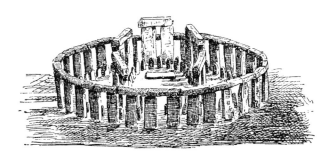

Stonehenge near Salisbury.

PREHISTORIC AND PRIMITIVE ORNAMENT.

Stonerelief from Yucatan
(Globus 1884).

ivided according to the periods of development during which it existed, Prehistoric Ornament extends over two great epochs: the Stone Age and the Metal Age. It is, however, characteristic not alone of all peoples who lived on the earth in Prehistoric times, peoples separated by thousands of years from each other, but even of people who exist at the present day. We find the Prehistoric Ornament not only amongst the remains of those races of people who lived along the Mediterranean over 6000 years ago, but also the primitive ornament amongst different people who inhabit certain parts of the earth at present but who have not yet advanced beyond that stage civilisation to which this style of Ornament is peculiar.

Prehistoric ornament embraces two periods: the Stone Age and the Metal Age.

The Stone Age is generally supposed to have begun at the end of the last period of the Tertiary Age, distinct proofs place it at the last epoch of the Diluvian Era. During the Paleolithic or Ancient Stone Age, stone was habitually used as the material from which tools were made; in the Neolithic or later Stone Age the tools were polished and given an artistic form, and vessels made of clay decorated with simple ornamentations were manufactured. Lake dwellings, the burying of the dead in caves, middens, barrows, cromlechs, and other numerous Megalithic monuments, the use and purpose of which are still matter of speculation, are all characteristic of this era. In the course of time these early inhabitants arrived at a stage of development which enabled them to make use of metals, bronze being first employed and later on iron, the different periods being designated as the Earlier and Later Bronze Age and the Earlier and Later Iron Age. The use of bronze was introduced from the East throughout the entire of Europe at about the year 1500 B. C. The Later Bronze Age extended only over the middle and north of Europe and dates from about 1000 to 600 B.C. Iron was however already worked during this period in the countries bordering on the Mediterranean, and was besides extensively known to the Assyrians in the ninth century before Christ. In all probability the use of iron was introduced from Assyria into Europe, where, in consequence of its introduction, new forms were given to arms, tools, and implements of all kinds. Iron was now used almost entirely for arms and tools, bronze being employed for artistic work. The Earlier or Ancient Iron Age is called also the Hallstadt Period, Hallstadt being a locality in the Salzkammergut where all the greatest and most important discoveries dealing with this period were made. The Later Iron Age, designated also as the La Tène Period in consequence of the discovery of remains found in the castle in the island La Tène in the Lake of Neuchatel, dates from 400 to 100 B. C., and is confined generally speaking to the Gallic races.

Even in those prehistoric times a very lively commercial intercourse existed between the different peoples. The locality, therefore, where a certain article has been discovered cannot by any means be accepted as the country of its origin. It could just as well have been manufactured by another people more advanced in civilisation, and have been brought by itinerant traders to the locality where it was eventually found.

The Stone and Metal periods, however, are not confined alone to those prehistoric peoples who have long since passed away, and of whose names or descent we have never been able to acquire the slightest knowledge. There are people in Asia, Africa, America, and Australia, at the present day, who have not even yet arrived so far as the Metal period. The inhabitants of America at the time of its discovery had not yet advanced beyond the Stone or Metal Age. Examples of their work are therefore included in the two plates dealing with these periods.

Prehistoric and the Primitive Ornaments may be said to be purely geometric ones, the artists of the time rising very seldom to such heights as to try and imitate in their work the figures of men, animals, or plants. Altough there cannot be any mention of "style" in connection with it as it was so disconnected, and so widely separated by time and space—still, Prehistoric ornament as such formed the foundation upon which genuine styles were constructed later on.

Plate 1.   PREHISTORIC ORNAMENT.   5

Plate 1.

Prehistoric Ornament.

Fig. 1. Ivory carving found in a cave in Lourdes (Hoerner, Urgeschichte).
,, 2. Ivory carving found in Arudy (Basses Pyrénées), France (Hoerner).
,, 3. Ivory carving found in Brassempoy, France (Hoerner).
,, 4. Clay statuette found in Budmir, Bosnia (Hoerner).
,, 5, and 6. Earthenware vessels found in Budmir, Bosnia (Hoerner).
,, 7. Vessel found in the pile-dwellings on Laibach Moor, later Stone Age (Hoerner).
,, 8. Bronze object from the first Iron Age found in Hungary (Hoerner).
,, 9. Bronze jewel found in Hungary (Hoerner).
,, 10. Bronze needle (Brockhaus, Konversationslexicon).
,, 11. Earthenware vessel found in Odenburg, first Stone Age (Hoerner).
,, 12. Urn found in West Prussia (Hoerner).
,, 13. Urn found in Borgstedfeld, Holstein (Hoerner).
,, 14. Bronze plate found in Glarinoc, Bosnia (Hoerner).
,, 15. Bronze greave found in Herzegovina (Hoerner).
,, 16. Weapon found in Hungary (Hoerner).
,, 17. Iron dagger found in the Lake of Garda (Hoerner).
,, 18. Fragment of an engraved bronze girdle found in Chodschali in Transcaucasia (Hoerner).
,, 19. Jewel from the gold-discoveries in Vettersfelde (Hoerner).
,, 20. Lance-head, Germany (Hoerner).
,, 21, 22, and 28. Wicker-work found in the Swiss pile-dwellings (Lübke, Die Kunst des Altertums).
,, 23. Border ornamentation of a bronze basin found in the Wies, Styria (Hoerner).
,, 24. Clay figure found in a Bœotian grave (Hoerner).
,, 25. Stone axe of Montezuma (Sir John Evans).
,, 26. Sword of the Bronze Age (Lübke).
,, 27. Needle of the Bronze Age (Lübke).
,, 29, and 32. Bronze Clasps (Brockhaus).
,, 30. Scabbard (Brockhaus).
,, 31. Figure of Charon on a bronze relief plate found in North Syria (Hoerner).
,, 33. Bronze fibula (Brockhaus).
,, 34. Double earthenware vessel found at Langenlebron in a grave of the Hallstadt period (Hoerner).
,, 35. Scissors (Brockhaus).
,, 36. Bronze wedge (Brockhaus).
,, 37. Neck ornament (Lübke).
,, 38. Needle (Lübke).
,, 39. Bronze sword (Lübke).
,, 40. Stone spear-head (Brockhaus).
,, 41. Bronze fibula (Brockhaus).
,, 42. Stone knife (Brockhaus).
,, 43. Stone sickle (Lübke).
,, 44. Iron spear-head (Brockhaus).
,, 45. Iron vestment pin (Brockhaus).

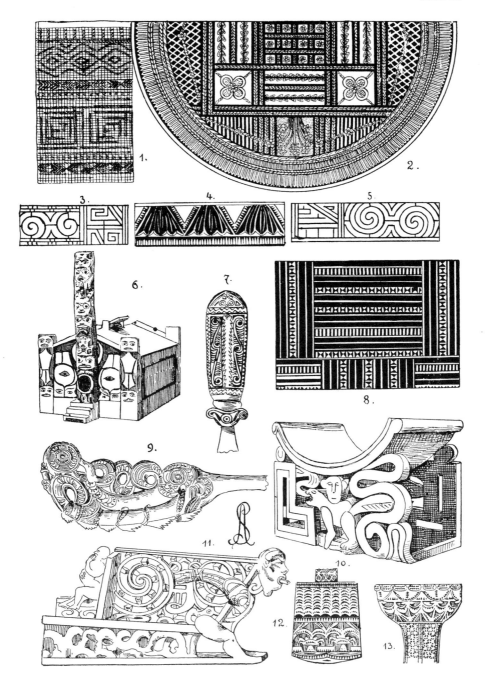

Plate 2.

Prehistoric Ornament.

Fig 1. **Ancient Peruvian Vase** (Brockhaus Konversationslexikon).
„ 2. **Granite Vase found in Honduras** (Brockhaus).
„ 3, 4, 26, 27, 41, 42, and 44. **Bronze weapons** (Lübke, Kunst des Altertums).
„ 5 **Urn found in the district of the Elbe** (Reichhold, Flachornament des Altertums).
„ 6, 23, and 30. **Knives found in the Swiss pile-dwellings** (Reichhold).
„ 7. **Relief on the Monolith Gate of Tiahuanaco** (Lübke).
„ 8, and 11. **Wedges of the Inkas period** (Brockhaus).
„ 9, 10, 12, and 14. **Earthenware vessels found in America** (Reichhold).
„ 13. **Relief from a Mexican temple** (Brockhaus).
„ 15. **Earthenware vessel found in the island of Cyprus** (Reichhold).
„ 16. **Sepulchral urn found in England** (Reichhold).
„ 17. **Sepulchral urn found in Sweden** (Reichhold).
„ 18. **Ornament from a building in Prinxillo** (Lübke).
„ 19, 20, 43, and 45. **Earthenware vessels from the Middle Rhine** (Reichhold).
„ 21. **Old Italian sepulchral urn with engraved ornamentations** (Reichhold).
„ 22. **Relief cut in the rocks in Izamal, Yucatan** (Brockhaus).
„ 24, 25, 28, 29, 31—34, and 36. **Bronze jewels** (Lübke).
„ 35. **Fragment of a column (American), found in Tula** (Brockhaus).
„ 37 to 39. **Metal-vessel ornamentations of the Bronze Age** (Lübke).
„ 40. **Idol.**

Plate 3.

Primitive Ornament.

Fig. 1. **Mat from the Southsea** (Finsch, Erfahrungen und Belegstücke aus der Südsee).
„ 2. **Fan screen of painted feathers from Australia** (Racinet, l'ornement polychrome).
„ 3, and 5. **Painting from an Australian canoe** (Racinet).
„ 4. **Painted Woodcarving from Central Africa** (Racinet).
„ 6. **Model of a house of the Haida, Queen Charlotte's Islands.** In the Anthropological Museum of Berlin.
„ 7. **Ebony spatula with incrusted work from New Guinea** (Reichhold, Kunst und Zeichnen).
„ 8. **Specimen of woven work from Australia** (Racinet).
„ 9. **Club from New Zealand** (Racinet).
„ 10. **Native chair, Camerun.** In the anthropological Museum of Berlin.
„ 11. **Woodcarving from a canoe in New Zealand.** In the Louvre (Racinet).
„ 12, and 13. **Terminal heads of paddles from Polynesia** (Glazier, A manual of Historic Ornament).

Door of the grand Theocalli of Uxmal, Yucatan (Gailhabaud, Denkmäler).
Frame: **Mexican Ceramic Ornaments in the British Museum** (Owen Jones,
Grammar of Ornaments).

ANTIQUITY.

Egyptian wood columns (Prisse d'Avennes, hist. d. l'art égyptien).

EGYPTIAN ORNAMENT.

Egyptian Dress (Lübke).

ong before civilisation was known in Egypt there existed at one time in Ancient Syria and Babylonia, countries once so rich and flourishing, a civilisation much older than that of Egypt. Proofs of this civilisation have been brought to light in the excavations carried out in recent years in these two countries. It is, however, Egypt that has supplied us with those series of monuments by means of which the most ancient historical facts now in our possession have been put together and verified. Even so far back as 4000 B. C. an extensive artistic spirid reigned throughout Egypt. The historic period of the country, which dates from about the year 3200 B. C. when Mena was king, comprise thirty dynasties, and is divided in accordance with the records of the priest Manetho into four principal periods, namely:

1. **The Ancient Kingdom** dating from about 4180 B. C. to about 3000 B. C. This period, reached its highest glory under Khan, the last king of the tenth dynasty. The city of Memphis in Lower Egypt flourished during this period.

2. **The Middle Kingdom** dates from 3000 to 1587 B. C. The principal centres were in Middle and Upper Egypt with the capital Thebes. The highest period of development characteristic of this epoch was reached about 2660 B. C. during the 12th dynasty, the decline and decay of this development being brought about by the conquest of the country by the Hyksos who had their centre of government in the city of Tanis.

3. **The Modern Kingdom** dates from the year 1587 to 702 B. C. The principal city was Thebes in Upper Egypt. The highest period of development was reached in the years 1516 to 1234 B. C. under Hat-Shepsut, Rameses, Seti, and Rameses II., of the 18th and 19th dynasties. The decline began about the year 950 B. C.

4. **The Later Period** dates from the year 664 B. C., the period of the restoration by Psammeticus with the capital Sais. The final development took place under the 26th dynasty between the years 663 to 525 B. C. when the country was conquered by the Persians, during whose occupation few buildings were erected. In 332 B. C. a revival took place under the rule of Alexander the Great which was continued by the Ptolemies from the year 323 B. C. and by the Romans from 31 B. C.

The life led by the ancient Egyptians was characterised by distinctly marked order and regularity, and to this is due the clearness, exactness and dignity, which distinguish Egyptian works cf art. They are deficient however in that warm spirit which animates Grecian art, and are in consequence cold and stiff. Owing to the scarcity of timber, all the great enclusures of temples, palaces, and domestic structures generally were built in unburnt brick, a material which necessitated a much greater thickness for the lower part of the wall at the base, and this type of construction would appear to have been the model on which all the great monuments in stone were based, thus accounting for the raking walls given to the pylcns and temples

Apart from a pure geometrical setting-out, Egyptian ornament consists of a rigidly systematic arrangement of plants native to the country. The well-known Egyptologist, Louis Borchardt, has arranged a clear classification of Egyptian plant-ornamentation, and the complete plants used as models being arranged by him as follows:

1. **The Lotus-flower,** Nymphaea Lotus L., Nymphaea Cerula L., and Nymphaea Nelumbo L.

2. **The Lily,** the botanical name of which has not yet been fixed.

3. **The Papyrus flower,** Cyperus papyrus L.

4. **The Date-palm,** Phoenix dactylifera L.

5. **Reeds and a kind of Withe*** were also cften employed as can be seen from certain fragments discovered in the excavations.

The lotus and papyrus flowers were, however, used the most often by the Ancient Egyptians in the ornamentation of all kinds of work, from the most colossal Egyptian columns down to the smallest objects. Borchardt denies that there is any constructive importance to be attached to the Egyptian plant-column. To the ancient Egyptians, the temple meant the world, the ceiling was the heavens, under which the columns, made to represent plants, rose up from a mound of

---

* Probably the leaf of the maize or Indian corn.

EGYPTIAN ORNAMENT.

earth. That the imitation of a plant was used as a support for the ceiling is an idea which cannot be accepted. As, however, supports for carrying the ceiling were necessary, there was placed, as connecting link between the supports and the burden, an abacus, which on account of the strong swell of the capital, was invisible from below. In this way, the idea of having again flowers under the open skies was realised. It is therefore, according to this, evident that the ornament was used as a support and not that the support was ornamented.

The principal features characterising the manner in which Egyptian artists wished to represent the lotus flower were, first, the elliptical form of the buds with stalks, then the calyx of the flowers rounded off above, and the intermediate petals rounded off in a similar manner. The lotus-flowers have no foot-leaves, these being peculiar to the papyrus-shaped columns only. There are closed and opened lotus and papyrus columns, as well as simple and compound ones.

Although stone is the material which predominates, columns and vessels in wood have also been discovered. Casting in metal, clay and even glass-blowing, were known to the ancient Egyptians, and they were adepts in the textile industry. In the ornamentation of Egyptian buildings, more especially in temples and tombs, painting was the predominant characteristic.

Plate 4.

Border: Column with closed lotus capital from a mural painting found in the tomb of the Kej of Bersche. It dates from the Middle Egyptian Kingdom (Borchardt).

Fig. 1. **Column with closed lotus capital from the Middle Kingdom, found in Beni-hasan. Horizontal section is also given.** (Lepsius, Tagebuch.) Like all lotus columns, this one has neither foliage nor entasis. From the stone base, on which the column is raised, rise 4 main stalks. These, and the 4 intermediate stalks, are held together by means of 5 chaplets. The capital is made up of 4 lotus-buds with longitudinal convex bands. The abacus is small and square.

" 2. **Closed lotus capital dating from the Ancient Egyptian Kingdom, found by de Morgan in the tomb of the Ptah-schep-ses near Aboukir. Horizontal section of the column is also given.** (Revue arch. 1894.) The column consists of 6 principal and 6 intermediate stalks, held together by 5 neck-bands. The capital consists of very sharp-pointed buds. The intermediate stalks end above in open lotus-flowers. The whole column is painted over in a naturalistic manner.

" 3. **Closed lotus capital from the Ptolemaic epoch, taken from the temple of Isis-us-ret in Philae** (Borchardt). Columns with closed lotus capitals did not exist in the Modern Kingdom. This kind of capital, like all capitals from the time of the Ptolemies, was peculiar in the fact that the stalks were allowed to appear below the bands of the necking. In this example, furthermore, the triple intermediate stalks do not rest between the main stalks. The shaft is smooth and completely covered with hieroglyphics.

Plate 4. EGYPTIAN ORNAMENT. 15

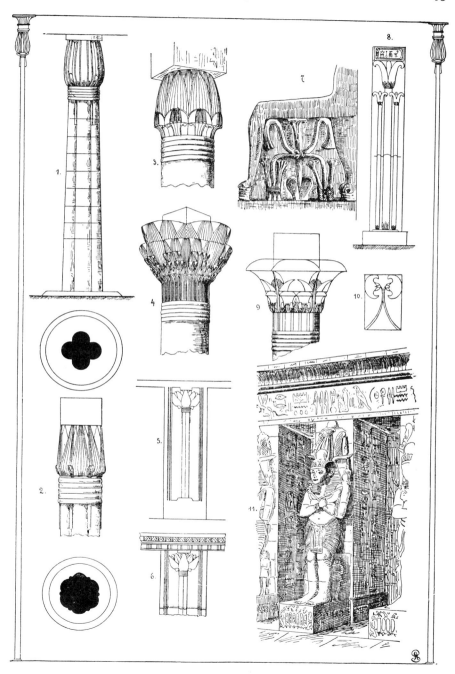

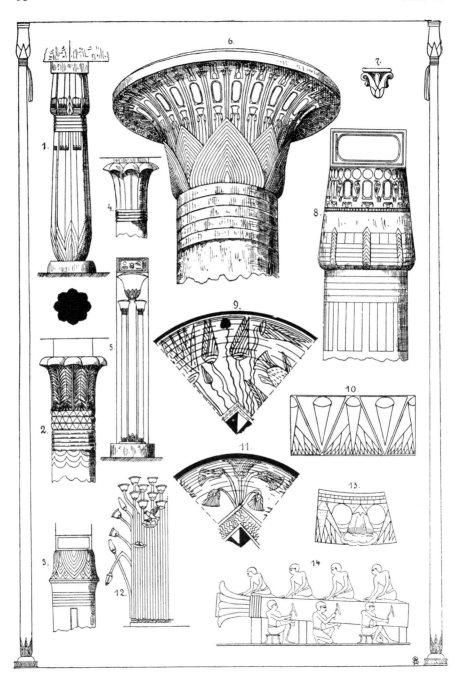

Fig. 4. **Open lotus capital in Edfu, dating from the time of the Ptolemies** (Prisse, Histoire de l'art égyptien). This capital consists of 4 large lotus-flowers standing close to each other. Between each pair of these flowers are 3 others—one large and 2 small ones—which rise from small intermediate posts, and between these 16 flowers are 16 other extremely small ones. Open lotus capitals of columns dating from the Ancient Kingdom have not yet been discovered in a perfect condition.

„ 5, and 6. **Open lotus capitals decorating piers from the Ancient Kingdom, found in the tombs 1 and 2 of the Hepi in Sawijet el Meitni** (Borchardt).

„ 7. **Symbol of the union of Upper and Lower Egypt from the throne of a Cephren statue in Gizeh** (Borchardt). The symbol of Upper Egypt was the lily, the botanical name of which cannot, however, be even yet fixed, and the Symbol of Lower Egypt the papyrus.

„ 8. **Thothmes pillar of granite dating from the New Kingdom, found in the sanctuary in Karnak** (Lepsius, Tagebuch).

„ 9. **Open papyrus capital in Philae dating from the time of the Ptolemies** (Prisse).

„ 10. **Papyrus ornament from a mural fresco found in a tomb in Beni-Hasan** (Prisse).

„ 11. **Osiride pillar from Medinet Habû** (Perrot and Chipiez, History of Art).

Plate 5.

Border: Papyrus column with closed capital from a mural fresco found in the tomb of Kha'-em-hêt at Gurna. This example dates from the Later Egyptian Kingdom (Borchardt).

Fig. 1. **Papyrus column with closed capital in front of the pyramid of Amenemhet near Hawara. This column dates from the Middle Kingdom** (Prisse). From the stone base on which the column rests, spring 8 stalks arranged in regular order. The horizontal section of the column given in the same figure will make this clear. As is the case with all papyrus columns, there are, at the foot of the stalk, sheathing leaves which enclose the lower portion of the column. Under the capital, the stalks narrow off, and are bound together by 5 fillets. Over these fillets, 8 closed buds, each with a head-foil, develop themselves. The section of the buds and stalks is triangular. Under the neck-band are 8 clusters each having 3 stalks. These capitals, however, gradually lost their characteristic form, until finally, they became completely changed as in fig. 8.

„ 2. **Palm-leaf capital of a column at Philae dating from the later Egyptian Kingdom** (Prisse). Here, also a space exists between the capital and the neck-band.

„ 3. **Capital in the Palace of Thothmes, 1541—1516 B. C. in Karnac** (Lepsius).

„ 4. **Palm-leaf capital of a column in Bersche dating from the Middle Kingdom** (Borchardt).

„ 5. **Papyrus column with open Flower capital from the granite pilasters in front of the Sanctuary in Karnac** (Lepsius).

„ 6. **Open papyrus flower capital at Karnac, dating from the Middle Kingdom** (Prisse). Pictures and inscriptions are worked in between the painted flower stalks.

„ 7. **Clay mould with lily from Tell-el-Amarna dating from the Middle Kingdom** (Petrie, Tell-el-Amarna).

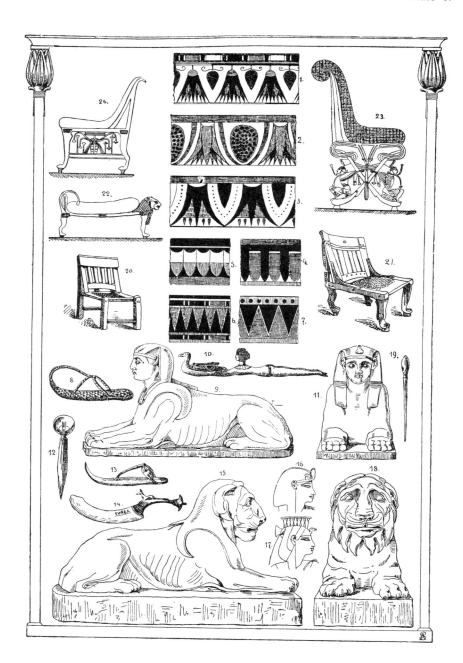

Fig. 8. Turned papyrus-capital of a column with closed flower, at Karnac, dating from the later Egyptian Kingdom (Prisse).

„ 9. Decoration of a figured dish in the British Museum (Borchardt).

„ 10. Figured frieze—flowers and buds from the same plant—from the palace of Amenophis' IV. in Tell-el-Amarna (Borchardt).

„ 11. Papyrus ornament on a figured dish in the British Museum (Borchardt).

„ 12. Papyrus thicket from the mural fresco of a tomb in Benihasan, dating from the Middle Kingdom (Borchardt).

„ 13. Withe from a painted wreath of a coffin, dating from the Middle Kingdom.

„ 14. Palm-shaped column in process of manufacture from a mural fresco at Gurna; dating from the Middle Kingdom.

Plate 6.

Border: Closed lotus capital from a mural fresco (Borchardt).

Fig. 1 to 7. Egyptian mural fresco (Uhde).

„ 8. Woven work sandals (Prisse, Hist. de l'art égypt.).

„ 9, and 11. Sphinx in red granite in the museum of the Vatican (Tatham, Anc. Ornam. Arch. in Rome).

„ 10. Scent-spoon from collection in the Louvre (Perrot and Chipiez).

„ 12. Egyptian dagger (Perrot and Chipiez).

„ 13. Leather sandals (Perrot and Chipiez).

„ 14. Egyptian bronze knife (Perrot and Chipiez).

„ 15, and 18. Egyptian lions in green basalt before the Capitol in Rome (Tatham Anc. Ornam. Arch. in Rome).

„ 16, and 17. Egyptian heads in relief dating from the Later Kingdom (Lübke).

„ 19. Egyptian sewing-needles (Perrot and Chipiez).

„ 20, and 21. Old-Egyptian wooden chairs (Koeppen und Breuer, Geschichte d. Möbels).

„ 22, 23, and 24. Egyptian furniture (Canina, arch. ant.).

Plate 7.

Border: Columns with open lotus-capital from a painted canopy in a tomb at Gurna, dating from the Middle Kingdom (Borchardt).

Fig. 1. Painted bouquet-column in the tomb of Sennundem. Dates from the Egyptian Middle Kingdom (Berlin Museum, Ph. 664).

„ 2. Breast-plate of gold with incrusted enamel bearing the name of Rameses II. (Perrot and Chipiez).

„ 3. Head of Nofret (Lübke).

„ 4. Egyptian clay jar (Libonis, Les styles).

„ 5. Egyptian amphora (Libonis).

Fig. 6. **Rhyton, an Egyptian musical instrument** (Libonis).
„ 7. **Ceiling ornamentation from Memphis and Thebes** (Prisse).
„ 8. **Winged sun, the symbol of royal dignity dating from the Ancient Kingdom of the Egyptians.**
„ 9. **Gold necklace** (Libonis).
„ 10. **Girl with guitar from a mural painting in Thebes** (Perrot and Chipiez).
„ 11. **Ornament** (Libonis).
„ 12. **Ring of Rameses II.** (Perrot and Chipiez).
„ 13. **Transporting a mummy, from a mural painting.**
„ 14. **Harness** (Prisse).
„ 15. **Engraved ring in the Louvre, Paris** (Perrot and Chipiez).
„ 16. **Egyptian doors of wood** (Prisse).
„ 17. **Bracelet of Prince Psat, dating from the New Egyptian Kingdom.**

Building a temple, from a mural painting found in a grave
at Abd-el-Gurna (Lübke).

BABYLONIAN-ASSYRIAN ORNAMENT.

Stone imbossed work, representing the surrender of Lachis to Sennachérib (Roger-Milès).

Along the banks of the Euphrates and Tigris, in the sacred land of Mesopotamia, and under the special influence of these two streams, a characteristic civilisation developed itself more than 5000 years ago — much the same as the civilisation which was developed in Egypt under the influence of the Nile. The results of the latest excavations in Tello, Niniveh, Nimroud, Koyunjik, Khorsabad, and other places, have afforded proofs of the existence, even as far back as 4000 B. C. of the Sumerians, a non-Semitic people who became afterwards united with the Assyrians. It may therefore be accepted as certain, that in this river valley a civilisation existed which was older than that of Egypt. The language cf the Sumerians long after it ceased to exist as a living tongue was spoken as a dead language by scholars. The Bible itself mentions the colossal buildings erected by the Babylonian and Assyrian kings at that remote period. In this particular country, there was such a mixture of peoples, one alternately subjugated by another, that the art of the epoch must be regarded as one common to the people as a whole. The people themselves appear to have been more of a sensible and practical, rather than of a peotic turn of mind. They were at once commercial as well as warlike, keeping material gain and their own supremacy above all other matters.

In the third thousand before Christ a number of small principalities . . . such as Shirpula, Ur of the Chaldees, Isin, Larsa, etc. . . . existed in South Babylonia, but were finally conquered by Khammunrabi, king of North Babylonia in the year 2232 B. C. After this conquest the city of Babylonia was made the capital. The kingdom of the Semitic Assyrians was founded and began about the year 2000 B. C., developing into a powerful state about 1300 B. C., the principal cities being Ashur and Nineveh. This kingdom reached its highest glory in the reigns of Assurnasipal (884—860 B. C.), Shalmaneser II. (860—824 B. C.), Sargon II. (722—705 B. C.), Sennachirib (705—681 B. C.), Esarhaddon (681—668),. and Ashur-bani-pal (Sardanapalus) (668—626). Under this latter monarch Assyria became the principal world-power, being however deprived of this supremacy by Nabc polassar of Babylonia and Cyaxaras of Media in the year 603 B. C. The new kingdom now established flourished for a short time, 605 to 561 B. C. under Nebuchadnezzar, being itself finally conquered by Cyrus King of Persia in this year 538 B. C.

While structures built of stone predominated in Egypt, in these districts on the Tigris and Euphrates the buildings were almost always constructed of air-dried bricks, which accounts for the fact that so few of them have remained intact. Walls made of these unburnt bricks were first coated with stone slabs, plaster, or asphalt, and then covered with mosaic-work formed of glazed pieces of terra-cotta. Most of the discoveries, therefore, made in this region, consist of these fragments of glazed terra-cotta, in which work these people excelled.

The specimens of sculpture which have come down to us are mostly all in relief, few of them being in cavo-relievo.

Many of the art objects discovered in recent excavations show Egyptian influence, but there is no proof of any kind at hand pointing to the supposition that such objects were brought into Assyria by Egyptian traders. As in Egypt, so here also the lotus-flower played a very important role in ornamentation.

There must be a distinction made between a specific Babylonian period and a specific Assyrian period, the ruins of which were discovered at different levels in the excavations in Nimroud, Khorsabad, Nineveh, and Koyunjik.

It must be regarded as certain, that, next to the Egyptian, Babylonian-Assyrian art exercised a very great influence, on the one side, towards the East and North, that is, India, China and Persia, and on the other side, towards the West, especially in the Mediterranean islands.

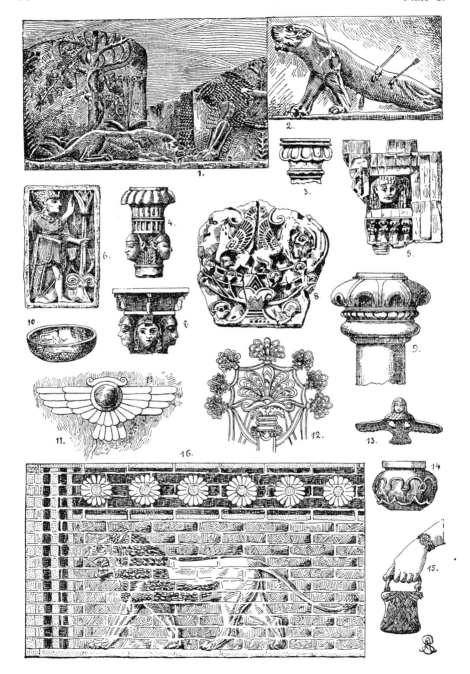

Plate 8.

Fig. 1. **Assyrian relief in alabaster from Nineveh,** taken from the palace of King Ashurbanipal (668—626 B. C.), after a photograph from the English excavations. What is very remarkable in this example is the extremely soft outlines of the lioness as she lies stretched at the feet of the lion; the lithe grace and lissomness of her body are in fine contrast with the strongly-marked, swelling, and powerful muscles.

,, 2. **Bas-relief showing a wounded lion** (Libonis). In the British Museum.

,, 3, 4, and 7. **Capital in ivory from the ruins of Nineveh.** In the British Museum. (Dieulafoy, l'Art antique).

,, 5. **Window with balustrade under cill,** from the ruins of Nineveh (Dieulafoy).

,, 6, and 8. **Relief in ivory from the ruins of Nineveh** (Dieulafoy). In the British Museum.

,, 9. **Capital of Baluster.**

,, 10. **Assyrian bowl** (Semper, Der Stil).

,, 11. **The Assyrian winged-globe** (Perrot).

,, 12. **The Assyrian mysterious tree** (Perrot).

,, 13. **Siren** (Babelon, Archeologie).

,, 14. **Assyrian pedestal** (Dieulafoy).

,, 15. **Vessel resembling a basket in the hand of a sacrificer** (Semper).

,, 16. **The Babylonian lion.** Bas-relief made of glazed bricks from the temple of Ninmach (Gurlitt). The Babylonian lion was white with a yellow mane, or yellow with a green mane, the background being light blue.

Plate 9.

Fig. 1. **Floor ornament from Koyunjik** (Lübke, Kunst des Altertums). The motif in this ornament appears to have been copied from a very ancient piece of textil-work, which, notwithstanding its antiquity, shows highly-developed artistic workmanship.

,, 2. **Capital or base of column at Khorsabad** (Uhde, Architekturformen des klassischen Altertums).

,, 3. **Mural decoration made of burned, glazed stone, from Nimroud** (Uhde).

,, 4. **Assyrian relief in alabaster, showing King Ashurbanipal** (688—626 B. C.) **hunting.** Taken from a photograph at the English excavations in Nineveh.

,, 5. **Assyrian wall decoration made of enamelled slabs** (Lübke).

,, 6. **From an Assyrian embroidery** (Perrot and Chipiez).

,, 7. **Bronze fragments of chairs found in Nimroud** (Uhde).

,, 8. **Ornamentation on glazed, coloured bricks from the wall of a court in the palace of King Nebuchadnezar at Babylon.** From a photograph taken in the recent German excavations in Babylon.

,, 9. **Assyrian standards** (Libonis).

,, 10. **Arched portal from Koyunjik** (Lübke).

,, 11. **Horse bridle** (Brockhaus).

,, 12. **Bronze lion from the palace of Sardanapalus** (Libonis).

,, 13. **Winged steer with human head, in the Louvre, Paris** (Libonis).

Plate 10.   BABYLONIAN-ASSYRIAN-ORNAMENT.   27

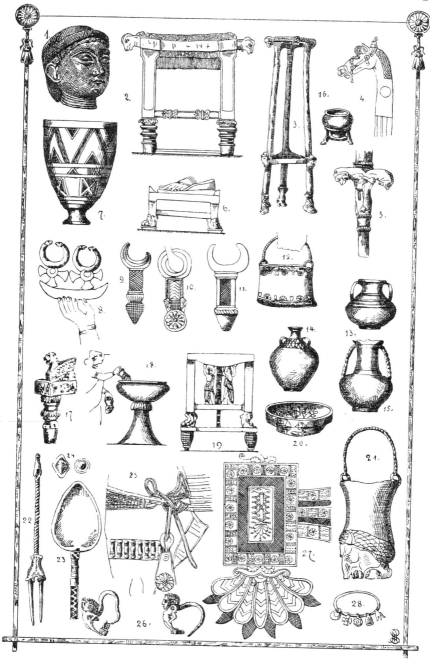

Plate 10.

Border: Flag-post on palaces (Uhde).

Fig. 1. **Ancient Babylonian female head in Diorite.** A genuine original is preserved in the Berlin Museum. A similar head was discovered in the excavations carried out by the French in Tello (South-Babylonia).

„   2. **Assyrian Chair** (Perrot).

„   3. **Bronze tripod in the Louvre** (Perrot).

„   4. **Carriage-pole** (Perrot).

„   5. **Bronze sword** (Perrot).

„   6. **Footstool** (Perrot).

„   7. **Beaker** (Perrot).

„   8. **Bracelet** (Perrot).

„   9, 10, and 11. **Ear-rings** (Perrot).

„   12. **Metal bucket** (Perrot).

„   13, 14, and 15. **Amphorae of clay** (Perrot).

„   16, and 18. **Goblets** (Semper).

„   17. **Bronze fragment from a chair of state** (Babelon).

„   19. **Washhand stand** (Semper).

„   20. **Dish** (Semper).

„   21. **Metal bucket** (Semper).

„   22, and 23. **Fork and spoon** (Smith, Assyrian Discoveris).

„   24. **Gold buttons, in the British Museum** (Perrot).

„   25. **Harness** (Perrot).

„   26. **Gold ear-ring** (Perrot).

„   27. **Embroidered breast-piece** (Layard, Monuments).

„   28. **Royal necklet of gold** (Perrot).

Assyrian fighting car (L'Art pour tous).

PERSIAN ORNAMENT.

Imbossed work, representing the king Xerxes upon the throne (Roger-Milès).

Disunion and a continual state of unrest were the conditions permanent in the south-western part of Asia in ancient times. The supremacy was ever changing and never fixed, and, as a consequence, the peoples who inhabited it were not in a position to develop any independent art distinct from each other. The conquerors or the conquered were always naturally influenced by the more advanced section of those with whom they were brought into contact. For these reasons, it is clear that Persian ornament can show but very little characteristic peculiarities, Egyptian, Assyrian and Hellenic influences being all plainly discernable.

The beautiful buildings of the Persian kings were erected by artists who were made prisoners in the wars in Babylonia, Egypt, and in the Grecian colonies in Asia Minor.

The first beginnings in Persian art were very probably made by the Medes, a people who conquered the kingdom of the Elamites with its capital city Susa

in the 7th century B. C. an then founded a powerful state making Egbatana the capital, but who were, later on themselves subjugated in the year 550 B. C. by the Persians under Cyrus. No remains, however, of a special Median art have ever been discovered. Persia developed into the most powerful empire in the world under the reigns of Cyrus (559—529), Cambyses (529—522), Darius 521—485), and Xerxes (485—465 B. C.), but was in its turn conquered by Alexander the Great in the year 330 B. C. From the years 312 to 284 B. C. it was under the sway of the Seleucidae, from 284 B. C. to 284 A. D. it was subject to the Parthians, and from 284 A. D. to 641 A. D. to the Sassanians. Under the sway of the latter a new Persian Empire was established which flourished until it finally became subject to Islamite supremacy. The Islamites when in decided power changed entirely the character of Art then flourishing, giving it an entirely new direction an turning it on to entirely different lines from those along which it had hitherto moved. Persian art, which continued to develop for about two centuries, is the last echo of the art of the Mesopotamian lands. With the destruction of the Persian Empire by Alexander the Great, Hellenic art, already flourishing at that period, won the upper hand throughout the East.

Plate 11.

Fig. 1. **Lion frieze in the Louvre** (Dieulafoy).
„ 2. **Lion and griffin frieze** (Dieulafoy).
„ 3, 4, and 11. **Columns from Persepolis** (Uhde).
„ 5, and 7. **Column in the hall of Xerxes in Persepolis** (Uhde).
„ 6. **Detail from the tomb of King Achemenides in the necropolis of Takhte-Djemschid** (Dieulafoy).
„ 8. **Floor of stairs in the palace of Artaxerxes** (Libonis).
„ 9. **Frieze, a winged steer** (Libonis).
„ 10. **Relief at Persepolis** (Lübke).
„ 11, and 12. **Persian bases** (Dieulafoy).

Plate 12.

Fig. 1, and 2. **Persian Wall decoration of glazed terra-cotta** (Libonis).
„ 3. **Head of a steer in the Louvre** (Perrot and Chipiez).
„ 4, 5, and 6. **Persian pottery** (Perrot and Chipiez).
„ 7. **From a bas-relief in the hall of the 100 columns, Persepolis** (Flandin et Coste, Perse ancienne).
„ 8. **Persian silver coin** (Perrot and Chipiez).
„ 9. **Bas-relief at Persepolis.**
„ 10. **Head-dress of Cyrus** (Dieulafoy).

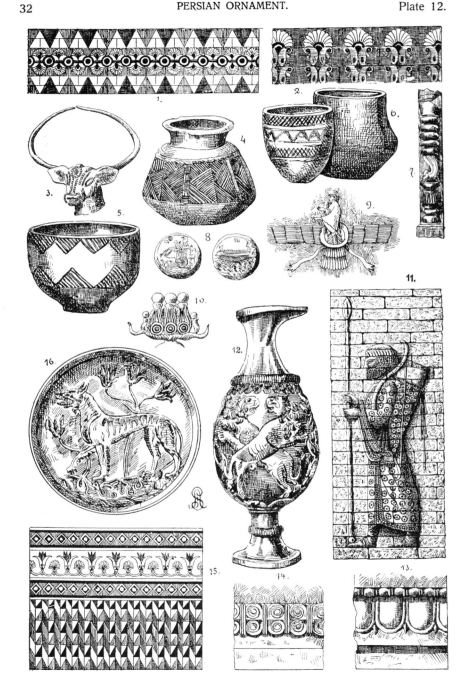

Fig. 11, and 12. **Fragment of an enamel bas-relief from Susa** (Dieulafoy).
„ 13, and 14. **Bas-reliefs from the graves of Naksche Roustem** (Dieulafoy).
„ 15. **Mosaic from the floor of stairs in the palace of Artaxerxes** (Libonis).
„ 16, and 17. **Utensils in chased silver.** Dating from the Sassanian period. In the Paris Medaillon-Cabinet (Havard, Histoire de l'orfèvrerie Française).

Curtain over the throne of Achemenides (Dieulafoy).

PHOENICIAN-HEBRAIC ORNAMENT.

A Phoenician in the time of King Thoutmes III
(Roger-Milès)

I n Phoenicia lived a distinctly commercial people, full of the spirit of trade, thinking of nothing but gain and commerce and keeping their commercial interests always above other interests of any kind whatever. In the second thousand before Christ they were already settled on the coast of Syria, had trading-stations and colonies in Greece, Italy, Gaul, Hispania, and Africa, and in their intercourse with the various peoples with whom they traded paid attention only to such matters as were best likely to forward their own commercial interests. To this commercial spirit is due the fact that there is no strictly Phoenician art. In the Phoenician Ornament evidences of all kinds of decoration can be recognised, Egyptian-Assyrian influence being specially predominant. The most characteristic examples of Phoenician art which have come down to us are their jewels. These imply that the Phoenicians lived in a high state of luxury, and prove also that they had reached a high state of development in the art of working in gold. The Hebrews in Palestine were entirely dependent on the Phoenicians for their technics and their art. The Mosaic law forbidding pictures and images prevented the free development of art amongst the Jews. In the reigns of David and Solomon, that is, about the year 1000 B. C., Hebrew Art was in its highest glory, and remained so until the destruction of Jerusalem by Nebuchadnezar in the year 586 B. C. The principal buildings of King Solomon's palace, and of the Temple, were however the work of Phoenician artists and artisans. Numerous tombs cut into rocks at this time and characteristic of this period are still preserved. In North Syria along the Upper Euphrates

Plate 13.   PHOENICIAN-HEBRAIC ORNAMENT.   35

and in Cappadocia lived a people called the Hittites who were neither of Aryan or Hebrew stock. They were settled here since the year 1500 B. C., and, from 1130 B. C. were continuously attacked by the Assyrians, being finally conquered and destroyed by Sargon in the 8th century B. C. These people had a special, characteristic style of their own, a style, however, which shows traces of Egyptian and Assyrian influence. The Art of the Hittites, however, on the other hand played an important part in and powerfully influenced the development of Persian art. Only very few remains of this civilisation are now in existence.

With regard to the other races who also lived in Asia Minor, it may be remarked that, the remains which have come down to us from these peoples are so few that it is no possible to deduce from them any distinct, characteristic style.

Plate 13.

Fig. 1. **Frieze hewn in stone** (Renan Mission, Libonis).
„ 2. **Capital found in Cyprus** (Vogüé Mission).
„ 3, and 4. **Phoenician capitals** (Libonis).
„ 5, 13, and 18. **Phoenician jewels** (Libonis).
„ 6, 9, 11, and 12. **Phoenician vases from Dali** (Lübke).
„ 7. **Vase from Larnaka** (Lübke).
„ 8. **Glass vase from Jerusalem** (Libonis).
„ 10. **Pigmy in burnt clay, in the Louvre** (Libonis).
„ 14. **Head of a sarcophagus in clay from Carthage** (Libonis).
„ 15, 16, and 17. **Phoenician vases from Alhambra** (Lübke).
„ 19. **Phoenician glass vases** (Libonis).
„ 20. **Phoenician altar** (Cippe), (Libonis).
„ 21. **Silver dish from Curium in Cyprus** (Graul, Bilderatlas).
„ 22. **Coffin plate** (Libonis).

**Painting from an old Cyprian clay vessel representing
tree adoration** (Seesselberg, Frühmittelalterliche Kunst).

INDIAN ORNAMENT.

t is generally believed that Indian civilisation dates back to a very remote period, it was not, however, till about the year 2000 B. C. that the Aryans who had emigrated from Central Asia settled in the South of India and reached the plenitude of their power. The archaeological discoveries made in India reach no further back than a few centuries before Christ. A close observation of Old-Indian ornaments shows

Bas-relief from Ellora. us that Indian art was by no means free of foreign influences, more especially Persian, and later on, Greek. India is but a purely geographical expression, and has no ethnographical signification whatever. It is inhabited by races of people so different and distinct from each other that to class them together as the Indian race would be incorrect. To speak of a homogeneous Indian art is therefore impossible, the more so, as each race which inhabited the country had its own art history.

The general history of Indian art may be divided into the following periods:

1. The Vedi-Brahman era extending up to the middle of the 3rd century B. C. There is perhaps no monument from this period in existence.

2. The Buddhist era which extends to the 7th century A. D., and began when Buddhism was raised to be the established state religion by King Asoka in the year 256 B. C.

3. The New-Brahman Period which began on the restoration of the Brahma religion in the 8th century and continued up into the 12th century A. D. This period reached its highest glory between the 8th and 12th centuries A. D.

4. The period of the dominion of Islam to the present time.

The spread of Buddhism helped most materially in giving a great impulse to the development of art. Indeed the progress made in art in other countries besides India has always been greatly influenced by religious fanaticism. The style of decoration used at this period, although worthy of admiration, was so fantastic and bizarre, that the form was completely overspread and hidden by the ornamentation. The oldest monuments from this period at present in existence date from the reign of King Asoka 272—236 B. C.

With the spread of Islam, Indian art took a new direction based on Arabian art. This part of the subject will be treated of later on when dealing with the art of the Mahommedans.

Plate 14.

Fig. 1. **Corner-pillar of the temple in Nijamizzur** (Uhde, Die Konstruktionen und die Kunstformen der Architektur).

„ 2, and 3. **Details from temple in Ahmedabad** (Uhde). Appears to have been made after textile samples.

„ 4. **Capital from the temple in Kumurpal, Palitana** (Uhde). This capital shows clearly defined traces of Grecian influence.

„ 5. **Isolated monolith column near the temple at Peroor** (Uhde). The use of metal in this example strengthens the impression that the ornamentation was copied from a textile sample.

„ 6. **Capital from Bharhut** (Lübke).

„ 7. **Isolated stone-column from the cave at Karli** (Uhde). Hewn out of the solid rock. The lion signifies the victoy of Bhuddism.

„ 8. **Pillars from the Chaitya cave in Karli** (Uhde).

„ 9. **Pilaster, with crest, from the temple in Bhagovati** (Rajendralalá Mitra).

„ 10. **West portal at Sanchi, Tope** (Uhde). This is one of the oldest stone monuments in India. It is however an imitation of wooden architecture.

„ 11. **Iron memorial column commemorating the victory of Buddhism** (Uhde). This column dates from the reign of King Asoka in the third century B. C.

„ 12. **Detail from the temple in Mukteswara** (Rajendralalá Mitra).

„ 13. **Column from the rock-temple in Lauka, Ellora** (Uhde).

„ 14. **Capital from the Kutub near Delhi** (Uhde). Dates from the later period 1191—93.

„ 15. **Column from the rock-temple of Indra in Ellora** (Canina, architectura antica).

„ 16. **Column from the Vihara in Ajunta** (Uhde).

„ 17, and 18. **Details from the temple at Bailur.** Appears to be copied from a carpet pattern.

Plate 15.

Fig. 1. **Window from the temple of Muktes'wara** (Rajendralalá Mitra. The other illustrations in this plate are all from the same authority).

„ 2. **Moulding from the temple of Bhagovati.**

„ 3. **Detail from the tower of Bhuvanes'war.**

„ 4. **Medaillion from the temple of Sárí Deül.**

„ 5. **Moulding from the temple of Muktes'wara.**

Fig. 6. Statue of the province from a niche in the temple of Bhuvanes'war.
„ 7. Relief from the same temple.
„ 8. Pillars from the rock-temple of Uday-agirí.
„ 9. Lotus ornament from the temple of Rájeráni.
„ 10. Relief from the temple of Bhuvanes'war.
„ 11. Base of a pilaster from the great tower of Bhuvanes'war.
„ 12. Cornice from the temple in Parásurámes'vara.

Plate 16.

Fig. 1, 4, 7, and 8. Old Indian furniture (Rajendralalá Mitra).
„ 2. Ornament worn by females of the middle class (Raj.).
„ 3. Club found in Bhuvanes'war (Raj.).
„ 5. Bas-relief from Bharhut representing an Indian of the 2nd century B. C. (Lebon).
„ 6. Club found in Puri (Raj.).
„ 9. Flag found in Sánchi (Raj.).
„ 10. Javelin from Cunningham's Bhilsa Topes (Raj.).
„ 11, 19, and 23. Tridents found in the same place (Raj.).
„ 12. Wooden jewel-case found in Amravati (Raj.).
„ 13. Wooden box found in Bhuvanes'war (Raj.).
„ 14. Antique fan (Raj.).
„ 15, and 16. Ear ornaments (Raj.).
„ 17. Four sided clay vessel (Raj.).
„ 18. Urn for holy water (Raj.).
„ 20. Guitar from Amravati (Raj.).
„ 21. Metal shield found in Konárak (Raj.).
„ 22. Short club (Raj.).
„ 24, and 27. Battle axes (Raj.).
„ 25. Crown for a goddess (Raj.).
„ 26. Gold bracelet (Raj.).
„ 28, 30, and 31. Clay vases (Raj.).
„ 29, and 34. Samples of antique textiles (Raj.).
„ 32, and 33. Bow and arrow (Raj.).

Painting in a grotto at Adochantá (after Grünwedel).

GREEK ORNAMENT.

Grecian Women at home
(Gerhardt, auserlesene Vasenbilder).

t has been clearly and defini-
tely proved, both from discoveries made in excavations,
as well as from certain signi-
ficant statements made by
Homer himself, that even in
prehistoric times several centres of art existed in Greece
and in the islands lying in its
neighbourhood. These centres
were chiefly found in the Pelo-
ponnessus, in Attica, in Miletus,
Ephesus, Chios, Samos, and many other islands, as well as also in Southern
Italy. The prehistoric Greek Ornament, which was brought to light by Schliemann
in the excavations undertaken by him in Troy, Mycenae and Tiryns, contains
so many Egyptian and Assyrian *motifs* that no doubt can be entertained, that
Egypt and Asia Minor exercised a most powerful influence on its early beginnings. That an intercourse existed between these countries is beyond doubt,
for, even in prehistoric times, the waters of the Mediterranean were alive with
craft trading in all directions.

In its primary stages of development, Greek art in the islands of the Aegean
Sea was subject to Oriental influences. The Greek style was developed from
wooden structures, the constructive forms, in many cases, changed into ornament
in the stone masonry.

The national character of the Greeks was very different from that of the Egyptians, the cold severity peculiar to Egyptian art was antagonistic to the sense of beauty characteristic of the Greeks, and the latter, consequently, soon changed the Egyptian form into one more genial, pleasing, and agreeable. Style is after all but the truthful expression of the character and perceptions of a people or of an historical epoch.

Greek art can be divided into four epochs:

I. The Mythical Period or the Heroic Epoch which continued up to the migration of the Dorians to the year 1104 B. C. The Aryans, a tribe of people of the same stock as the Hellenes and designated by the latter under the general title of Pelasgians, were without doubt the original inhabitants of Greece. This period is confined to that prehistoric era when stone and copper predominated, and to the Bronze Age of the Mycaenean epoch. The principal centres of the artstyle of this period were found on the coasts and islands of the Aegean Sea but especially in Argos and Crete.

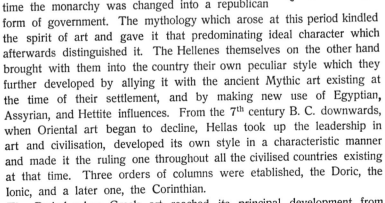

II. The Doric, or Archaic Period, from 1104—470 B. C. The national Hellenic period began about the year 1000 B.C., when the Hellenes had taken up permanent residence in the country, at which time the monarchy was changed into a republican form of government. The mythology which arose at this period kindled the spirit of art and gave it that predominating ideal character which afterwards distinguished it. The Hellenes themselves on the other hand brought with them into the country their own peculiar style which they further developed by allying it with the ancient Mythic art existing at the time of their settlement, and by making new use of Egyptian, Assyrian, and Hettite influences. From the 7th century B. C. downwards, when Oriental art began to decline, Hellas took up the leadership in art and civilisation, developed its own style in a characteristic manner and made it the ruling one throughout all the civilised countries existing at that time. Three orders of columns were etablished, the Doric, the Ionic, and a later one, the Corinthian.

III. The Period when Greek art reached its principal development from 470 to 338 B. C., during which time the Doric and Ionic Orders exercised their influence mutually one on the other. The centre of this flourishing period was that reached at Athens under Pericles in the years 469—429 B. C., when the Doric and Ionic styles, which developed together, evolved the Attic-Doric and Attic-Ionic styles. The latter excelled in elegance, the former in manly strength. The Erechtheion which was begun in the year 425 B. C. but not completed till 408 B. C., is one of the most beautiful monuments of Greek art in existence.

IV. The Alexandrian Period from 338 to 146 B. C.; this included ·the development of the Corinthian style down to the destruction of Corinth, which was followed by the downfall of Greek independence and the union of Grecian with Roman art.

Although the two great styles of Greek construction were developed simultaneously still the general employment of each separate style enables a chronological division to be made. The Doric must be described as the oldest style, but its strongly marked, earnest character, unsuitable for rich ornamentation, failed to give pleasure to the gay spirit of the luxurious Athenians who lived at the time of Pericles when Greek art was in its glory. The Doric was, therefore, partly superseded by the Ionic, and, later on, by the Corinthian style. The ornamentation in these two styles allowed more play to the artist's fancy, and was not so binding in its rules as the Doric. The quiet harmony peculiar to the Doric was, however, lost, ornamentation became predominant and, later on, tended to mask the masonic form in Roman art.

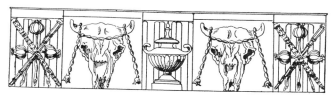

Late Doric Frieze found in the wall of a church at Athens.

Plate 17.
Greek Pre-historic Ornament.

Fig. 1. **Mural frescoes in the palace of Tiryns** (Schliemann).
„ 2, 4—12, 16, and 17. **Gold jewels found in graves in Mycenae** (Schliemann).
„ 3. **Bronze plate from Olympia** (Lübke).
„ 13. **Dipylon vase** (Baumeister).
„ 14. **Cyprian coin.**
„ 15. **Capital of Column from the Tomb of Agamemnon** (Canina).
„ 18. **Kyanos frieze from Tiryns** (Schliemann).
„ 19. **Ceiling in relief from Orchomenos** (Schliemann).

Plate 18.
Doric Ornament.

Fig. 1. **Angle of Pediment of the temple in the island of Aegina.** (Mauch, Architektonische Ordnungen). This temple is an example of the Doric Order architecture at the period of its highest splendour, that is, after the defeat of the Persians, and when Pericles stood at the head of the government of Athens. Pericles fully understood, at this period, the great importance of Art and its influence on the state. All the works of art designed by him were carried out by Phidias the renowned sculptor, with the assistance of Ictinus and Callicrates, the best architects of the time. These men succeeded in bringing Greek architecture in all its parts to the highest perfection.

The temple was erected, probably in the 75th Olympiad, and was dedicated to Aphaea. The columns have an entasis of ¹/₈₀ of the lower diameter, and present much more pleasing proportions than those from Paestum. This is especially so in the capital; here, the strong, sharp-angled projection produced by a swelled cushion is avoided, and the capital formed of cornicelines which rise delicately and gracefully from the flutings. In this way, an echinus is formed, which, while being strong, is not bent and swollen out under its burden, and in which the effects of light and shade are most attractive. The fillet under the echinus displays that delicate formation peculiar to the time of Pericles, the ehannels in the neck alone being the only parts which remind one of the ancient columns from Paestum. The profile of the cyma over the sloping gable-cornice is very beautiful, and was painted with an ornament which the Greeks called anthemion. The griffin on the roof of the gable has been reconstructed after discovered fragments. The whole structure was built of polished and painted sandstone. Traces of yellow and green foil have been found on the architrave.

The taenia was painted in vermilion, the regula, triglyphs, and mutule, in blue. The plain bands were red, with traces of scrolls having been painted on. The cymatium above these was decorated with red and blue foil, the same colours being given to the flowers on the cyma. The back ground of the pediment was blue.

„ 2. **Angle of Pediment from the temple of the Apollo Epicurius near Phigaleia in Arcadia.** (Mauch, Architektonische Ordnungen.) This temple, which was built by Ictinus, the Architect of the Parthenon in Athens, was with the exception of the temple of Tegea, one of the most beautiful throughout the entire Peloponnesus. It was constructed of bluish-white limestone, the sculptured frieze inside being of white marble. The entire proportions resemble those from the time of Pericles in Attica. The cyma over the gable-cornice is, however, entirely different. It is ornamented with the acanthus-flower in relief.

Fig. 3. **Capital from the temple of Ceres in Paestum** (Mauch, Architektonische Ordnung). This temple was in all probability built under the rule of the Sybarites, about the year 530 B. C. Certain peculiarities point to Etruscan influence.

„ 4. **Ante-fix from temple of the Apollo Epicurius near Phigaleia in Arcadia** (Mauch, Archit. Ordn.). This ornament is beautifully sculptured in marble. (See Fig. 2.)

„ 5. **Acroterium of the pediment of the temple on the island of Aegina** (Mauch, Archit. Ordn.). See Fig. 1.

„ 6. **Profile of the capital from the same temple** (Mauch, Archit. Ordn.). See Fig. 1.

„ 7. **Under surface of the corona from the Parthenon in Athens** (Mauch, Archit. Ordn.).

„ 8. **Ante-fix from the Parthenon in Athens** (Mauch, Archit. Ordn.).

„ 9. **Capital found in Paestum** (Mauch, Archit. Ordn.). This capital shows undoubted evidences of Etruscan influence.

„ 10. **Anta-capital in Athens** (Mauch, Archit. Ordn.). The cymatium of this capital is painted with the foil peculiar to the ancient Doric Anta capitals.

„ 11. **Anta-capital from the temple of Nemesis in Rhamnus** (Mauch, Archit. Ordn.).

„ 12. **Doric cymatium** (Lübke; Kunst des Altertums).

Plate 19.

Ornamental Mouldings.

(From Uhde, Architekturformen des klassischen Altertums.)

Fig. 1—5. **Ancient Bead and reel.**

„ 6—8. **Ogees from the Ptolemeion.**

„ 9, and 10. **Ogees from the Erechtheion.**

„ 11. **Painted Ogees from the Theseum Athens.**

„ 12, and 13. **Painted Ogees from the Propylaea.**

„ 14. **Ogee from Mausoleum at Halicarnassus.**

Plate 20.

Ionic Ornament.

(From Mauch, Architektonische Ordnungen.)

Fig. 1, 2, 4, and 5. **Pilaster-capitals from the cella of the temple of Apollo Didymaeus near Miletus.** Fig. 1 shows the front view of half such an Ionian capital, and fig. 5, the side view. Figs. 2 and 4 are ornaments of the space between other capitals with the same cella.

„ 3, 8, 9, and 12. **Angle columns from the temple of Minerva Polias at Priene.** This temple is one of the most beautiful examples of Ionian architecture. Fig. 8 is the section of the column at the neck, with the capital, seen from below. Fig. 9 is the pedestal with four-cornered plinth. This description of base is rare, being found only in the Ionic column. Fig. 12 shows the ornament on the under side of the cornice. Details as to the helicoid of the Ionic capital will be found in "Speltz, Säulenform der Schneckenlinie des jonischen Kapitäls".

„ 6. **Capital and plan from the temple of Apollo Didymaeus near Miletus.**

„ 7. **Capital of the central column of the temple of Minerva Polias in Priene, with plan.**

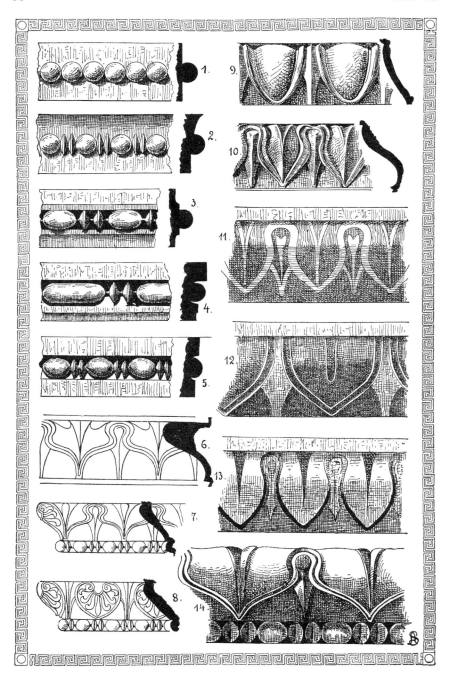

Plate 20. GREEK ORNAMENT. 51

Fig. 10. Capital from the aqueduct of Hadrian at Athens, with plan.
„ 11. Ornament between the Capitals in the cella of the temple of Apollo Didymaeus near Miletus.
„ 13. Side-view of a capital in the Propylaeum of the temple of Minerva Polias at Priene.
„ 14, and 15. Side and front-views of a pilaster-capital at Priene.

Plate 21.

Ionic Ornament.

Fig. 1, and 4. Capitals and pedestals of columns in the Temple of Minerva Polias at Athens (Mauch).

In the Acropolis at Athens were erected numerous buildings of which the Parthenon and the Erechtheion were the most important. The columns in the latter, with their energetic, double-fluted volutes, the braided torus over the echinus, the latter being visible in its entire round, the finely moulded cushion, and the delicately ornamented neck, display structure of the purest and most refined style.

Instead of the Sanctuary which formerly stood here, and was destroyed during the Persian war, the Erechtheion was erected, but was not completed until after the year 409 B. C. In the back wall of the North Portico, was the celebrated beautiful door, details of which are given in Figs. 3, 6, and 7. At the west end o the south side is the Caryatide Portico. This Portico, which is covered with marble tiles, is carried on 6 supports, called Caryatides (Fig. 10). They probably represent Pan-Athenaic virgins. The entablature over these figures has no frieze.

„ 2. Pilaster-capital from the hexastyle or Eastern portico of the Erechtheion, Athens (Mauch).
„ 3, 6, and 7. Details from the door of the Erechtheion in Athens (Mauch).
„ 5. Capital from the interior of the Temple of Apollo at Bassae, near Phigaleia (Mauch).
„ 8. Capital from the temple of Neandria (Lübke).
„ 9, 11, and 12. Grecian antefix of the time of Pericles (Libonis).
„ 10. Caryatid of the Erechtheion at Athens (Mauch).
„ 13, and 14. Capital and anta from the temple of Minerva Polias at Athens (Mauch).
„ 15, and 16. Grecian coins (Lübke).

Plate 22.

Corinthian Ornament.

Fig. 1. Capital of temple at Patara (Semper).
„ 2. Capital from the Tower of the Winds in Athens (Mauch).

This Corinthian capital, which is of the simplest kind, has been found with but very slight changes all over Greece. It was even employed in Byzanthine architecture.

„ 3. Capital and entablatures from the monument of Lysicrates at Athens (Mauch).

This tower-like structure, which dates from the year 334 B. C., is built of Pentelic marble, and is still in existence although in a very damaged condition. A six-columned circular pseudo-peripteral, rests on a substructure built in the form of a podium. On the roof are three caulicoloe (Plate 23, Fig. 11) with central finial

Plate 23. GREEK ORNAMENT. 55

or crest (Plate 22, Fig. 9 and 10). This crest, which is of one piece, is one of the most wonderful examples of Greek sculpture. The three wide projecting scrolls of the same were at one time supported by consoles, but these have now entirely disappeared. The capital approaches more to the real Corinthian capital than that of the Tower of the Winds.

Fig. 4. **Capital of a column from the ruins of the temple of Apollo near Miletus** (Mauch).

" 5. **Upper part of the Tower of the Winds in Athens** (Mauch).

This is an octagonal tower of Pentelic marble, on the sides of which, under the cornice, the figures of the eight winds are shown in relief. On the pyramidal top of the roof was a brazen Triton which served as a weather-cock. The tower itself contained a clepsydra or water clock.

" 6. **Base of a column of the Lysicrates monument at Athens** (Mauch) (Fig. 3).

" 7. **Capital of portico of the Temple of Jupiter Olympius at Athens** (Mauch).

" 8. **Pilaster capital from Paestum** (Mauch).

" 9. **Upper part of the Lysicrates monument in Athens** (Mauch) (Fig. 3).

" 10. **Crest of the same monument** (Mauch) (Fig. 3).

" 11. **Plan of the capital in Fig. 3.**

" 12. **Capital at Eleusis** (Mauch).

Plate 23.

Fig. 1. **Terra-cottas from Olympia** (Bötticher, Olympia).

" 2. **Frieze from a portico on the island of Delos, built at the time of Philip of Macedon 346—337 B. C.** (Uhde).

" 3. **Mosaic flooring in the Temple of Zeus at Olympia** (Graul).

" 4. **Lion from the tomb of Mausolus, in the British Museum** (Roger-Milès).

" 5. **Bronze plate, representing the dispute on the tripod** (Roger-Milès).

" 6, and 7. **Fragments of a Grecian frieze in the Villa Albani in Rome** (Tatham).

" 8, and 9. **Columns from portico on the island of Delos, front and side views** (Uhde).

" 10. **Head of Zeus in bronze from Olympia** (Lübke).

" 11. **Roof of the monument of Lysicrates in Athens** (Mauch). See Plate 21, Figs. 3, 6, 9, and 10.

" 12. **Painted clay antefix** (Reichhold).

Plate 24.

(From C. Thierry, Classische Ornamente.)

Fig. 1, and 3. **Bas-reliefs** from the Kircher's Museum, Karlsruhe.

" 2. **Bas-reliefs** from the National Museum, Karlsruhe.

Plate 25.

Fig. 1. **Bas-reliefs suggesting** oriental influence (Thierry).

" 2. **Marble ornament** from Branchidae (Thierry).

" 3. **Marble bas-relief** in the Villa Poniatowsky in Roma (Thierry).

" 4. **Painted terra cotta dish** (Dolmetsch).

" 5. **Marble seat or throne** (Thierry).

Plate 26.

GREEK ORNAMENT.

Plate 26.

Principal examples of the Grecian Vase from Baumeister.

The principal centres of pre-historic ceramics was in Troy and in the islands of Cyprus and Mytilene.

The real Grecian ceramics are distinguished as follows:

1. Vessels of the geometric style (about 1000—700 B. C.), which have been discovered principally near the Dipylon Gate in Athens, hence the title Dipylon Style. The colouring is dark-brown on yellow clay.

2. Vessels showing Oriental influences, dating from the 8th to the 6th century B. C., the principal centre being in Corinth.

3. Attic black-coloured vessels which were developed in Athens from the 6th century B. C. downwards, the clay is red.

4. Red-coloured vessels which were developed from the fore-going style in the fifth century B. C., the entire vessel being painted over with black varnish, thus enabling red figures to be made on a black ground. The ceramic art entirely disappeared from Greece about the year 300 B. C., being afterwards revived in Lucania, Campania, and Apulia.

Fig. 1. **Vase from the island of Mytilene,** dating from the beginning of the last millenium, B. C. The surface is gray, painted of a dull brown.

„ 2. **Vase, lacquered, from the Greek Islands,** of Mycaenean origin.

„ 3. **Athenian vase** from the 7th century B. C.

„ 4. **Phaleronian jug from Attica,** found in grave near Phaleron.

„ 5. **Attic amphora** from the 7th century B. C.

„ 6. **Vase of later date from the island of Rhodes.**

„ 7. **Corinthian vase.**

„ 8. **Chaldaean vase.**

„ 9. **Vase of Gamedes from Boeotia.**

„ 10. **Vase on three feet, Boeotia.**

„ 11. **Attic Amphora.**

„ 12. **Black figured Amphora, Athens.**

„ 13. **Attic Oinochoe.**

„ 14. **Attic Kylix.**

„ 15. **Amphora by Nicosthenes.**

„ 16. **Krater or mixing bowl for wine.**

„ 17. **Pyxis or toilet box.**

Plate 27.

Frescoes and Vase-painting.

Fig. 1, 3, 5—7, 9—12, 20, 26—28, 33, 35, 36, 39, 41—43. **Greek vase paintings** (Libonis, Reichhold, Meyer).

„ 2, 4, 13—16, 21—25, 34, 38. **Fret-work fillets, principally from Greek vases** (Meyer, Reichhold).

„ 8. **Team of carriage horses** from the older Grecian period, from a black figured vase (Gerhard, Äusserliche Vasenbildung).

„ 17. **Grecian war-ship** from a vase-painting (Baumeister).

„ 18, 30—32, 39. **Coffer-work from the ceiling of the Propylaea in Athens** (Meyer).

„ 19. **Vase-painting, Ceramic work from the Grecian islands** (Reichhold).

„ 29. **Ornamental work on the ears of a Greek vase** (Reichhold).

„ 37. **Ornamental work on the neck of a Greek hydria** (L'art pour Tous).

„ 40. **Ornamentation of a coffered work ceiling from the Parthenon, Athens** (Meyer).

Plate 28.

Fig. 1. **Grecian mirror** (Reichhold). This is given as an Etruscan mirror, bout it would perhaps be more correct to consider it as having been produced in Greece.

„ 2. **Female apparel dating from the time when Greece stood at its highest splendour** (Reichhold)

„ 3, and 17. **Furniture inlay from the Greek colonies in the Crimea** (Semper).

„ 4. **Marble chair of state** (Baumeister).

„ 5. **Bronze leg of an arm chair** (Reichhold).

„ 6, 10, 16, 18. **Chairs** (Racinet and Baumeister).

„ 7. **Bronze tripod from he geometrical ornament period** (Reichhold).

„ 8. **Fans** (Racinet).

„ 9. **Kylix or dish found near Kertsch** with engravings showing the furniture of Greek lady's boudoir (Antiq. d. Bosph., Cymm.).

„ 11—13. **Lyres** (Racinet).

„ 14. **Drinking-horn** (Racinet).

„ 15. **Small table** (Racinet).

„ 19. **Marble arm-chair** (Dörpfeld and Reich, Theater).

„ 20. **Couch with table** after copy from the Industrial Art Museum in Dresden.

Plate 29.

Fig. 1. **Helmet from Samnium** (Baumeister).

„ 2, and 6. **Helmets of gladiators** (Baumeister).

„ 3, and 4. **Relief, arms and armour** (Baumeister).

„ 5. **Dagger** (Baumeister).

„ 7. **Iron helmet** (Baumeister).

„ 8. **Bronze figure from a carriage-pole,** in the Museum Dutuit, Paris.

„ 9. **Relief, weapons, from Pergamon** (Baumeister).

„ 10. **Iron helmet with silver ear-laps** (Baumeister).

„ 11. **Bronze greaves** (Baumeister).

„ 12. **Bronze shield** (Libonis).

„ 13. **Helmet from the time of Homer** (Racinet).

„ 14. **Bronze tripod from Metapontum** (Reichhold).

„ 15. **Bronze handle of a looking-glass,** from the Dutuit Museum, Paris.

„ 16. **Spear-head** (Baumeister).

„ 17. **Coins stamped with the Olympian Zeus, from Elis** (Lübke).

„ 18. **Fragment of statue of a woman, from the Acropolis in Athens** (Lübke).

„ 19. **Stele of Aristion by Aristocles, Athens** (Lübke).

„ 20, and 21. **Arrow heads** (Baumeister).

„ 22, and 23. **Theatre masks for men and women** (Baumeister).

„ 24. **Box, from a vase-painting** (Gerhard, etruskische Spiegel).

Plate 30.   GREEK ORNAMENT.
                                                                    65

Plate 30.

Fig. 1—5, and 8. **Ornaments** (Libonis).

„　　6, and 7. **Foot-gear** (Renard).

„　　9. **Cymbals** (Renard).

„　10. **Gold belt-clasps** (Libonis).

„　11. **Tambourine** (Renard).

„　12, and 13. **Sacrificial knives** (Renard).

„　14. **Sunshade** (Baumeister).

„　15. **Girl with embroidery-frame** (Baumeister).

„　16, 17, 21, and 22. **Coiffures with ornamentation** (Racinet).

„　18. **Torch** (Renard).

„　19. **Horse-bridle** (Racinet).

„　20, and 23. **Necklaces** (Havard). The first is considered by some to be Etruscan work, it is, however, in all probability Grecian.

„　24. **Silver vase with relief in gilt** (Havard).

Greco-Phoenician Bust.
(L'Art pour tous.)

ETRUSCAN ORNAMENT.

Scene of a banquet
(Martha, l'Art Étrusque).

Etruscan was the name given to a people who lived in what is now called Tuscany at the time when Rome was founded. It is impossible to trace the origin of their descent, but it appears as if they had wandered down from the north east and took forcible possession of the country about the twelfth century, B. C. in which they afterwards settled and which was inhabited by Samnites, Umbrians, Pelasgian and other races. The period of the highest development of the Etruscans dates from 800 to 400 B. C. They were subjugated by the Romans, after which they gradually disappear from history, the only traces of their once having existed being some few architectural monuments, chiefly tombs, which have come down to us. Although the monuments left behind by the Etruscans show most decided traces of Grecian influence, still, the hypothesis that the Etruscans were of Grecian origin cannot be accepted on that account. The racial differences between them and the Grecians were so marked, they were so totally different in their physical constitution from the latter, that it is impossible to regard the Etruscans as of Hellenic origin. It is possible that in their wanderings towards Italy they came into intimate contact with the Grecians, and thus brought with them the elements of Grecian art into their adopted country. Their art was in all probability subject to influences proceeding from Phoenicia and Carthage, but more especially to ancient Ionic influence. They understood, however, how to change all these influences in such a way as to give them the stamp of their own national art.

At the period of their subjugation by the Romans, the Etruscans had brought their own art to such a high state of development that it was able to exercise an influence by no means small on the development of Roman art which was at that time in its infancy. Roman art came afterwards, of course, entirely under the influence of Grecian art.

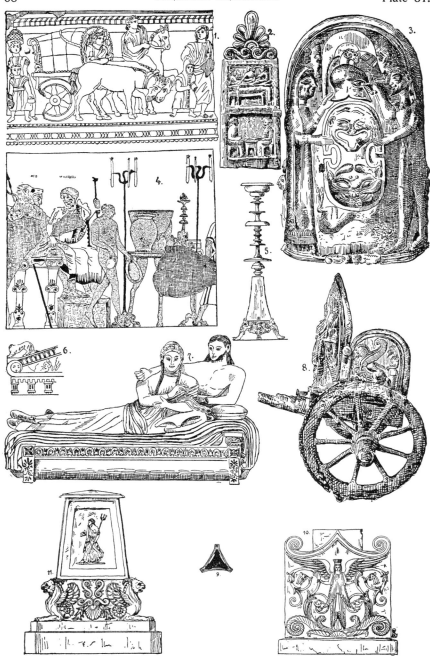

Plate 31.

Fig. 1. **Relief, travelling-carriage** (Baumeister).
„ 2. **Antefix of a tomb** (Martha).
„ 3, and 8. **Etruscan bigas with bronze casing.** These were found in Norchia and purchased by the Metropolitan Museum in New York.
„ 4. **Etruscan frescoes** (Martha).
„ 5. **Bronze candelabrum** (Martha).
„ 6. **From the facade of a tomb in Norchia** (Lübke).
„ 7. **Clay sarcophagus from Cervetri,** in the Louvre (Lübke).
„ 9, and 11. **Marble altar** from the collection in the Villa Borghese near Rome (Tatham).
„ 10. **Terra-cotta altar** (Tatham).

Plate 32.

Fig. 1, and 6. **Swords** (Baumeister).
„ 2, and 5. **Helmets** (Libonis).
„ 3. **Link for the handle of a bucket.** 6th century B. C. (Reichhold).
„ 4, 16, 17, 19, 20, 22, and 25. **Ornaments** (Libonis).
„ 7, 12, and 14. **Greaves** (Libonis).
„ 8. **Fibula** (Libonis).
„ 9. **Fighting warriors** (Racinet).
„ 10. **Etruscan peasant** (Racinet).
„ 11. **Razor** (Libonis).
„ 13. **Etruscan mirror** in the numismatic collection in Paris (Gerhard, Etruskische Spiegel). This is considered by some to be Grecian work.
„ 15. **Tripod** (Reichhold).
„ 18. **Tripod** (Martha, l'Art Étrusque).
„ 21. **Dagger** (Baumeister).
„ 23. **Heating-stove** (Martha).
„ 24. **Antique bronze cist** (Gerhard).
„ 26. **Spear-head** (Baumeister).

Etruscan tomb in Cervetri (Renard).

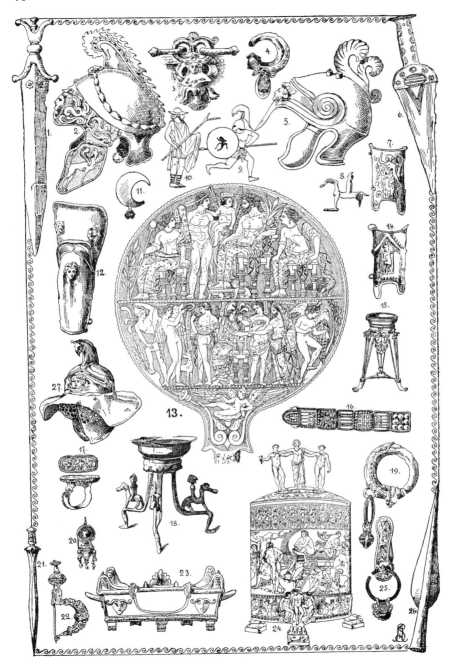

ROMAN ORNAMENT.

ith their art the Greeks conquered the world, the Romans with their politics and their legions. The whole civilized world at the present day is striving to emulate the works of art of the former, the laws of the latter are considered throughout the world as the foundation upon which all laws must be established. In these facts lie the difference in character between the two peoples. Those Romans who lived at the beginning of Roman history were unable to develop an independent art of their own, for all their endeavours were directed to amassing wealth, and increasing their lands. They were obliged therefore to take the motifs for their art from Etruria and continued to do so until Grecian art became predominant. Becoming more accustomed to luxury from the conquests which they made, the Roman began gradually to form a national art of their own under the guidance of Greek teachers. The practical spirit of the Romans and their taste for monumental work are naturally to be seen best exemplified in their architecture, a science in which they have performed most magnificent work especially in connection with the monumental development of temples, basilicas, thermae, theatres, etc. The Romans furthermore took up and accomplished the task of combining numerous elements in a homogeneous whole, and of developing them further. In this latter art they became the teachers of future generations. The Romans adopted the three columnar Orders of the Greeks retaining however at the same time the Etruscan column. To these four orders they added the Composite Order.

Besides bringing architecture to a high state of development, the Romans also succeeded in bringing the art of sculpture to a great degree of perfection.

In this latter, however, they had the assistance of Greek artists. The manner, however, in which the Romans enriched their ornament was detrimental to the characteristic Greek outlines, and the insatiable luxury predominating during the time of the Caesars finally destroyed completely the exquisite harmony of Greek art—the form was entirely overgrown by the ornament. The art of mosaic work, which had its origin in the Orient, was brought to its highest perfection by the Romans, all the old Roman mosaics now in our possession prove this beyond any question.

The fall of the Roman Empire, and the victory of Christianity, marked also the decline and fall of classic art, for this art could no longer appeal to those Christian barbarians who now poured into the country from all sides. The eastern Roman Christian Empire exercised a very great influence on the development of a new art amongst the Christian States which rose from the ruins of the Western Roman Empire.

From the so-called Early Christian and Byzantine Style shortly afterwards developed, the Romanesque Style which from the 9th to the 12th centuries spread through all the newly constituted States.

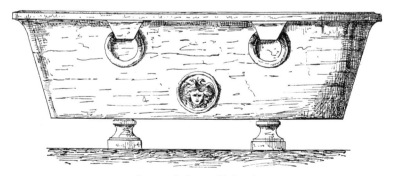

Roman Labrum (Tatham).

Plate 33.

ROMAN ORNAMENT.

Plate 33.

Fig. 1, 4, 9, 19. **Capitals and entablatures of the Doric Order, found in Albano, near Rome** (Mauch). It appears as if Vignola organised his Doric Order according to this fragment. The entablature produces a specially fine effect by means of the under aspect of the corona soffit, Fig. 19. There are two fascias to the architrave, the upper one projecting infront of the lower. Figure 4 gives a view of the capital seen from below, and Fig. 9, the base of the column.

„ 2, 5, 17. **Doric Capitals and entablatures from the Thermae of Diocletian** (Mauch) which were erected about 300 B. C. The delicate profile of the cornice, the decorated members, and the fretwork denticulations in meander form, belong really more to the Ionic order. Figure 5 shows the capital seen from below, and Fig. 17, the soffit of the corona.

„ 3. **From a white marble altar in the Vatican Museum** (Tatham).

„ 6, 18. **From a white marble altar in the Museum of the Capitol in Rome** (Tatham).

„ 7, 8, 10, 11, 13, 14. **Foil for cyma** (Mauch).

„ 12. **Bead-moulding** (Mauch).

„ 15. **Arch with rustication from the Amphitheatre in Pola.** Completed 150 A. D. (Uhde).

„ 16. **Frieze ornament** (Tatham).

Plate 34.

Fig. 1, 2, 5. **Square angle pier with principal cornice from the Thermae of Diocletian in Rome** (Mauch). This pier, which is of the Ionic order, and was placed on an angle, is an example of the questionable inconsistency of employing the capital of a column on a square pier. This is seen in the fact that the echinus, which is rounded above, is forced, below, together with the astragal, to sink into the straight lines of the body of the column. The Frieze is pulvinated, a form often used by the Romans. Figure 2 shows the base of the pilaster, and Fig. 5 a view of the capital seen from below.

„ 3, 4, 6. **Columns and entablatures from the temple of Fortuna Virilis in Rome** (Mauch). This temple was Tetrastyle Pseudo-peripteral with a portico two inter-columniations deep. Its erection took place towards the close of the Republic. The entablature is by no means free from objections, for, besides other errors, the bed moulding is heavy, the frieze and the architrave poor. Figure 3 shows the base of the column, and Fig. 6, the capital seen from below.

„ 7. **Column in the court of saint Hieronymus in Rome** (Piranesi).

„ 8. **Capital of a house on the Bridge of Gratianus in Rome** (Piranesi).

„ 9. **Capital from the temple of Procedis** (Piranesi).

„ 10. **Capital from the basilica of San Clemente** (Piranesi).

„ 11. **Capital from a house in Rome** (Piranesi).

„ 12. **Capital from the Palace Pionetti in Rome** (Piranesi).

„ 13. **Capital from the temple of Priscae in Rome** (Piranesi).

„ 14. **Capital of a column in the Villa Negronia in Rome** (Piranesi).

Plate 35.

Fig. 1. Soffit of the corona from the temple of Castor in the Forum Romanum (Mauch).

„   2, 10, 11, 12. Capitals and entablatures from the interior of the Pantheon in Rome (Mauch).

This building is still well preserved it was built by Hadrian 124 A. D. on the north side of the Thermae of Agrippa. Figure 10 gives a view of the capital from below, Figure 11, the base of the column, and Fig. 12 an under view of the corona.

„   3. Fragment from the Villa Borghese in Rome (Piranesi).

„   4, 5, 7. Fragments found near S. Gregorius (Mauch).

„   6. Fragment from the Villa Albani (Piranesi).

„   8. Fragment from the Villa Borghese (Piranesi).

„   9. Capital from the temple of Castor in the Forum Romanum (Mauch).

Plate 36.

Fig. 1, 6. Capitals and entablatures from the arch of Septimius Severus in Rome (Mauch).

This is an example of the composite order. Figure 6 is a view of the Capital from below.

„   2. From a Roman sacrificial altar (Piranesi).

Marble Fragment from Rome (Tatham).

Plate 37.   ROMAN ORNAMENT.   79

Fig. 3, 4, 7, 8. **Base, capital, and entablature from the Temple of Vesta in Tivoli** (Mauch).

This temple was circular and peripteral with 18 columns, 10 of which are still in good condition. The columns are not perpendicular but inclined to the axis in such a manner that the inner lines on the tapering shaft receive almost a vertical direction, thus increasing not only the apparent but the real stability of the whole. In order to produce this effect, the fillets under the base and above the capital are somewhat wedge-shaped. The capital, which differs in form from the usual normal capital of the Corinthian order, has a very pleasing shape with a large central-flower between the volutes. The leaves also bear more resemblance to the curled cabbage rather than to the acanthus. Figure 4 shows a section through the corners of the capital and one at the roots of the leaves. Figure 7 gives an oblique view of the capital. The base on podium in Fig. 8 has no plinth, possibly on account of the circular form in which it is constructed. The frieze is most effective being decorated in a naturalistic manner with ox head, rosettes, festoons, and patera, instead of the usual ox-skull.

„   5. **Roman egg and dart moulding** (Mauch).

Plate 37.

Fig. 1 and 8. **Pedestals from the Villa of Cardinal Alexander Albani before the Solarian Gate in Rome** (Piranesi. The remaining examples are all from the same authority.)

„   2. **Base from the Villa Barberini.**
„   3. **Base from the Temple of Nero.**
„   4. **Base from the Mausoleum of Augustus.**
„   5. **Capital from the Villa Farnese.**
„   6. **Base from the Church of S. S. Quattro Coronati.**
„   7. **Base from the Basilica of S. Bartolomeo all' Isola.**
„   9. **Pedestal from the Church of S. Prassede.**

Plate 38.

Fig. 1, 5. **Pilasters of veined marble in the cloister of the Convent of Ara coeli near Rome** (Tatham).

„   2. **Fasces from a bas-relief in the Massimi Palace in Rome** (Tatham).
„   3. **Ancient marble altar from the collection in the Villa Borghese in Rome** (Tatham).
„   4. **Fasces from a bas-relief in the Capitol** (Tatham).
„   6. **Fragment of an antique frieze found in Tivoli** (Tatham).
„   7. **Fragment of a frieze in high-relief from the Villa Aldobrandini in Rome** (Tatham).

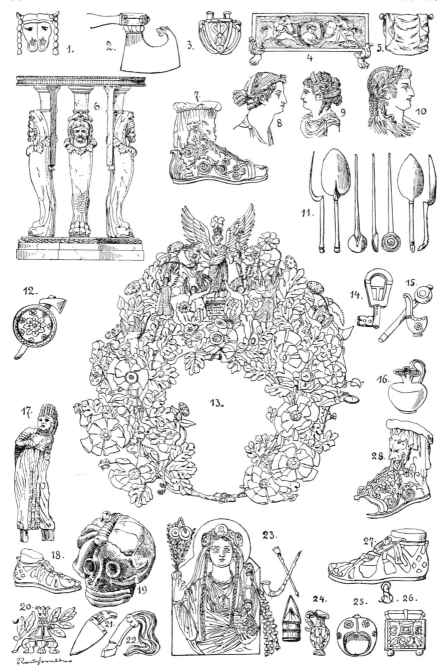

Plate 39.
Roman Chairs and Seats after Tatham.

Fig. 1. White marble arm-chair from Rome.
„ 2, 4. Foot of a white marble sarcophagus in the Vatican Collection. Front and profile.
„ 3. Half of a green marble tripod from the Vatican Collection.
„ 5, 8. Ancient bronze arm-chairs from the Museum in Portici. The covering is modern. Front and profile.
„ 6. Ancient marble stool from Rome.
„ 7, 9. Ancient bronze stools from Rome. Front and profile.
„ 10, 11. Chairs of state in white marble from the Vatican Collection. Front and profile.

Plate 40.
Roman Sculptures after Piranesi.

Fig. 1. Marble tripod in the Capitol Museum at Rome.
„ 2. Marble vase in the Farnese Palace.
„ 3. Terra-cotta vase in the Vatican Library. The chimerical figure has reference to human life.
„ 4. Marble candelabrum in the Piranesi Museum.
„ 5, 6. Marble vases from the Villa of Hadrian.

Plate 41.

Fig. 1. Skull Ornament (Baumeister).
„ 2. Copper axe (Racinet).
„ 3. Sheath for the sacrificial knife (Baumeister).
„ 4. Incense box (Racinet).
„ 5. Handkerchief of the sacrificer (Baumeister).
„ 6. Marble table from Rome (Tatham).
„ 7, 18, 27, 28. Ancient foot-gear (Racinet).
„ 8, 9, 10. Female coiffures (Racinet).
„ 11. Silver spoons (Baumeister).
„ 12. Sacrificial axe (Baumeister).
„ 13. Memorial wreath of gold plate, from Lower Italy (Baumeister).
„ 14. Key (Racinet).
„ 15. Priest's ladle (Baumeister).
„ 16. Wine-jug of clay used in religious rites (Racinet).
„ 17. Ivory figure of an actor (Baumeister).
„ 19. Weight in form of skull (Dutuit).
„ 20. Fumigating altar (Baumeister).
„ 21. Sacrificial knife (Baumeister).
„ 22. Sprinkler (Baumeister).
„ 23. Priests of Cybele in full canonicals with sacrificial implements (Baumeister).
„ 24. Wine-jug for use in sacrifice (Baumeister).
„ 25. Priest's mask (Baumeister).
„ 26. Incense-box for use in sacrifice (Baumeister).

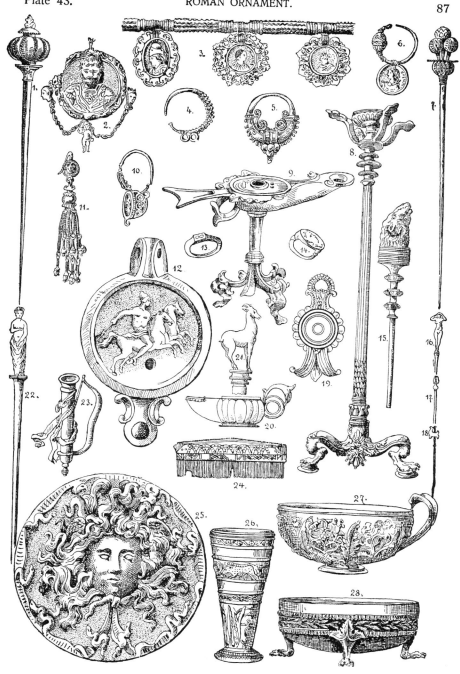

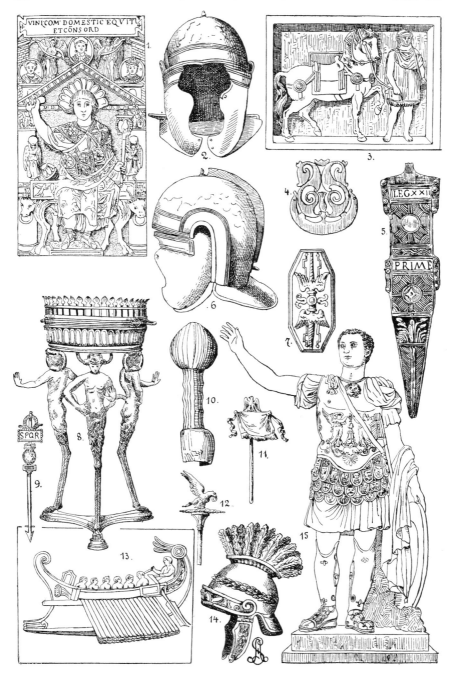

Plate 42.

Fig. 1. Marble candelabrum (Canina).
„ 2, 6. Marble table (Canina).
„ 3. Fragment of a bronze candelabrum from Naples (Libonis).
„ 4. Silver dish found in the silver discoveries in Hildesheim (Havard).
„ 5. Marble candelabra (Canina).
„ 7. Roman scales (Dutuit).
„ 8. Roman satyr (Baumeister).
„ 9. Amulet with head of Mercury (Dutuit).
„ 10. Roman sedan chair (Baumeister).
„ 11. Portrait of Julia, daughter of Titus ⎫
„ 12. Portrait of Augustus ⎬ on Cameos, found in Florence (Libonis).
„ 13. Clay oil-lamps (Libonis).
„ 14. Bronze toilet-vase (Dutuit).
„ 15. Roman coins 1 As (Baumeister).
„ 16, 19, 21. Silver forks (Baumeister).
„ 17. Vase in chased silver (Martha, Manuel d'archéologie Etrusque et Romaine).
„ 18. Bronze from Naples showing Hercules fighting with the snakes (Baumeister).
„ 20. Bronze wine-jug (Baumeister).

Plate 43.

Fig. 1, 7, 15. Hair pins (Libonis).
„ 2. Medallion with picture of Hercules (Libonis).
„ 3. Massive gold necklace (Libonis).
„ 4—6, 10, 11. Ear-rings (Libonis).
„ 8. Bronze candelabrum from Naples (Libonis).
„ 9. Bronze lamp in the Louvre (Libonis).
„ 12. Terra-cotta lamp (Libonis).
„ 13, 14. Rings (Renard).
„ 16—18, 22. Pins (Renard).
„ 20. Needle (Renard).
„ 23. Quiver with bow (Renard).
„ 24. Bronze comb in the Mayence Museum (Renard).
„ 25, Head of Medusa (Libonis).
„ 26, 27, 28. Silver vessels discovered in Hildesheim (Havard).

Plate 44.

Fig. 1. Costume of a Consul from the later period (Baumeister).
„ 2, 6. A Roman helmet found in Germany (Baumeister).
„ 3. Relief from the Mayence Museum showing a rider leading his horse (Baumeister).
„ 4. Bronze ribbon brooch or clasp (Lindenschmitt).

Fig. 5. **Iron dagger-sheath in the Mayence Museum** (Baumeister).
„   7. **Shield** (Renard).
„   8. **Bronze tripod from Naples** (Libonis).
„   9, 11, 12. **Roman military badges** (Raciner).
„ 10. **Ivovy sword-pommel** (Baumeister).
„ 13. **Bas-relief from Puteoli, showing a Trireme** (Baumeister).
„ 14. **Helmet of a Centurion** (Libonis).
„ 15. **Marble statue of Titus in State armour, in the Louvre** (Baumeister).

Ancient Chimaera in white Marble, Rome
(Tatham).

POMPEIAN ORNAMENT.

n the neighbourhood of Mount Vesuvius on the Bay of Naples stood the cities of Pompeii, Herculaneum and Stabiä. These three cities were destroyed by an eruption of Vesuvius in the year 79 A. D., and were so thoroughly and completely buried that for centuries no trace of where they stood could be found. Their position was, however, accidentally discovered in the year 1748. The city of Pompeii became subject to the Romans in the 4th century B. C., and, having been thoroughly Romanised, grew to be the favourite summer residence of the wealthier classes. The characteristic tendency of the Romans towards luxury soon made Pompeii a special centre, Greek artists were introduced, style was given to classic art, and, finally, a special Pompeian Style grew into existence. The small arts and work in metal were brought to a very high state of perfection. The remains of objects of this class at present preserved in the museum at Naples, more especially those vessels found in the silver discoveries in Boscoreale, are extremely beautiful and worthy of the highest admiration.

Peculiarly characteristic of Pompeian art are the mural paintings and the coloured stucco ornamentation. Similar work might of course have also existed in other Roman cities, all traces having disappeared in the course of time. Four distinct and regularly consecutive periods can be distinguished in these mural paintings, the incrustation style, already used in Hellenic-Oriental art, consisting of imitations of many-coloured marble ashlar-work combined with ornament worked in stucco. After this came the pictorial architectural style which consisted in exhibiting, in perspective, on smooth surfaces, paintings of fantastic architectural pictures. The wall was divided into panels in free ornamental style and decorated with small figurative centre pictures. The type which appears to have been in most general use was the prospect style, here, the straight wall, was so changed by a rich play of delicate stone architecture that the chamber had the appearance of being larger than it really was. These types, as far as their collective arrangement goes, show decided leaning towards Hellenic proto-types from Alexandria, at the same time, however, very many single Ornaments show, in their pure naturalistic style, very great artistic independence. Although the al fresco mural paintings, which were coloured by simple hand-workers, are of a most dazzling brillancy of colour, still, the gradations are toned off so regularly and legitimately that the effect of the whole is soothing and pleasing to the eye. This style of art was, in all probability, well known to a large circle.

It is impossible to form an exact picture of Roman life in any Roman city, but this is more especially the case with Pompeii which was completely over-whelmed in one night. It is impossible also to differentiate exactly Pompeian from Rom art, for it is highly probable that many objects discovered in Pompeii were manufactured in other parts of the Empire, and that other articles disco-vered in various other cities had their origin in Pompeii.

Plate 45.

Fig. 1. **Column from the house of the Tragic poet in Pompeii** (Uhde).
„ 2. **Mural ornamentation from the house of M. Lucretius in Pompeii** (Uhde).
„ 3. **Mural ornamentation from the house of Modestus in Pompeii** (Uhde).
„ 4, 6. **Capitals from the basilica in Pompeii** (Uhde).
„ 5, 7. **Pilastercapital, and column from the house of the Colours in Pompeii** (Uhde).
„ 8. **Capital from the house of the Faun in Pompeii** (Uhde).
„ 9. **Capital of column from the house of Actaeon in Pompeii** (Uhde).
„ 10. **Podium from the tomb of Naevoleia Tyche in Pompeii** (Uhde).

Plate 46.

Fig. 1. **Mosaic from Pompeii, showing a theatrical scene** (Libonis).
„ 2. **Mural frescoes from Pompeii** (Reichhold).
„ 3, 6, 8. **Mosaic floors** (d'Espouy).
„ 4. **Mural fresco, the holy marriage of Zeus and Hera** (Baumeister).
„ 5. **From a mural fresco, illustrating Mediation** (Roux ainé).
„ 7. **Mural fresco with theatrical mask** (Baumeister).

Plate 45.   POMPEIAN ORNAMENT.   93

Plate 47. POMPEIAN ORNAMENT. 95

Plate 47.

Fig. 1. Marble table from the house of Cornelius Rufus in Pompeii (Bühlmann, die Bauformenlehre).
,, 2, 3, 4, 7. Vessels in embossed silver from the discoveries of Boscorcale (Libonis).
,, 5. Bronze table in the Museum at Naples (Buhlmann).
,, 6. Bronze candelabrum (Libonis).
,, 8, 9, 10, 16. Ornaments (Lübke).
,, 11. Bronze figure of a Triton (Collection Dutuit).
,, 12. Lamp (Collection Dutuit).
,, 13. Pompeian glass vase (Libonis).
,, 14, 15, 17. Bronze tripods (Lübke).

Plate 48.

Fig. 1—5, 9, 16, 20, 21. From Pompeian mural frescoes (Roux ainé).
., 6, 7, 8, 10, 11, 18, 19. Bronze candelabra (Mauch).
,, 12, 13, 15, 17. From Pompeian mural frescoes (Reichhold).
,, 14. Later Sphinx of bronze (Baumeister).

Plate 49.

Fig. 1—10. Various mural frescoes in Pompeii (Roux ainé, Herculanum et Pompeii).

Figure of bronze (Roux ainé).

CELTIC ORNAMENT
(FRANCE AND GERMANY)

Frankish Warrior
(Hottenroth).

oubts no longer exist as to the fact that before they came into contact with the Romans, the Celts and Germans had their own characteristic national art, even, although the same had not advanced beyond the bronze and iron periods. It is difficult to strictly separate Celtic from Germanic ornament, the connections between the two races were so varied and so intimate, that what was characteristic of the one was transplanted to the other. The Celts, who had occupied the whole of Europe, were after a time driven out from Germany and Austria by the Germans, there must have been therefore ample opportunity, before the Romans came into contact with the Germans, for Celtic and Germanic art to exercise mutual and abiding influence on each other. The Romans became, afterwards, the instructors of both in ornamentation, and under the influence of Roman art, Celtic and Germanic art came closer to each other, the relationship developing into a most intimate connection at that period when the Germans held possession of the Western Empire of the Romans.

After the fall of the Roman Empire, Byzantine influence predominated, and as the Roman style became developed, a new art period made itself manifest. Pure Celtic ornament, far purer than in France, existed in the British Islands up into the 12th century. This part of the subject, however, is dealt with in the next chapter, although it would be perhaps more correct chronologically to refer to it in treating of the art of the Middle Ages.

Germanic Ornament was entirely confined to the decoration of weapons and useful articles. Nothing was known of architecture, not even of architecture in wood, even rites and ceremonies were never held within doors, but in the open air under a tree.

In their first attempts at architecture, which were made soon after the introduction of Christianity, the Celtic artists confined themselves almost entirely to the building of wooden churches and oratories. All their splendid triumphs as seen in the development of the Celtic Church Architecture were achieved a few centuries later.

Gallic Warrior (Racinet).

Plate 50.

Fig. 1, and 3. **Breton embroidery from Pont l'Abbé, Finisterre** (Racinet).
„ 2. **Bronze ornament,** found in Castel near Agen, in the Cluny Museum (Racinet).
„ 4. **Bronze buckle,** Cluny Museum (Racinet).
„ 5. **Belt-buckle,** Cluny Museum (Racinet).
„ 6. **Bronze brooch,** Cluny Museum (Racinet).
„ 7. **Neck ornament of bronze** (Racinet).
„ 8, 9, and 10. **Belt buckles from the Merovingian Period** (Racinet).
„ 11. **Bronze fibula,** in the Louvre (Racinet).
„ 12. **Bronze fibula from the Merovingian Period,** Cluny Museum (Racinet).
„ 13. **Bronze belt-buckles,** Cluny Museum (Racinet).
„ 14, and 15. **Heads of Gallic chieftains from the time of the Romans, after bronze medals** (Racinet).
„ 16. **Silver brooch from Goldborough in Yorkshire** (Racinet).
„ 17. **Remnant of a reliquary of iron with bronze and silver ornament from Cashel,** Co. Tipperary, Ireland (Racinet).
„ 18. **Brooch with granate and gold filigree-work,** found near Abingdon (Racinet).
„ 19, and 20. **Bronze fibulae** (Racinet).
„ 21. **Bronze brooch with silver ornamentation,** found near Lincoln (Racinet).
„ 22. **Bracelet from Pont-Audemer** (Havard).
„ 23. **Bronze brooch found in the churchyard at Blasion** (Havard).
„ 24. **Buckle found in the churchyard at Chisell-Down,** in the Isle of Wight (Racinet).
„ 25. **Bracelet, found in Réallon, Hautes Alpes** (Havard).
„ 26, and 27. **Bracelets from Caranda** (Havard).

Plate 51.

Fig. 1. **Frankish weapons,** from the Museum at St. Germain (Barrière-Plany, Les Arts industrials peubles barbares de la Gaule. All the following Figures in this plate are from the same author).

„ 2. **Burgundian ornament from Elisried** (Canton Bern).

„ 3. **Necklet, same origin.**

„ 4. **Neck ornament in the Museum at St. Germain.**

„ 5. **Burgundian ornament from Delle near Belfort.**

„ 6. **West Gothic buckle from Jean-le-Pouget,** in the Museum at Cluny.

„ 7. **Burgundian buckle from Flerier near Tonniges** (Haute Savoie).

„ 8. **Frankish glass bottle from Achery-Magot** (Aisne).

„ 9. **Burgundian clay vessel from Tournus** (Saone et Loire).

„ 10. **Frankish glass dish from Anguilcourt-le-Sort** (Aisne).

„ 11. **West Gothic clay vase from Herpes** (Charente).

„ 12. **Frankish comb.**

„ 13. **Burgundian clay vase from Charnay** (Saone et Loire) in the Museum at St. Germain.

„ 14. **Anglo-Saxon knife.**

„ 15. **West-Gothic buckle from Figoret-Guzarques** (Hérault).

Plate 52.

The Merovingian Period.

Fig. 1—5, 8—13, 15, and 16. **Ornaments** (Havard).

„ 6. **Sword of the Childerich** (Roger-Milès).

„ 7. **Cross from St. Martin, Limoges,** made by Saint Éloi (Havard).

„ 14. **Chair of Dagobert, made of gilt bronze** (Havard).

Plate 53.

Fig. 1, and 2. **German sword in the Mayence Museum** (Lindenschmitt, Aus der heidnischen Vorzeit. The following are all according to the same authority).

„ 3. **Silver needle from the Frankish graves near Neuhofen.**

„ 4. **Frankish fibula.**

„ 5. **Half-drawn dagger from the graves at Hallstadt.**

„ 6. **Frankish bracelet,** Museum in Mayence.

„ 7. **Bucket with bronze mounts and iron handles from the Frankish graves near Monsheim,** in the Mayence Museum.

„ 8. **Bucket with bronze mounts found in the graves on the Schiersteiner Wege.** Wiesbaden Museum.

„ 9. **Ear-ring from the graves near Wörrstedt.**

„ 10. **Dagger from Sprendlingen,** Rheinhessen.

„ 11. **German ribbon clasp,** Mayence Museum.

„ 12. **Fibula from the graves near Nordendorf.**

„ 13. **Necklet from a grave in Wurmlingen,** Württemberg.

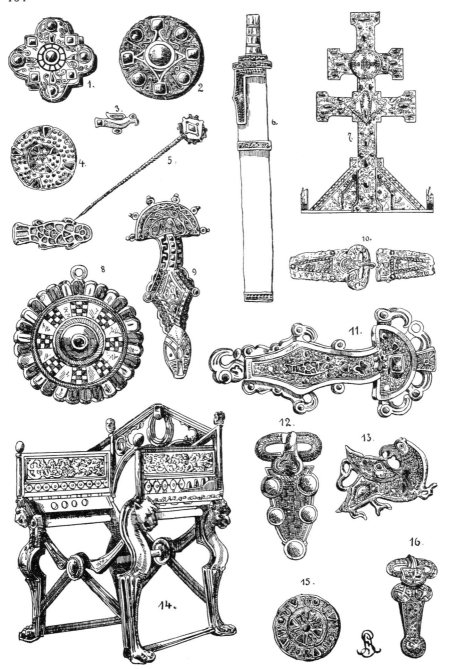

Plate 53.　　　　　CELTIC ORNAMENT.　　　　　105

Fig. 14.   **Ear-ring in the Wiesbaden Museum.**
„   15.   **Shoe found in the turf moor Friedeburg,** West Friesland.   Hannover Museum.
„   16.   **Frankish belt-buckle,** Mayence Museum.
„   17.   **Glass vase found in grave near Kreuznach.**
„   18.   **Clay vase found in grave near Ulm.**
„   19.   **Clay vase found in graves at Osthofen,** Mayence Museum.
„   20, and 22.   **Coffins of Gypsum.**
„   21.   **Clay urn found in graves near Remingen.**
„   23.   **Ring from the Mayence Museum.**

Anglo-Saxon Baptismal Font
(Müller and Mothes).

CELTIC ORNAMENT
(GREAT BRITAIN AND IRELAND).

Initial from the 7th century
(Owen Jones).

rnamental art, such as was developed in the British Isles, but more especially in Ireland, even during the sway of heathenism, was, without any doubt, a pure Celtic art of its own, without any traces of Byzantine or South European influences. The very same ornamental work which we find in the old heathen stone coffins are also to be seen in the manuscript paintings of the Celtic monks of the sixth century. Celtic artists show a most astonishing and extraordinary skill and variety in the delineation of ornamental tracery, in which the bodies of birds, dogs, snakes and fantastic animals are most skillfully interwoven. Vegetable ornaments were entirely absent in the earlier specimens of this work, appearing first in the 9th century, very probably as the result of Roman influence. The very great similarity existing between Scandinavian and Celtic ornament points to a very close connection between the two styles of art, a fact which is all the more evident when we remember that Christianity was introduced into Norway and Sweden by Irish missionaries.

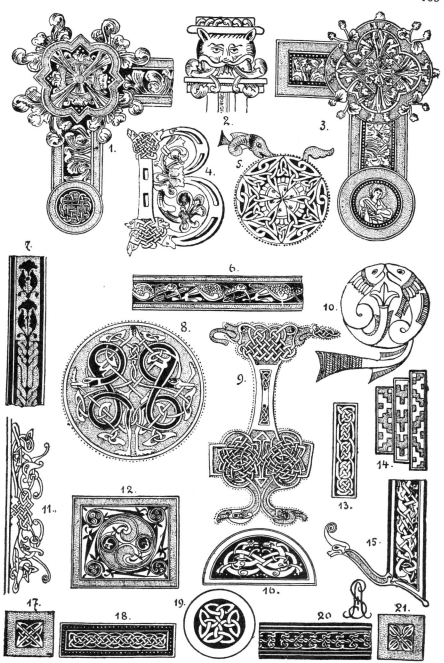

CELTIC ORNAMENT.

Plate 54.

Fig. 1. Manuscript painting from the 10th century (Dolmetsch).
„ 2. Initial from a Psalter, 11th century, at present in Trinity College, Dublin (Owen Jones).
„ 3, and 4. Manuscript paintings from the 10th century (Owen Jones).
„ 5. The Aberlemno cross (Owen Jones).
„ 6. Initial from the 7th century (Dolmetsch).
„ 7—11. Manuscript paintings of Celtic-Anglo-Saxon origin (Owen Jones).
„ 12. Ornament from base of cross in the church of Eassie, Angusshire (Owen Jones).
„ 13. Ornament from base of cross in the church at St. Vigean, Angusshire (Owen Jones).
„ 14. Ornament from base of cross in the church at Meigle, Angusshire (Owen Jones).

Plate 55.

Fig. 1, 3, 4, and 8. Specimens of manuscript paintings from the 10th century (Dolmetsch and Owen Jones).
„ 2. Manuscript paintings from the 11th century (Dolmetsch).
„ 5, 6, and 10. Manuscript paintings from the 8th century (Dolmetsch).
„ 7. Manuscript painting from the 9th century (Dolmetsch).
„ 9. Initial from the Franco-Saxon bible at St. Denis, from the 9th century (Owen Jones).
„ 11—21. Specimens from manuscript paintings of Celtic-Anglo-Saxon origin (Owen Jones).

Plate 56.

Fig. 1—3. Specimens of manuscript paintings from the 7th century (Dolmetsch).
„ 4. Manuscript painting from an Irish Gospel of the 10th century. The border is copied from the Gospel of St. Cuthbert now in the British Museum, and known as the Book of Durham, a book which was written between the years 698 and 720. (Henry Shaw, Mediæval Alphabets and Devices.)

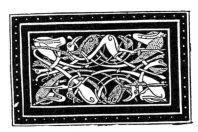

From an Irish Spelling-Book (Mothes and Müller).

Plate 56 CELTIC ORNAMENT. 111

Roman Marble Vase (Piranesi).

The Middle Ages

Window from Monastery St. Juan de los Reyes, Toledo (Monumentos de España).

EARLY CHRISTIAN ORNAMENT.

**From a
Carolingian Gospel
in the British
Museum**
(Müller and Mothes).

radually, as the political supremacy of a country begins to decline, Art in that country begins also to decay. The decline of classic art was the natural consequence of the political weakness and final decay of the Western Roman Empire, as well as of the decisive victory which Christianity finally obtained over Heathenism. In all the old historic styles there exists an intimate connection between religion and art. Art developed under the aegis of religion and was so strongly influenced by it that a style of art produced under the influence of a certain religion could never harmonise with any other religion except that from which it sprung. When, therefore, Christianity received into its hands the remains of classic art, it was obliged to change and harmonise them into a style in unison with Christian ideas, tastes, and necessities, without a the same time entirely freeing itself from classic influences. On the ruins, therefore, of the Western Roman empire, the Christian States erected a new civilisation changing everything they found to fit the new condition of affairs, and making use of the peculiar elements of Byzantine art, then in its full glory to form a new style of art of its own. The Byzantine influence was so powerful at that time, that it is often a matter of real difficulty for the art historian to say whether certain works of art belong to the Early Christian or to the Byzantine style. The antiquities discovered in the ancient city of Ravenna show most remarkable traces of Byzantine influences.

Early Christian art may be regarded as a period of transition the tendency of which was to free itself alike from Classic and Byzantine influence. It was only when this latter influence had been entirely overcome, when, about the year 900 A. D., the Romanesque style of architecture began to develop itself, that art began again to move along secure lines.

The attempts to change classic art into forms more suitable to Christianity were, however, not confined to the Western Roman empire. Attempts in this direction were also made in Asia Minor, but were finally rendered unavailing by the spread of Islamism.

Before their contact with the Romans, the art of the Celts, if we exclude Architecture and Sculpture, even though primitive, was still a thoroughly characteristic, peculiar one. The Eastern Goths, who ruled Italy from 493 to 555, but who soon lost their peculiar individuality, did not cherish this style of art as the Lombards did. These latter, who settled in Northern Italy under Alboin in the year 568, preserved it carefully, and to such an extent that it actually exercised a very remarkable influence on the development of Italo-Romanesque art.

Mural painting from the Coemeterium Majus, Rome
(Wilpert, Malereien der Katakomben Roms).

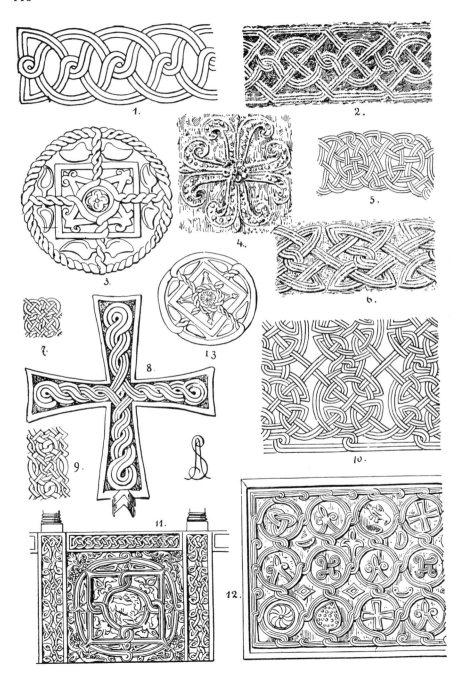

Plate 58. EARLY CHRISTIAN ORNAMENT. 117

1.

2.

3.

4.

5.

6.

7.

8.

Plate 57.

Lombardo-Byzantine Ornament in Italy.

(E. A. Stückelberg, Longobardische Plastik.)

Fig. 1. Circular pattern braided work from Ventimiglia.
„ 2. Diamond pattern braided work from Ravenna.
„ 3. Bottom of a basked from Rome.
„ 4. Relief from Ventimiglia.
„ 5, and 13. Interlaced work from Milan.
„ 6. Relief from Spalato.
„ 7. Interlaced work from Como.
„ 8. Processional Crucifix from Milan.
„ 9. Interlaced work from Valeria.
„ 10. Lattice work from Milan.
„ 11. Church altarscreen from Aquileja.
„ 12. Relief from altar in Orvieto.

Plate 58.

Lombardo-Byzantine Ornament in Italy.

(After Professor Karl Mohrmann and Dr. Eugen Ferd. Eichwede, Germanische Frühkunst.)

Fig. 1, 2, and 5. Capitals from the church of S. Ambrogio, Milan.
„ 3. Fountain, in the Museum at Venice.
„ 4. From a balustrade in the cathedral at Aquileja.
„ 6—8. Portals from the church of S. Ambrogio, Milan.
„ 9. Capital of column from the church of S. Ambrogio, Milan.

Crucifix in the Museum at Ravenna (Dehli).

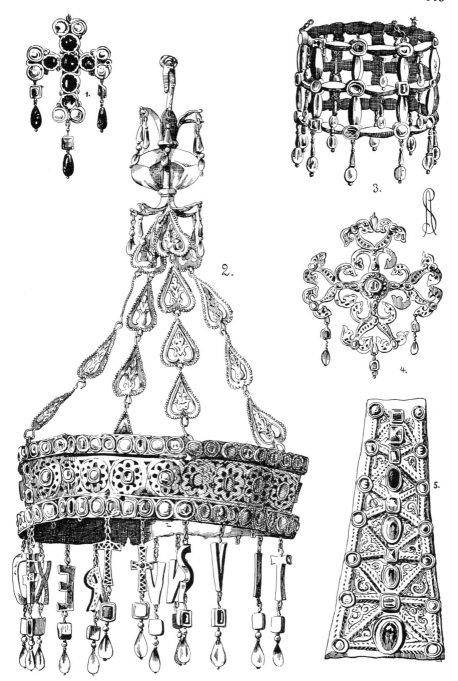

Plate 61.   EARLY CHRISTIAN ORNAMENT.

121

Plate 59.

Visigothic Ornament in Spain.

(After Monumentos de España.)

Fig. 1. Cross from the crown of Receswint.
„ 2. Crown of Suinthila.
„ 3. Votive crown.
„ 4. Votive cross.
„ 5. Arm of a processional crucifix.

Plate 60.

Italo-Byzantine Ornament in Italy.

Fig. 1. Frieze from the church at Dana in Syria (Vogüe, La Syrie Centrale).
„ 2. Capital from the church of St. Apollinare Nuovo, Ravenna (Dehli).
„ 3, 4, and 5. Capitals from the church of St. Vitale in Ravenna. The church of St. Vitale in Ravenna was founded by the treasurer Julianus Argentarius being moved thereto be the exhortations of Bishop Ecclesius (524—534 after Christ). The strongly marked Byzantine character of this church is easily explained when it is remembered that very intimate relations existed at that time between Ravenna and Byzantium (Dehli).
„ 6. Marble panel from Ravenna (Bilderatlas).
„ 7. Monogram of Christ in a sarcophagus in the church of St. Apollinare-in-Classe, Ravenna (Dehli, Selections of Byzantine Ornament).

Plate 61.

Frankish Ornament.

Fig. 1. Gospel of Charles the Bald in the National Library in Paris (Havard).
„ 2. Sword of Charlemagne in the Imperial Treasury in Vienna (Havard).
„ 3. Chair of the statue of St. Foy in the treasury at Conques (Havard).
„ 4. Gold crucifix, presented to the monastery of St. Denis by Charles the Bald (Havard).
„ 5. Crown of Charlemagne in the Imperial Treasury in Vienna (Havard).
„ 6. Crown of the statue of St. Foy in the treasury at Conques (Havard).
„ 7. Reliquary medallion of Charlemagne in the monastery at Aix-la-Chapelle (Havard).
„ 8. Throned Christ from a gospel of Charlemagne (Müller and Mothes).
„ 9. Hunting horn of Charlemagne in Aix-la-Chapelle (Müller and Mothes).
„ 10. Madonna from the catacomb of St. Calixtus in Rome (Müller and Mothes).

Plate 62.

Fig. 1. Diptych from the 6th century, supposed to be the Cathedral of Maxentius (Libonis).
„ 2. Sarcophagus of the Exarch Isaac, representing the adoration of the Three Magi (Libonis).

Plate 62.　　EARLY CHRISTIAN ORNAMENT.

123

Fig. 3. **Ambo in Salonica** (Gagarin, Russische Ornamente).
  „   4. **Bookcase in church in Ravenna** (Havard).
  „   5. **Chalice,** presented to the monastery of Kremsmünster in 780 by Duke Tassilo (Müller and Mothes).
  „   6. **Reading desk of St. Adelgundi** (Libonis).
  „   7, and 8. **Sarcophagi in Ravenna** (D'Espouy).
  „   9. **Mosaic flooring from the church of St. Vitale in Ravenna** (D'Espouy).
  „ 10. **The Empress Theodora and her suite.** Mosaic from the church of St. Vitale, Ravenna (Libonis).

Altar in the Museum at Ravenna (Dehli).

BYZANTINE ORNAMENT.

yzantine is the title given to that conglomerate style of art which was developed in the Eastern Roman Empire from all the different styles which were in existence at that early period. The first impulse to the development of a Byzantine style was given in the year 330 A.D., when Byzantium or Constantinople became the seat of the royal residence of the emperor Constantine, and when Christianity was made the established state religion. Byzantine Art may be said to have reached its highest standard in the 6th century when it spread throughout the whole Empire and extended to North Africa.

Initial from a breviary in the Mazarin Library (Libonis).

Its influence however was not confined to those regions for already in the same century it had reached as far north and west as Scotland and Ireland, in which countries it is found intermingled with Celtic Art. It also penetraded through the Balkan States and Italy, and, from the 9th century when under the influence of the Macedonian Empire, it took fresh life, down to the middle of the 12th century, it permeated the ornament of all the Romanesque Styles of Europe, whilst even in Constantinople when taken by the Turks, in 1453, the Church of Sancta Sophia became the model on which all the Turkish Mosques were based, so far as their main features are concerned.

Plate 64. BYZANTINE ORNAMENT. 127

It was in fact the political influence which the Byzantine Empire enjoyed during the period of its supremacy, together with the low standard of civilization existing at that period in the Christian States of the West, which caused the new Christian Art, whose development had already commenced, to be strongly influenced by the Byzantine Style, more especially in its ornament.

Plate 63.

Fig. 1.   Arch and column of the lower gallery in the church of St. Sophia, Constantinople. (Salzenberg, Altchristliche Baudenkmale von Konstantinopel.) This church, erected in place of a basilica destroyed by fire, was built under Justinian in the years 532—537, after plans designed by Anthemios of Tralles assisted by Isidorus of Miletus. The church has been used as a mosque since 1453.

„   2—4.   Details from the façade of the church of St. Marks in Venice (Gagarin). The church of St. Marks, although a prototype of Romanesque architecture, contains many features peculiar to Byzantine art. Though founded about 830 A. D. the five domes were not commenced till 1063 A. D. and the sumptuous marble decoration not completed till two centuries later.

„   5.   Bronze door in the church of St. Marks, Venice (Gagarin).
„   6.   Arch and capital in the baptistery of the church of St. Marks, Venice (Gagarin).
„   7, 8.   Capitals in the church of St. Marks, Venice (Gagarin).

Plate 64.

Fig. 1.   Arch from a gallery in the church of St. Sophia, Constantinople, from the 6th century (Gagarin).
„   2, 3.   Bronze knockers from the door of St. Marks, Venice (Dehli, Byzantine Ornament).
„   4.   Capital from the church of St. Marks in Venice (Dehli).
„   5—10.   Capitals from the church of St. Marks in Venice (Gagarin).

Plate 65.

After Dehli, Selections of Byzantine Ornament.

Fig. 1.   Stone panel from the Atrium of St. Marks in Venice.
„   2.   Baptismal Font in the Vendramin palace, Venice.
„   3.   Sarcophagus from the church of St. Antonio, Padua.
„   4.   Relief from the church of St. Pietro in Verona.
„   5.   From transept of St. Marks, Venice.
„   6.   Frieze over door of the Zeno Chapel in St. Marks, Venice.

Plate 65.   BYZANTINE ORNAMENT.   129

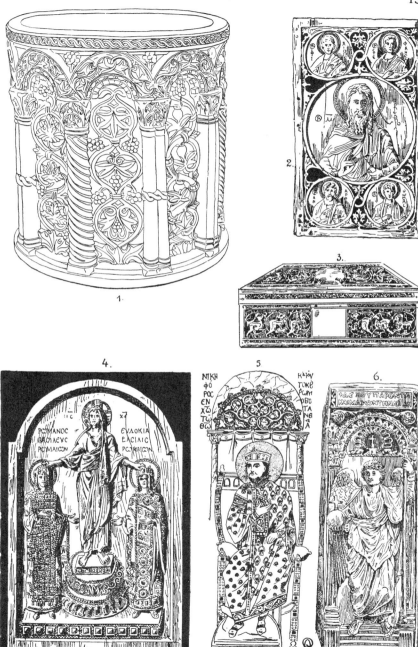

Plate 66.

Fig. 1. Gold ring from the collection of Rollin and Bourdent (Libonis).
„ 2. Border of a manuscript of the 10th century (Libonis).
„ 3. Stone panel in the gallery of the church of St. Marks, Venice (Dehli).
„ 4. Ivory Bookcover in the South Kensington Museum (Libonis).
„ 5. Marble mosaic (Libonis).
„ 6. Mosaic panelling in the triforium of the church of St. Sophia, Constantinople (Bilderatlas zur Geschichte der Baukunst).
„ 7—9. Marble mosaics from the church of St. Marks in Venice (Dehli).
„ 10. Letters from a manuscript (Libonis).
„ 11. Stone relief from the church of St. Sergius in Constantinople (Krauth und Meyer, Steinhauerbuch).

Plate 67.

Fig. 1. Well head from Venice, now in the South Kensington Museum (Dehli)
„ 2. Cover of an ivory reliquary in the South Kensington Museum showing John the Baptist between Saints Philip, Stephen, Thomas, and Andrew (Libonis).
„ 3. Byzantine ivory coffer.
„ 4. Cover of book of the four gospels owned by St. John of Besançon, showing the crowning of Romanus IV and Eudoxia. Dates from the 11th century, at present in the National Library, Paris (Libonis).
„ 5. Byzantine miniature-painting (Libonis).
„ 6. Leaf of a diptych in the British Museum showing Michael the Archangel (Libonis).

Plate 68.

Fig. 1—6, 8—10. Miniature paintings from manuscripts in the National Library, Paris (Gagarin).
„ 7. Lectern, from a manuscript in the National Library, Paris (Gagarin).
„ 11. Byzantine crown (Hottenroth, Trachten).
„ 12—15. Byzantine coiffures (Hottenroth).
„ 16. Reliquary (Hottenroth).
„ 17. Chalice (Hottenroth).
„ 18, 19, 20. Arm chairs (Hottenroth).
„ 21. Consular chair of state.

Plate 69.

Byzantine Ornament in Spain.

(After Monumentos de España.)

Fig. 1. Ruins of the ancient cloister of San Roman in Hornija.
„ 2. Capital from the same cloister.
„ 3. Fragment of parapet, preserved in the cathedral of Cordova.

Plate 68.　　　　BYZANTINE ORNAMENT.　　　　133

Plate 70.   BYZANTINE ORNAMENT.   135

Fig. 4. **Outer cornice of the Camara Santa in the Cathedral of Oviedo.**
„ 5—7, and 13. **Window from the church of San Salvator in Valdedios.** Concejo de Villa Viciosa.
„ 8, and 12. **Capitals from the hermitage of Santa Christina in Lena, Oviedo.**
„ 9. **Medallion from the same church.**
„ 10. **Pulpit parapet from the same church.**
„ 11, 14—16. **Capitals from the church of San Salvator in Valvedios.**

Plate 70.

Byzantine Ornament in Spain.

(After Monumentos de España.)

Fig. 1, and 3. **Fragments from a building — called the Cisterna — in Mérida.**
„ 2. **Fragment from the Basilica in Cordova.**
„ 4. **Enamelled work from a reliquary in the cloister of San Domingos de Silos.**
„ 5, and 6. **Pillar from the transept of the Church of St. Miguel de Lino, Oviedo.**

Decorative Frieze (Libonis).

ROMANESQUE ORNAMENT.

Initial from a
German XIIth century
manuscript (Dolmetsch).

O soon as Charlemagne had succeeded to a certain extent in consolidating his empire, he selected Aix-la-Chapelle as his place of residence, and called around him in that city artists of all kinds both from the former Western as well as from the Eastern Roman empires. These artists were engaged in decorating and adorning his palaces, and it was here that a new style, the Romanesque style, based upon classic architecture, and very strongly influenced by Byzantine art, which stood then at its highest glory slowly developed itself. At first, after the death of Charlemagne, art could not make much progress in the empire, a circumstance due to the fact that Charlemagne's successor was an incapable ruler under whose dominion the land lay diseased and dormant, awaiting with dulled apathy the end of all things. It was not until the year 1000 had come that new life began to be again manifest, and later on when the religious zeal was stirred up by the Crusades that some really great and genuine works of art were produced. The Romanesque style of architecture, whose earliest architects were priests and monks, the lay element being introduced later on, is a genuine Orthodox style. In the beginning this style was heavy, but it soon developed, and reached its highest standard in the 12th and 13th centuries. The aftergrowths of the Romanesque style in Germany were produced by a combination of the same with the Gothic, a style which came in from France, resulting in the pointedarch style which sprung into existence. The Romanesque style itself spread rapidly into all those countries which were included in the former Western Roman empire, its character becoming changed in accordance with the character of the inhabitants

of each particular country. In France Spain and England the Romanesque style developed into the Gothic, and some time afterwards, towards the middle of the 13th century, Germany, following the example of France and using the French Gothic as a standard, began also gradually to develop, the Gothic style of architecture.

Romanesque Ornament in Germany.

Plate 71.

(Heideloff, Ornamentik des Mittelalters.)

Fig. 1. Keystone of a vault in the church of St. Sebald, Nüremberg.
„ 2, and 3. Arch frieze with consol from the same church.
„ 4, and 7. Bases of columns, from the convent church in Heilbrunn, Bavaria.
„ 5. Capital from the church of St. Sebald, Nüremberg.
„ 6. View and ground plan of large column in the vestibule of the cathedral in Schwäbisch-Hall.
„ 8. Shaft of column from the portal of the Burggraf Chapel in the Augustinian Cloister, Esslingen.
„ 9. Capital from the same church.
„ 10. Capital from the Benedictine Abbey in Murrhard.
„ 11. Capital from the convent church in Faurudan near Göppingen.
„ 12. Cornice on the tower of St. John's church in Schwäbisch-Gmünd.

Plate 72.

Fig. 1. Abacus from the church of St. Michel in Hildesheim, 12th century (Raguenet, Matériaux et documents). This church, which was begun by Bishop Bernward of Hildesheim in the year 1001, and completed in the year 1033, marks the transition from the Early to the Late Romanesque Style.
„ 2. Abacus from the church of Marmoutiers in Alsace (Raguenet).
„ 3. Capital from Rosheim near Strassburg, dating from the 11th century (Raguenet).
„ 4. Stone cross in the market-place at Treves (Raguenet).
„ 5. Capital and base from Eger (Gruber, Kaiserburg in Eger).
„ 6. Capital from the cathedral in Limburg (Opderbecke, Bauformen). This church was built by Konrad II in the years 1030—1042, and dedicated in 1046 in the reign of Henry III. The building operations were conducted by the Cluniac Abbot Poppo von Stoblo.
„ 7. Signature tablet from the 11th century (Müller and Mothes).
„ 8. Door-knocker in the cathedral at Aix-la-Chapelle from the 8th century (Raguenet).
„ 9—12. Mural paintings from the cathedral in Brunswick (Gailhabaud l'architecture).
„ 13. Frieze from Mary's Chapel in the cathedral in Gandersheim (Raguenet).

Plate 73.

Fig. 1. **Frieze from the Burg at Münzenberg in Hessen** (Opderbecke, Bauformen des Mittelalters).

„   2. **Frieze from the church in Denkendorf,** 12th century (Lübke).

„   3. **From a stall in the cathedral at Ratzeburg** (Joseph).

„   4. **Ornamentation on shaft of a column from Buchenberg near Goslar,** 12th century (Opderbecke).

„   5. **Capital from the church in Brenz, Württemberg,** 12th century (Opderbecke).

„   6. **Base from the abbey church in Laach,** 12th century (Opderbecke).

„   7. **Archivolte from the doorway of Worms cathedral,** 12th century (Opderbecke).

„   8. **Capital from the Scottish church of St. Jacob in Ratisbon,** 12th century (Opderbecke).

„   9. **Window from the church at Laach** (Opderbecke).

„ 10. **Window-column from the cathedral at Worms,** 12th century (Opderbecke).

„ 11, and 14. **Doorway from the church at Gelnhausen,** 12th century (Opderbecke).

„ 12. **Tympanum from St. Michael's Church in Schwäbisch-Hall,** 12th century (Opderbecke).

„ 13. **Base from the church at Arnsberg,** 12th century (Opderbecke).

Plate 74.

Fig. 1. **Throne of Emperor Henry II,** after a miniature in the monarch's own Book of Gospels which is at present in the Court Library in Munich (Müller and Mothes).

„   2. **Flagon in the Royal Imperial Numismatic Cabinet in Vienna** (Müller and Mothes).

„   3. **Comb of Henry I** (Hefener-Alteneck, Trachten).

„   4. **Wrought-iron candlestick** (Hottenroth).

„   5. **Seven-branched candlestick in Brunswick cathedral** (Müller and Mothes).

„   6. **Bronze candlestick** (Hottenroth).

„   7. **Bishop's crozier from the Church Treasuries in Deutz** (Müller and Mothes).

„   8. **Two-handled chalice from the Marienstern Cloister in Saxony** (Muller and Mothes).

„   9. **Candelabrum from the cathedral in Aix-la-Chapelle** (Hottenroth).

„ 10. **Reliquary of oak with gilt reliefs in lead,** dates from the year 1300, at present in the Nüremberg Museum.

„ 11. **Glass painting from** 12th **century in Neuweiler, Alsace** (Müller and Mothes).

Plate 75.

Fig. 1. **Wooden coffer,** 10th century (Hottenroth).

„   2. **Initials from the time of Joseph XIII** (Müller and Mothes).

„   3. **Candlestick,** 12th century (Hottenroth).

„   4. **Bishop's crozier,** 11th century (Hottenroth).

„   5. **Chalice,** 11th century (Hottenroth).

„   6. **Fragment of a small crystal bottle,** 10th century (Hottenroth).

„   7. **Initials from the Bremer Gospel,** from the year 1050 (Müller and Mothes).

„   8. **Thurible of gilt copper,** 12th century (Müller and Mothes).

Plate 76.   GERMAN ROMANESQUE ORNAMENT.   145

Fig. 9. **Writing-desk,** after a manuscript in the National Library at Paris (Gagarin).
„ 10. **Bronze church lamp,** 11th century (Müller and Mothes).
„ 11. **Stool** (Hottenroth).
„ 12, and 13. **Beds,** 12th century (Hottenroth).
„ 14. **Fighting warrior,** 13th century (Hottenroth).
„ 15. **Cup** (Hottenroth).
„ 16. **Bishop's chair** (Hottenroth).
„ 17. **Imperial shoe** (Hottenroth).
„ 18. **Clasp of Imperial mantle** (Hottenroth).
„ 19. **Sprinkler** (Hottenroth).
„ 20. **Cover of the prayer-book of St. Elizabeth** (Müller and Mothes).
„ 21. **Bed,** 12th century (Müller and Mothes).

Plate 76.

North-German Brickwork.

(After Stiehl, Backsteinbau romanischer Zeit.)

The Romanesque style of brick architecture was introduced into the Altmark, at Jerichow, and into parts of Mecklenburg, Holstein, and Pomerania, during that period of time when these Wendic lands were being germanised. These districts being poor in stone and very rich in clay, necessitated the employment of burnt bricks. The origin of brick architecture has been traced to Lombardy by Herr O. Stiehl, Government architect, who carried out a series of careful and searching inquiries into this question (O. Stiehl, Der Backsteinbau romanischer Zeit, besonders in Oberitalien und Norddeutschland). From Lombardy it was introduced into the Wendic districts by missionaries. As the Romanesque style of architecture was the prevalent one at that period, the brickwork was constructed in accordance with it.

Fig. 1—3. **Capitals from the convent church at Arendsee.**
„ 4. **Capital from the church at Jerichow.**
„ 5. **Capital from the church of St. Maria auf dem Damme at Jüterbog.**
„ 6—8. **Arched doorway and capitals from the church of St. Nicolas in Treuenbrietzen.**
„ 9. **Capital from the cathedral at Brandenburg.**
„ 10. **Capital from the church at Gadebusch.**
„ 11. **Arched Corbel Table from the church at Mölln.**
„ 12. **Rib mouldings from the convent church at Dobrilugk.**
„ 13, and 14. **Bases of piers from the cathedral at Ratzeburg.**
„ 15, and 16. **Compound piers from the church at Altenkrempe.**
„ 17. **Window from the village church at Großmangelsdorf.**
„ 18. **Capital from the convent church at Dobrilugk.**

Plate 77.

German Enamel Work in the Middle Ages.

(After v. Falke and Frauberger, Deutsche Schmelzarbeiten des Mittelalters.)

The Historic Art Exhibition held in Dusseldorf in the year 1902 contained a most beautiful and unequalled collection of German Enamel-Work from the Romanesque Art-epoch. The different works of art contained in this collection have since been reproduced by Otto von

Falke and Heinrich Frauberger in their beautifully illustrated work „Deutsche Schmelzarbeiten des Mittelalters". There can be hardly any doubt but that the German artistic enamel-work has its origin in the Byzantine empire. In Germany itself certain centres for this art were established in a few cities, the masters giving instruction each according to his own particular school. One of the most celebrated centres was at Cologne, where the great and celebrated master Frederick taught. Celebrated schools were also established in Treves, Coblenz, and a few other places.

Fig. 1. **Plate from angle column of the Mauricius Shrine in Cologne by Frederick;** dates from the year 1180.

„   2, 3, 4, and 8. **Enamel plates from the Ursula Shrine in Cologne,** done by Frederick in the year 1170.

„   5. **The Benignus Shrine in Siegburg.** Made in Cologne, in the year 1190.

„   6. **Bronze pillars from the Anna Shrine in Cologne,** 1183.

„   7. **Reliquary plate in Fritzlar,** from the second half of the 12th century.

„   9. **Crest of the Albinus Shrine in Cologne,** from the year 1186.

„ 10. **Crest of the Anna Shrine in Siegburg.** Made in Cologne in the year 1183.

„ 11, and 12. **Crest of the Mauricius Shrine in Cologne,** by Frederick in the year 1180.

Painting from Bamberg Cathedral (Heideloff).

Romanesque Ornament in France.

In the provinces of France, the Romanesque style of architecture developed itself in a somewhat peculiarly characteristic fashion, while the Roman classic predominated in the south, more especially in Provence, but the Byzantine style held sway in the south-west. In the north of France, and in Normandy, the two styles were blended together.

Plate 78.

Fig. 1. Doorway of the church of St. Ursin, Bourges, 12th century (Opderbecke).
„ 2. Column from the church of Saint Pierre, Chauvigny (Havard, Histoire et philosophie des Styles).
„ 3. Doorway of the church at Surgères, 11th century (Opderbecke).
„ 4. Column from the church of St. Lazare, Avallon, 12th century (Opderbecke).
„ 5. Base from the church at Cusset, 12th century (Opderbecke).
„ 6. Ornament on Doorway of the church at Suger, 12th century (Opderbecke).
„ 7. Base from the church at Poissy, 12th century (Opderbecke).
„ 8. Shaft of column from the cathedral at Chartres, 12th century (Opderbecke).
„ 9. and 10. Base and carved string from church at Vezelay, 12th century (Opderbecke).
„ 11. Corbel table from a chapel in Lâon, 11th century (Opderbecke).
„ 12. Corbel table from apse of the church et Léognon, 11th century (Opderbecke).

Plate 79.

Fig. 1. Frieze in relief from cloister at Moissac (Havard).
„ 2. Frieze from the cathedral at Bourges (Raguenet).
„ 3. Frieze from the museum at Toulouse, 12th century (Raguenet).
„ 4. Corbel table from the church at Aulnay, Charente inférieure (Raguenet).
„ 5. Cross from Notre Dame du Port, Clermont-Ferrand, 11th century (Raguenet)
„ 6. Abacus from the museum at Toulouse (Raguenet).
„ 7. Abacus from the cloister of St. Trophime, Arles (Raguenet).
„ 8. Capital from the cathedral at Senlis, 12th century (v. Pannewitz, Formenlehre der romanischen Baukunst).
„ 9, and 12. Capitals from Toulouse (Heideloff).
„ 10. Base from the church of Semur in Brionnais, Burgundy (Raguenet).
„ 11. Capital from the church of St. Severin, Toulouse (Joseph).

Plate 80.

Romanesque Ornament in Provence.

(After M. Henry Revoil, Architecture Romane du midi de la France.)

Fig. 1, and 6. Column and arch from the cloister of St. Sauveur, d'Aix, Bouche du Rhône.
„ 2. Capital and principal cornice from the chapel of St. Gabriel, Bouche du Rhône. Transition from the classic to the Romanesque style.
„ 3, 5, and 10. Principal cornices.

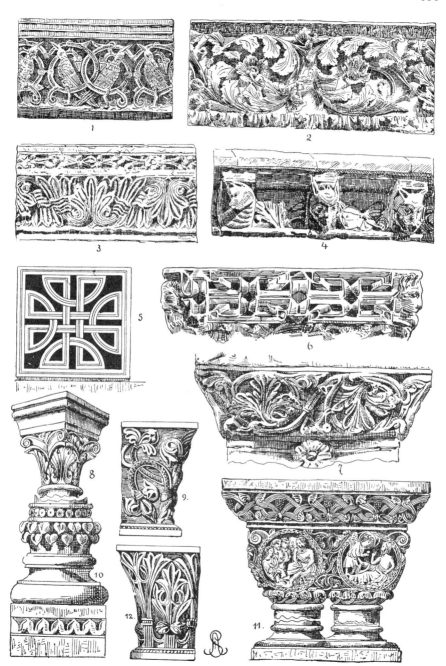

Plate 81.   FRENCH ROMANESQUE ORNAMENT.   153

Fig. 4. Compound pier from the abbey of Montmajour.
„ 7, 9, and 11. Compound piers from the castle of Simiane, Basses-Alpes.
„ 8, 12. Pilaster from the church at Thor, Vaucluse.

Plate 81.

Norman-Romanesque Ornament.

(After V. Ruprich-Robert, l'architecture Normande.)

Fig. 1, and 2. Pillar capital from the church of Montevilliers, Seine inférieure.
„ 3. Doorway of the church of Anisy, Calvados.
„ 4. Capital from the church of Montevilliers.
„ 5. Tympanum from a door of the church at Marigny, Calvados. Dates from the year 1150, and represents the old custom of Tree-worship.
„ 6. Doorway of the church at Beaumais, Calvados.
„ 7. Window of the church at Saint-Contest.

Plate 82.

Norman-Romanesque Ornament.

(After V. Ruprich-Robert, l'architecture Normande.)

Fig. 1. Painted capital from the church of St. Georges de Bocherville, 13th century.
„ 2. Capital from the church at Mont Saint Michel (Manche).
„ 3. Capital from the church at Breteuil (Oise).
„ 4, 6, 9, and 11. Columns from the church of St. Gervais, Rouen, 11th century.
„ 5. Norman alphabet, 11th century, after M. de Caumont.
„ 7. Column from the Chapter hall of the Abbey of Hambe (Manche).
„ 8. Capital from the crypt of the cathedral of Bayeux.
„ 10. Cross from the church Sainte Trinité in Caen.

Plate 83.

Fig. 1. Iron Grille from the church of St. John of Malta in Aix, Provence (Havard).
„ 2. Wrought iron hinge on the sacristy door of the cathedral at Noyon (Havard).
„ 3. Glass painting from the cathedral of Chartres (Havard).
„ 4. Baptismal font in the church at Besme, Champagne (Raguenet).
„ 5. Bishop's crozier (L. Roger-Milès, Comment discerner les styles).
„ 6. Grisaille in the church at Bonlieu, Creuse (Havard).
„ 7. Cloth fabric from the Abbey Saint Germain-des-Prés, Paris, 11th century (Roger-Milès).
„ 8. Crozier of Archbishop Abaldos, who died in the year 933, in the cathedral at Sens (Roger-Milès).
„ 9. Gold embroidered silk (Roger-Milès).
„ 10. Iron grille in the museum at Rouen, 13th century (Raguenet).
„ 11. Iron grille from the cathedral at Puy, 9th century (Raguenet).

Plate 84. FRENCH ROMANESQUE ORNAMENT. 157

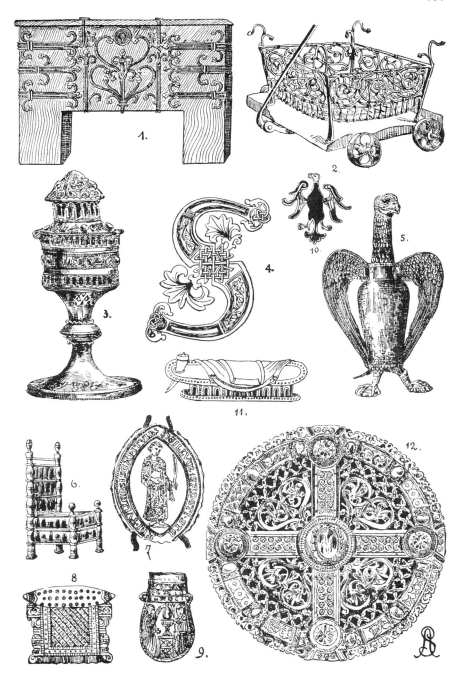

Plate 84.

Fig. 1. Wood coffer from the sacristy of the cathedral of Noyon (Havard).
„ 2. Chafing-dish from the Archbishop's palace in Narbonne, 13th century (Müller and Mothes).
„ 3. Chalice and cover from the cathedral of Saint-Omer (Havard).
„ 4. Initial letter from the prayer-book of Charles the Bald (Roger-Milès).
„ 5. Holy mass flagon from the church treasury of St. Denis (Müller and Mothes).
„ 6. Wooden arm-chair (Roger-Milès).
„ 7. Seal of the Capitol of Toul, 1127—1218 (Ary Renan, le costume en France).
„ 8. Stool (Roger-Milès).
„ 9. Jewel of the Holy Tear of Vendome (Havard).
„ 10. Eagle from hilt of a sword, 10th century (Roger-Milès).
„ 11. Small-writig-desk for writing on the knees (Roger-Milès).
„ 12. Paten of open-worked silver, chased and gilt, 13th century (Havard).

Plate 85.

French Enamel-work in the Middle Ages.

In the Middle Ages, certain centres of art were formed in France as well as in Germany, one of the most celebrated art-schools in the 12th century being established at Verdun. The Verdun Altar is the most renowned work of art during this epoch. It was prepared by Nicholas of Verdun in the year 1191, and is at present in the religious establishment at Klosterneuburg near Vienna (Karl Dreschler, Der Verduner Altar).

Fig. 1. Enamelled plate from the Verdun Altar.
„ 2—16. Details of borner, etc., from the same.

Frieze from the church of St. Pierre de Maguelonne (Hécourt).
(Revoil, Architecture Romane dans le midi de la France.)

Romanesque Ornament in Upper and Middle Italy.

The Lombard-Romanesque style shows evidences of Germanic influence but does not evince such a high degree of development as the German-Romanesque style. In Tuscany and Venice, this style had to give way before the Florentine and Byzantine style.

Plate 86.

Fig. 1. **Pulpit in the cathedral at Bitonto** 11th century (Raguenet)
„ 2. **Portion of arcade in museum at Brescia** (Mohrmann).
„ 3. **Carved string in museum at Brescia** (Mohrmann).
„ 4. **Rose-window from the church at Pomposa** (Mohrmann).
„ 5. **Fragment of column in museum at Brescia** (Mohrmann).

Plate 87.

Fig. 1. **Blind Arcade from Verona** (Mohrmann).
„ 2. **Relief from the cathedral in Matera** (Raguenet).
„ 3. **Capital from the cathedral of Torcello near Venice,** 11th century (Raguenet).
„ 4. **Italian rose-window after Rosenkranz** (Bilderatlas der Baukunst).
„ 5. **Window from the church of St. Abondio, Como** (Joseph).
„ 6, and 8. **Capital and archivolt from the church of St. Zeno, Verona** (Mohrmann).
„ 7. **Doorway from the church of the Fathers in Padua** (Raguenet).

Plate 88.

(After Prof. Karl Mohrmann and Dr. Eugen Ferd. Eichwede, Germanische Frühkunst.)

Fig. 1, and 2. **Doorway from the church of St. Stefano in Bologna.**
„ 3. **Lion plinth from the principal doorway of the cathedral at Verona.**
„ 4, and 5. **Lion plinths on the doorway of the church in Modena.**

Saracen-Norman Ornament in Sicily and Lower Italy.

The Normans where originally a northern tribe which had settled in Norway, and who afterwards, being forced through over-population to leave their Scandinavian home, founded a colony in Normandy. They conquered Sicily and Lower Italy and established also colonies in these countries. In the 11th century a characteristic Romanesque style had developed in Normandy. In the Norman colonies in Lower Italy, this style, being very strongly influenced by the Islamite style of the Saracens, developed further into another most characteristic style, which reached its highest standard in the 12th century. From this combination of Oriental and Christian art, the only exemple perhaps of the kind in history, from this union of quick Oriental fancy with the courage, strength, and power of the Northman, have sprung works of art whose delightful, and entrancing beauty charm the beholder and excite his wonder and admiration.

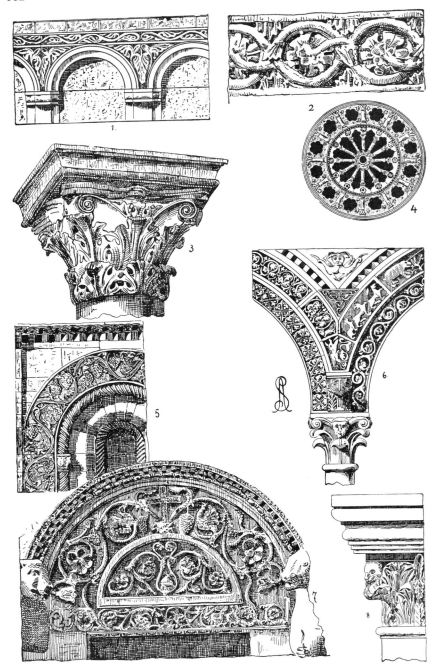

Plate 88.   ITALIAN ROMANESQUE ORNAMENT.   163

Plate 89.

Fig. 1, 4, 6, and 7. **Nave arches and superstructure of the Cathedral at Monreale** (J. J. Hittorff et L. Zanth Architecture moderne de la Sicile).

,, 2, and 3. **Ceilings from the same cathedral** (Hittorff).

,, 5. **Arcade from the cathedral at Monreale** (Camillo Boito, Architettura del medio evo in Italia). This church was built between the years 1173 and 1182, and restored between the years 1816—1859.

,, 8. **Arch from the cathedral at Monreale** (Hittorff).

Plate 90.

(After Kutschmann, Meisterwerke der sarazenisch-normannischen Kunst in Sicilien und Unteritalien.)

Fig. 1. **Relief on the front side of the altar of St. Cataldo.**

,, 2. **Baptismal font in St. Cataldo.**

,, 3—5. **Window archivolts from the palace of St. Antonio, Palermo.**

,, 6. **Ear-ring from the coronation hood of Queen Constance II.**

,, 7. **Mosaic from the Capella Palatina, Palermo.**

,, 8. **Inlaid frieze from the same church.**

,, 9. **Mosaic from a window reveal, same church.**

,, 10, and 11. **Mosaic friezes from the cathedral at Monreale.**

,, 12. **Mosaic from the church of the Martorana, Palermo.**

Plate 91.

Fig 1, and 3. **Mosaics from the church of the Martorana, Palermo** (Kutschmann).

,, 2. **From the ceiling of the cathedral at Monreale** (Hittorff and Zanth).

,, 4, and 5. **Fragments from archivolt in the side aisle of the Capella Palatina at Palermo** (Kutschmann).

,, 6. **Mosaic from arch soffit in the same church** (Kutschmann).

,, 7, and 9. **Mosaics from the cathedral at Monreale** (Kutschmann).

,, 8. **Painting from the cathedral of Messina** (D'Espouy).

Mosaic from Monreale Cathedral
(Hittorff and Zanth).

Plate 91. ITALIAN ROMANESQUE ORNAMENT. 167

Romanesque Ornament in Spain.

Romanesque church architecture in Spain was influenced by Moorish architecture of which there are many remains.

Plate 92.
(From Monumentos de España.)

Fig. 1. Window from the church of San Isidoro, Leon.
„ 2, and 3. Strings from the same church.
„ 4. Capital from the same church.
„ 5, and 6. Capital and base from the church of St. Lorenzo, Segovia.
„ 7. Soffit from the same church.
„ 8, and 9. Capital and base from the Gate of Mercy in the same church.
„ 10. Fragment from the old cathedral of Salamanca.
„ 11 Capital, corbel and base from the church of St. Peter and Paul, Barcelona.

Plate 93.
(From Monumentos de España.)

Fig. 1. Doorway from the church of San Millan in Segovia.
„ 2. Arch mouldings of doorway of church of San Martin, Segovia.
„ 3, and 8. Plan and elevation of window from the ancient cathedral of Salamanca.
„ 4. Capital from the Pantheon San Isidoro, Leon.
„ 5—7. Panels from frieze in the church of San Lorenzo, Segovia.
„ 9. Stone Sarcophagus in the Pantheon San Isidoro, Leon.

Plate 94.
(From Monumentos de España.)

Fig. 1. Arcade in the interior of the apse of the church Santa Maria de Villa Mayor, Concejo del Infiesto.
„ 2, and 6. Capital and base from the tower on the Cámara Santa of the cathedral at Oviedo.
„ 3, and 4. Corbel table from the church of Santa Maria de Villa Mayor.
„ 5. Capital from tower in no. 2.
„ 7. Sarcophagus probably of King Alphonzo the Wise, in the cloister of Santa Maria la Real de las Huelgas, Burgos.

Corbel table of doorway of San Lorenzo in Segovia (Monumentos de España).

Plate 94.   SPANISH ROMANESQUE ORNAMENT.

171

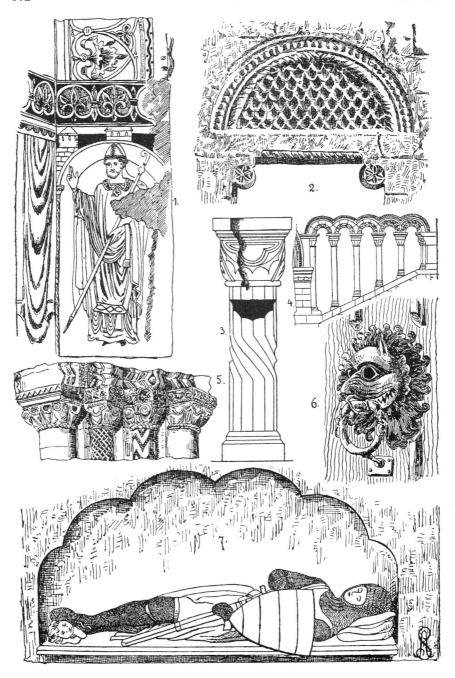

Romanesque Ornament in England.

The art of the early Middle Ages in England can be divided into two periods:
1. *The Anglo-Saxon period* from 449 to 1066. The art of this period consisted in an attempt to reproduce the remains of Roman architecture in the country, or in Italy.
2. *The Norman-period* from 1066 to 1189. The art of this period was an imitation of the Norman French, developing gradually into a characteristic national style.

Plate 95.

Fig. 1. **Norman mural paintings on the altar of Our Lady of Pity, Durham cathedral.** Dates from the year 1154 (Antiquarian Gleanings in the North of England by William B. Scott).
,, 2. **Door in Peterborough cathedral,** 12th century (Raguenet).
,, 3. **Column from Canterbury cathedral,** from the year 1070 (Pannewitz).
,, 4. **Arcade from the schools at Canterbury,** from the year 1115.
,, 5. **Capitals in the church of St. Peter at Northampton** (Graul, Bilderatlas).
,, 6. **Door-knocker from Durham cathedral** (Scott).
,, 7. **Tomb of an English knight,** 12th century (Hefener-Alteneck).

Plate 96.

Fig. 1. **Capital and base from the church at Lastingham, Yorkshire,** 12th century (Pannewitz).
,, 2. **Capital from the same church** (Pannewitz).
,, 3. **Capital from the church at Dunfermline, Scotland** (Pannewitz).
,, 4. **Capital from the church of St. Peter-at-Gowts, Lincoln,** Anglo saxon (Baldwin Brown, The arts in the early England).
,, 5. **Capital from Canterbury cathedral** (Pannewitz).
,, 6. **Capital from Waltham Abbey** (Pannewitz).
,, 7. **Capital from the white tower of the Tower of London.**
,, 8. **Double window of the east façade of the tower at Deerhurst** (Baldwin Brown).
,, 9, and 10. **Pyxes** (Hottenroth).
,, 11. **From the chasuble of St. Thomas A'Beckett** (Hottenroth).
,, 12. **Coffer from the Church at Brampton, Northamptonshire,** 12th century.
,, 13. **Norman ornaments from St. Saviour church, Southwark** (Pugin, Gothic Ornament).
,, 14. **Late-Romanesque tiles, yellow and red, from the church at Bloxham,** 13th century (Dolmetsch).

Plate 97.

(After V. Ruprich-Robert, Architecture Normande du XI et XII siècle en Normandie et en Angleterre.)

Fig. 1. **Triforium Arches of Rochester cathedral, Kent.**
,, 2. **Archivolt of doorway, Peterborough cathedral, Northamptonshire.**
,, 3, and 5. **Window shafts in the Abbey church of St. Albans, Herefordshire.**
,, 4. **Baptismal font in Sculthorpe church, Norfolk.**

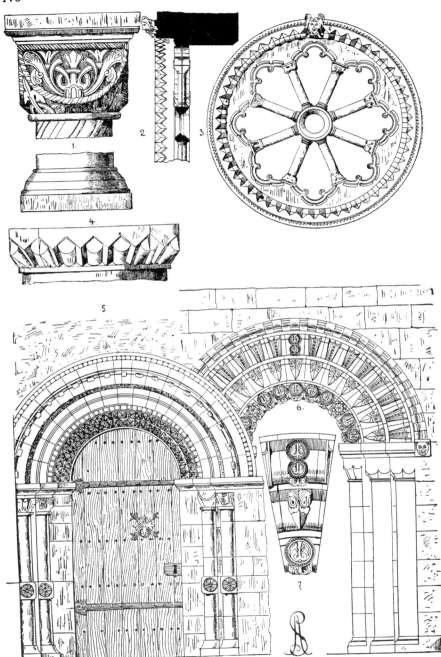

Fig. 6, and 9. Baptismal font in Winchester Cathedral, Hampshire.
„ 7, and 8. Mural paintings from same cathedral.
„ 10. Archivolt of doorway of St. Peter's Church, Northampton.
„ 11. Column from the crypt of Canterbury Cathedral, Kent.

Plate 98.

(After James K. Colling, Details of Gothic Architecture.)

Fig. 1. Capital and base from the crypt of vestry in Canterbury Cathedral.
„ 2, and 3. Rose window from Patrixbourne Church, Kent.
„ 4. Capital from the church at Walsoken, Norfolk.
„ 5. South doorway of the small church at Gt. Totham, Essex.
„ 6, and 7. West-Doorway in the tower of the church at Etton, Yorkshire.

Plate 99.

Fig. 1—12. From Norman cornices (Parker's Glossary of Architecture).
    Fig. 1. Lincolnshire, c. 1120, Deeping St. James.
    „ 2. St. Contest, Caen, Normandy.
    „ 3. Corbel table, St. Peter at Gowts, Lincoln.
    „ 4. Transept of Winchester Cathedral, 1090.
    „ 5. Billet, Canterbury Cathedral.
    „ 6. Beak Head, St. Ebbe's Oxford.
    „ 7. Double square Westminster Hall, c. 1097.
    „ 8. Chevron, North Hinksey, Berks.
    „ 9. Rose, Iffley, Church Oxon.
    „ 10. Segmental Billet, Abbaye aux Dames, Caen.
    „ 11. Double Cone, Stoneleigh Church, Warwickshire.
    „ 12. Embattled, Lincoln Cathedral, c. 1140.
„ 13. Grille in Winchester Cathedral (Bailey Scott Murphy, English and Scottish Wrought Ironwork).
„ 14—16. Capitals and base in the western tower of the church at Great Hale, near Sleaford, Lincolnshire (Baldwin Brown, The Arts in Early England).

Plate 100.

Fig. 1. Canon's staff (Hottenroth).
„ 2. Ship in which Duke William came over to England (Hottenroth).
„ 3. Anglo-Saxon pyx (Hottenroth).
„ 4. Anglo-Saxon sword-hilt (Hottenroth).
„ 5, and 8. Pyxes (Hottenroth).
„ 6. Norman shield (Hottenroth).
„ 7. Mitre of Thomas A'Beckett (Hottenroth).
„ 9. Norman sedan chair (Hottenroth).
„ 10. Anglo-Norman woman with water-jug (Hottenroth).
„ 11. Cross from Monasterboice Abbey, Ireland, dates from the year 924 (Margaret Stokes, Early Christian Art in Ireland).

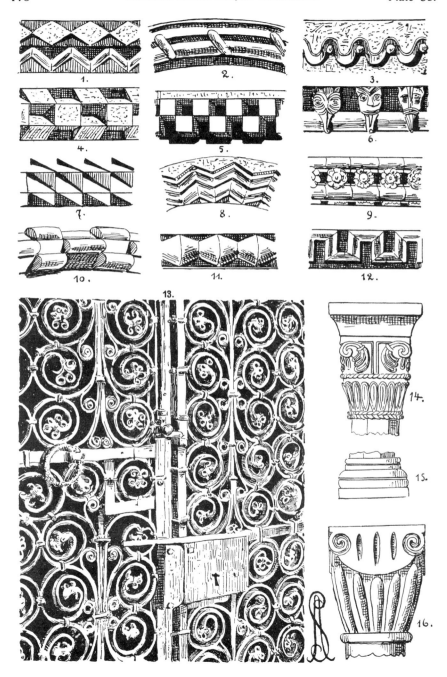

Plate 100. ENGLISH ROMANESQUE ORNAMENT. 179

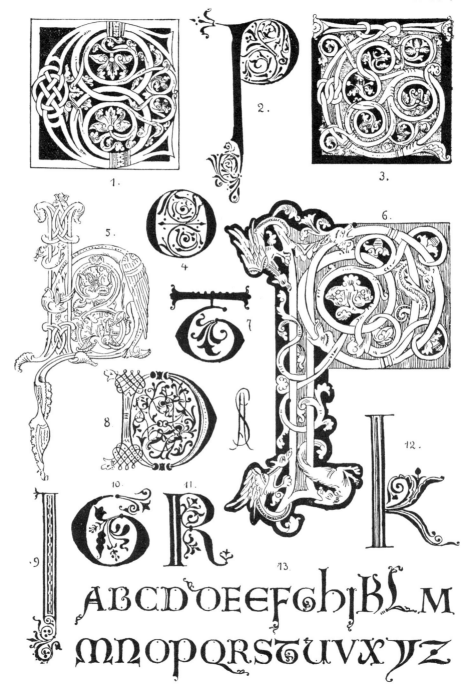

Fig. 12. **Anglo-Saxon dagger,** from the 10th century (Hottenroth).
,, 13, and 15. **Candlesticks** (Hottenroth).
,, 14. **Coronation spoon** (Hottenroth).
,, 16. **Dragon ship,** 11th century (Hottenroth).
,, 17. **Lantern** (Hottenroth).
,, 18. **Norman knight in chain armour** (Hottenroth).

Plate 101.

(H. Shaw, Mediaeval Alphabets and Devices.)

Fig. 1, 3, 5, 6. **Letters from the works of Josephus and other Mss.** 12th century.
,, 2, 4, 7—13. **Letters** from the same period taken from manuscripts in the British Museum.

Arched doorway from the church at Framlingham, Norfolk.
From the middle of the 12th century (V. Ruprich-Robert).

Plate 103.   SCANDINAVIAN ROMANESQUE ORNAMENT.   185

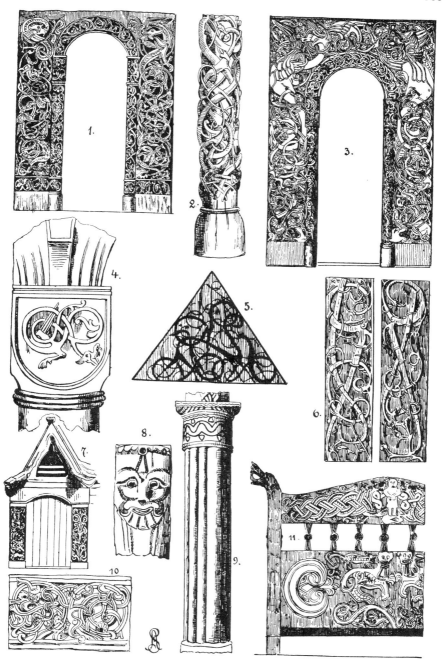

Plate 105.   SCANDINAVIAN ROMANESQUE ORNAMENT.

187

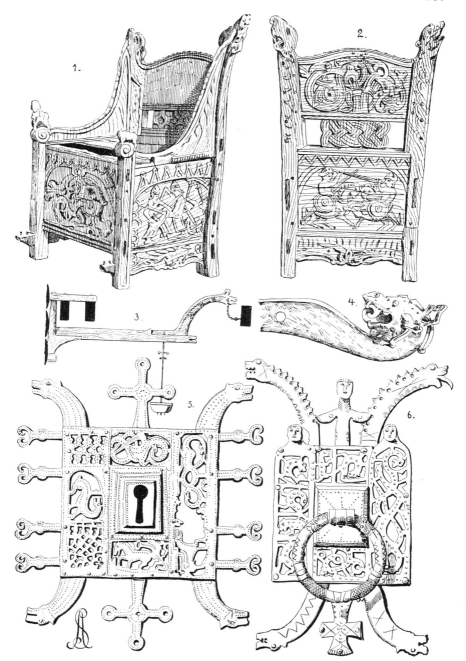

Fig. 2, and 4. **Column and capital from the church at Urnes,** one of the most interesting of Irish wooden churches. It is very ancient.

„ 3. **Doorway of the Andreas Church in Bourgund.** This church lies on the road leading from Christiania to Bergen, and dates apparently from the year 1150 after Christ.

„ 5. **West gable of the church at Urnes.**

„ 6. **Remains of a ruined Irish church in Hopperstad.**

„ 7. **Doorway from the church at Hitterdal,** dates probably from 14th century.

„ 8. **Mask from a wall pillar in the church at Hegge.** This church was first made mention of in the year 1327.

„ 9. **Column from the aisle of the church at Hitterdal.**

„ 10. **Unrolled cylindrical capital from the church at Hegge.**

„ 11. **Part of a chair from the church at Hitterdal.**

Plate 104.

(After Dietrichson and Munthe.)

Fig. 1. **Half of the outer west-doorway of the church at Hegge in Valdres,** bishopric of Hamor.

„ 2. **Half of the doorway of the church at Hemsedal in Hollingdal,** bishopric of Christiania.

„ 3. **Half of the doorway of the church at Hitterdal in Thelemarken,** bishopric of Christianiasand.

„ 4. **North doorway of the same church.**

„ 5. **Doorway of the church at Rennebo, Orkedal,** bishopric of Drontheim, in the museum at Drontheim.

„ 6. **Doorway of the church of Tönjem, Sogn,** bishopric of Bergen, in the museum at Bergen.

Plate 105.

Fig. 1, and 2. **Arm chair in the museum at Christiania.**

„ 3. **Hanging bracket in the same museum** (V. Ruprich-Robert).

„ 4. **Prow of ship in the same museum** V. Ruprich-Robert).

„ 5. **Door Lock in the museum at Bergen** (Mohrmann).

„ 6. **Door Handle in the Hedal church** (Mohrmann).

Plate 106.

Romanesque Ornament in Sweden.

(After Mohrmann.)

Fig. 1, and 4. **Baptismal fonds in the museum at Stockholm.**

„ 2. **Ornament from a baptismal font in the same museum.**

„ 3. **Capital from the crypt of church in Dalby, Sweden.**

„ 5. **Inscription on a baptismal font in the museum at Stockholm.**

„ 6—8. **Columns from the crypt of the church in Dalby, Sweden.**

Plate 107.

Romanesque Ornament in Denmark.

(After Mohrmann.)

Fig. 1—5, and 7. Incised border from altarplate in the church at Sal, Jutland.
,,   6. Doorway of the church at Ripe, Jutland.
.,   8. Altar of the church at Sal.

Stone Ornament from the Cathedral at Lund
(Sesselberg).

RUSSIAN ORNAMENT.

Initial from a Gospel in the Rumjantzow-Museum in Moscow (Dolmetsch).

artaric influence — which dates chiefly from 1237 to 1480, when the Tartars were in power—may be regarded beyond any doubt as the chief cause why the pure Byzantine style originally established in Russia came to be changed later on into the Ornament special to that country. There, as into every other country where they appeared, the Christians brought with them a new style of art, which developed itself afterwards in accordance with the national character of the people. The commencement of Russian Art may be said to date from the end of the 10th century under the reign of Vladimir the Great. In the latter part of the Middle Ages and towards the beginning of the Modern period, Italian artists were invited in great numbers into the country and were engaged in the construction of numerous monumental buildings. The influence of Oriental Art, however, was already so very great, that even Italian Art was not powerful enough to entirely eliminate it from the country. Wooden architecture plays a great part in Russian ornament. There exist at present in Russia some Old-Slavonian manuscripts dating from the 10th century.

Plate 108.

(After E. Viollet le Duc, l'Art Russe.)

Fig. 1. Arch of a doorway in the cathedral of St. Dimitri, Vladimir.
„ 2. Russian capital.
„ 3. Cupola of the cathedral of St. Basil.
„ 4. Russian column.
„ 5. Stucco ornament.

Plate 109.

(After Gagarin, Russische Ornamente.)

Fig. 1. From St. George's church in Jurjeff-Polsky, Government of Vladimir; dates from 13th century.
„ 2. Wood carving on an Ikon, 16th century.
„ 3. Relief decoration of a stone wall in the church of St. George, Jurjeff-Polsky, Government of Vladimir.
„ 4. From a silver mounting of a picture of Christ in Antschishat, Tiflis, 14th century.
„ 5, and 6. Entrance porch of St. George's Church in Jurjeff-Polsky, 13th century.

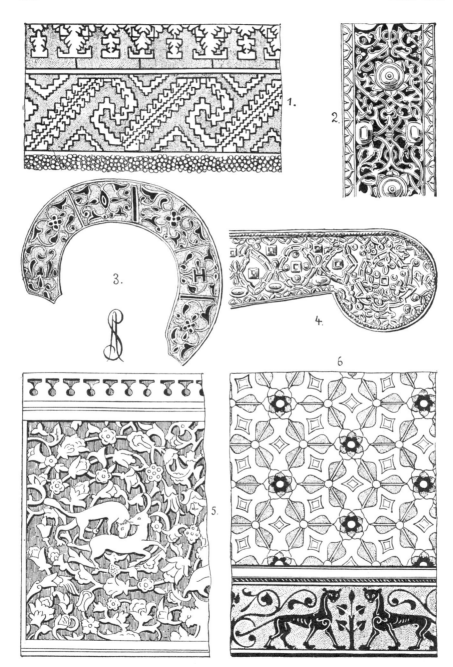

Plate 110.

Fig. 1, and 4. **Painted ornamentations from an Old Russian Psalter,** in the Imperial Public Library at Moscow (Dolmetsch, Ornamentenschatz).

„ 2. **From a Psalter,** in the library of the Holy Trinity, Moscow (Dolmetsch).

„ 3. **From a prayer-book,** in the Miracle-Cloister at Moscow (Dolmetsch).

„ 5. **From a prayer-book,** 15th century, in the Bjaloserski Cloister in Moscow (Dolmetsch),

„ 6. **Club in chased iron** (Libonis).

„ 7. **Old Russian helmet** (Libonis).

„ 8. **Chalice of St. Anthony of Rome** in the Cathedral of the Assumption, Moscow. Dates from 12th century (Libonis).

„ 9. **Krubok (beaker) belonging to Prince John III.** (Libonis).

„ 10. **Spoon belonging to Bishop Antonius,** in Moscow, 12th century (Libonis).

„ 11. **Eagle with victim in claws,** made of Siberian gold, at present in the Museum of the Hermitage (Moscow).

„ 12. **Altar in Antschishat in Tiflis,** 14th century (Gagarin).

„ 13. **Pew of the Czar in the Cathedral of the Assumption, Moscow.** This church was re-built in the years 1475—1479. by an Italian architect named Aristotle Fioravanti, which accounts for the Italian Renaissance influence observable in the Ornament.

„ 14. **Details from the Figs. 12.**

Plate 111.

(After E. Viollet le Duc, l'Art Russe.)

Fig. 1. **Embroidery from a Russian shirt.**

„ 2, 4, and 5. **Ornaments from throne of the Czar Alexis Mikailowitch.**

„ 3. **Diadem in enamel-work,** 16th century.

„ 6. **Mural painting.** The custom of Tree-worship, transmitted from very remote periods, is here plainly discernible.

From a Gospel in the Cloister at Novgorod (Dolmetsch).

MAHOMETAN ORNAMENT.

Decorative fragment fromb tomb of the Sultan El-Ghoury (Prisse).

In ancient times, art was the expression of the religious feelings of a people. When, therefore, a new religious faith was proclaimed, the development of a new art commenced. The proclamation of the peace of the church by Constantine in 323 A. D., led not only to new requirements to meet the demands of the new religion, but to great changes in design, and eventually to a style which differed materially from that which had gone before. The early Christian style in Rome and the West, and the Byzantine style in the East gradually transformed the ancient classic art. A similar change took place shortly after Mahomet carried the Islamic faith through Egypt, Syria and Persia. At first the conquerors and their new convents contented themselves with the structures then existing in the various countries subdued and converted, or, having no preconceived styles of their own, employed the native workmen to build for them, making use of the materials at hand, such as existed in profusion in the Pagan temples and the Coptic and Byzantine churches. In course of time these resources were no longer available, and then commenced the gradual development of the Mahometan style. This style varied in the several countries according as it was influenced by local traditions, and also in the periods when it commenced and when it reached its fullest developments. Thus in Syria, North Africa and Persia, the chief elements of the style are found towards the close of the 8th century. In Egypt it was nearly a century later, as also in Spain, where it was introduced from Kerouan in Tunis, in Asia Minor under the rule of the Seljuk

Turks of Rum it began to flourish toward the close of the 11ᵗʰ century, in India, at about the same time, but only in a small portion of the country, and in Constantinople toward the close of the 15ᵗʰ century. In all these countries there was one universal rule which was rarely departed from, viz, the absolute prohibition of naturalistic representations of men, animals or plants. This led from the first to a purely conventional type of leaf design, which often served as backgrounds for the magnificent inscription in Arabic characters, and to geometrical designs of immense variety, the followers of Mahomet being the greatest geometricians of the world; and at a later period to the decorative treatment of constructional features, such as are shewn in the elaboration of the voussoirs of an arch and more especially in the so-called stalactitic vaulting, which, except in India, prevails throughout the Mahometan style. Originally evolved from constructive features of small materials, such as brick, it was imitated in stone throughout Syria, Egypt, Asia Minor and Constantinople, in plaster in Spain and in all countries in wood.

The titles of the several developments of the Mahometan style vary in the different countries: thus in Persia, it is recognised as Persian, in Syria and Egypt as Saracenic, or Arabian; in Tunis, Morocco and Spain as Moorish, in Turkey as Ottoman, and in India as Indo-Saracenic. In Persia, Syria, Egypt, and Asia Minor, and to a certain extent in India, the pointed arch, first introduced as an important constructional feature in the Mosque of Ibu Tûlûn in Cairo 870 A. D., became eventually an emblem of the faith. In Syria and Egypt the pointed arches were also horse-shoe, that is to say, the arched from was continued below the level of the springing or centres. In Persia and Asia Minor the arches were generally four centred and not horseshoe and the same is found in India. In Tunis, Morocco and Spain the horseshoe arch with semicircular head would seem to have prevailed, this would appear to have originated at Kerouan in Tunis and was carried into Spain by the Moorish followers of Mahomet. To the Moors, however, is due another development of the greatest importance from the ornamental point of view, they were the first to cusp the arch, in 970 A. D., in the sanctuary of the mosque of Cordova, and this, so far as decorative form goes, constitutes the leading characteristic of the Moorish style in Spain.

Plate 113.

MAHOMETAN ORNAMENT.

Arabian Ornament.

Towards the middle of the 9th century the Islamites developed in Egypt a characteristic style of art of which the pointed arch was the distinguishing feature.

Plate 112.

Fig. 1—5. Columns and capitals from Cairo, 17th century (Prisse d'Avennes, la décoration Arabe).

„ 6, and 13. Windows from the mosque Thélây-Abou-Rezyq, 12th century (Prisse d'Avennes).

„ 7. Parapet of the mosque of the Sultan Ibn Kalaom (Owen Jones, Grammar of Ornament).

„ 8. Archivolt ornament from the same mosque (Owen Jones).

„ 9, and 10. Wrought-iron door knocker from Cairo (Owen Jones).

„ 11. Soffit from the mosque El Nasw (Owen Jones).

„ 12. Stalactite ornaments from Cairo (Dolmetsch).

„ 14. Frieze from the mosque Thélây-Aboy-Rezyq (Prisse d'Avennes).

Plate 113.

Fig. 1—4, 8—10, and 13. Decorative details from the interior of the mosque of Ahmed-ibn-Túlûn, 9th century (Prisse).

„ 5, 12, and 16. Wooden trellis work, 12th and 13th centuries (Prisse).

„ 6. From a wooden ceiling in the mosque at Qous (Prisse).

„ 7, and 11. Wooden trellis work from the mosque Thélây-Abou-Rezyq, 12th century (Prisse).

„ 14. From the mosque Tekieh Cheikh Hacen Sadaka, 14th century (Prisse).

„ 15. Interior window decoration from the mosque Queyçoum, 14th century (Prisse).

Plate 114.

Fig. 1. Window of open-worked plaster in the Mosque of El-Ashraf, 15th century (Prisse).

„ 2. Sample of stuff in the museum at Utrecht, 14th century (Prisse).

„ 3. Wall decoration in the mosque Shêkhun, 14th century (Prisse).

„ 4. Wall decoration in the palace of Ismail Bey, 16th century (Prisse).

Plate 115.

Fig. 1—3. Samples of mosaic work, 16th century (Prisse).

„ 4, 9, and 12. Helmet and arms from Toman-Bey (Libonis).

„ 5. Lamp from the mosque of Kalaom. In the Cairo museum (Libonis).

„ 6. Lamp from the mosque El-Ghûri. In the Cairo museum (Libonis).

7. Mosaic frieze from the tomb of Bursbey, 15th century (Prisse).
8, and 13. Decorative fragment from the tomb of the Sultan El-Ghûri (Prisse)
10, and 16. Wood carving from the mosque at Quos, 17th century (Prisse).
11, and 14. Border of wall-tiles, 16th century (Prisse).
15. Carved joist from the hospital of the Muristan, 13th century (Prisse).

Enamelled glass lamp from the mosque of Sultan Barkûk
14th century (Prisse).

Moorish Ornament.

In the wonderful buildings of the Moorish kings in Spain from the 9th to the 14th centuries, more especially in the Cathedral at Cordova, the Alhambra in Granada, and in the Alcazar in Seville, Mahometan Ornamental work may by seen in its highest splendour. In the artistic interlacing and interwaeving of geometric and arabesque Ornament, Moorish artists show extraordinary talent, and give free rein to the wonderful powers of fancy and imagination which they possessed in such a high degree. Despite the exuberance of the ornamentation and the rich and vived coloured of the painting, Moorish Ornament never wearies or confuses the eye, the technical drawing and the colouring of each single system of Ornament beeing so clearly defined and so distinct, that each can be distinguished from the other easily and clearly. The fine arabic lettering was often used by the Moors as Ornament.

Plate 116.

Ornament from the Caliphate in Toledo.

In the old Synagogue, new the Church of St. Maria de la Bianca, Toledo.

Fig. 1. Capital from the central aisle.
„ 2. Capital of the lower story.
„ 3. Stucco ornament from the arch of the central courtyard.
„ 4—6. Console under the tie beams of the aisle.
„ 7. Capital and springing of the arch.
„ 8. Console of the gallery at the entrance.
„ 9. Capital from the upper story.

Plate 117.

Ornament from the Caliphate in Granada.

Fig. 1, and 2. Arch panellings in the Alhambra (Junghändel).
„ 3. Capital from the Alhambra (Junghändel).
„ 4, and 5. Decorative details from the Alhambra (Junghändel).
„ 6. Capital from the Alhambra (Dolmetsch).
„ 7. Wall panelling from the Alhambra (Do'metsch).
„ 8. Taken from portal of the mosque in Tangiers (Uhde).
„ 9. Beginning of arch in the Alberca Court, Alhambra (Uhde).
„ 10. Beginning of arch in the Myrtle Court of the Alhambra (Uhde).
„ 11. Corbels from Toledo. In the Archaeological Museum, Madrid (Uhde).
„ 12. Cresting from the Alhambra (Uhde).

Plate 118.

Ornament from the Caliphate in Granada.

Fig. 1. Wall panelling from the Alhambra (Dolmetsch).
„ 2, and 3. Decorative details from the Alhambra (Junghändel).
„ 4—6. Wall panellings from the Alhambra (Owen Jones).

Plate 118. MAHOMETAN ORNAMENT. 209

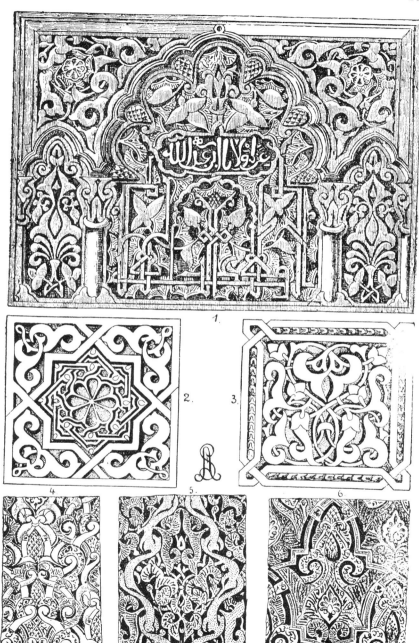

Plate 119

(After Monumentos de España.)

Fig. 1—3. Tile facings in the Hall of the Ambassadors, Granada.

„   4. Taken from the lower part of the Mirador de Lindaraja in the royal Alkazar of the Alhambra, Granada.

„   5—7. Tile facings from the royal chamber of Santo Domingo in Granada.

Plate 120.

Fig. 1. Door from the Alhambra (Uhde).

„   2. Boabdil's sword (Libonis).

„   3, 10, and 11. Mosaic borders (Owen Jones).

„   4, and 5. Plastic wall-border decorations (Owen Jones).

„   6, and 8. Enamelled glass bottles (Libonis).

„   7. Glass lamp from a mosque (Libonis).

„   9. Corner ornaments (Owen Jones).

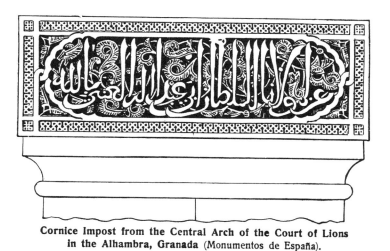

Cornice Impost from the Central Arch of the Court of Lions in the Alhambra, Granada (Monumentos de España).

Saracenic Ornament.

The Saracens, who originally came from Northern Arabia, like the Moors of Hamitic origin, were both for a long time the chief standard bearers of Islam art. When Sicily was conquered by the Normans, the Saracens placed their art at the disposal of the conquerors, in many cases Christian churches were ornamented and decorated by Mahometan artists. In this manner a peculiar Saracen-Norman style of art developed itself in Italy (see page 161). Unfortunately, there are so very few remains of Saracenic art in Sicily now existing that we cannot form any general view of what it really was.

Plate 121.

(After Kutschmann, Meisterwerke der sarazenisch-normannischen Kunst in Sizilien und Unteritalien.)

Fig. 1. **Fragment of a wooden ceiling in the National Museum at Palermo.**
„ 2, and 3. **Panellings of a wooden door in the Martorana at Palermo.**
„ 4. **Door soffit in the National Museum at Palermo.**

Ottoman Ornament.

The term Ottoman is given to the Mahometan style as practised by the Turks in Constantinople. It has, however, a much earlier origin, having been fully developed by the Seljuk Turks, who towards the close of the 12th century had conquered a considerable portion of Mesopotamia, Syria and Asia Minor. One of their earlier buildings is the Medresseh, or Collegiate Mosque at Erzeroum, dating from the middle of the 12th century. All the arches are pointed and the capitals of the columns carrying them are decorated with stalactites.

In this mosque and generally in those found at Konia, Nigdeh, Kaisariyeh and other towns, the principal feature is the entrance porch, which is surrounded by numerous borders, either elaborately carved with conventional designs and inscriptions, or covered with Persian tiles of brilliant colours in some cases probably exported from Persia, so that the influence of their design is noticeable in most of their work. Sometimes their mosques are preceded by an open arcade, with pointed arches, the voussoirs of which are alternately of black and withe marble At Kaisariyeh in the mosque erected by Houen in 1238 A. D., slightly horseshoe and ogee arches are found, but here, as also at Nigdeh, the most beautiful features are the octagonal tombs, in the former of the founder Houen and at Nigdeh of Havandah, the wife of Ala-ed-din of the 13th century. These tombs are enriched in profusion with elaborate carving; with stalactite cornices and conical terminations. Other Seljukian monuments are the four mosques at Sivas, built between 1211 and 1212. Amasia with 13th and 14th century examples, and Divrik, where the entrance doorway with its boldly relieved ornamentation is of great beauty. The power of the Seljuks lasted till their conquest by Timur in 1400 A. D., who devastated the country, which eventually in 1453 A. D. passed into the possession of Mohamet II the conqueror of Constantinople.

The Turks followed the example of all Mohametan rulers and adopted the architectural forms of Constantinople, the Church of Sta. Sophia, built by Justinian becoming the model on which all their mosques in future were based. Previous to the conquest of Constantinople, the Osmanli Turks had already taken possession of Nicaea in 1330 A. D., where tere were many Seljuk mosques, to which they added and enlarged. It was, however, at Brusa, which they took in 1326, that they erected their finest mosques, such as the Great Mosque 1360—1413, the Green Mosque 1420 A. D., a title given to it on account of the green glazed tiles with which its minarets and porch are covered, the tomb of Mohamet I, 1421 A. D. and other structures, in some of which there is certain evidence of Byzantine influence, possibly due to the fact that Greek architects were employed. The employment of tiles encasing the porches and minarets gives a Persian character to all these mosques.

The first great mosque built in Constantinople was the mosque of Mohamet II, built in 1663—69 A. D. on the site of the church of the Holy Apostles, this was designed by Christodoulos, a Greek architect. This was followed by the Bayezidiyeh, built 1497—1505; the Selimiyeh 1520—26; the Suleimanie (1550—56) designed by Sinan, who is said to have been an Armenian architect, and the Ahmediyeh erected by Sultan Ahmed 1608—14 A. D.

In all these mosques a central dome with great apses forms the chief feature, as in Sta. Sophia. The pointed arch, however, was adopted throughout and the details were all based on the Seljukian style with stalactitic capitals, conventional foliage decoration, and inscriptions in fine cufic characters. In the 18th century western Rococo architecture commenced to influence the design, and although, as in the Tulip Mosque 1760—67, the central dome is fine in its contour, its details are of the most debased character. — The Seljukian style was followed in the palace and public monuments, amongst which the numerous drinking fountains, with their rich ornamental decorations in inlaid marble are the most remarkable. In the cemeteries adjoining Constantinople the tombs, consisting of vertica slabs of stone richly carved with ornament, are interesting examples of the Ottoman style.

Tomb Stone at
Constantinople (Normand).

Plate 123.   MAHOMETAN ORNAMENT.   217

1.

2.

3.

4.

5.

Plate 122.

Elements of Ottoman Architecture.

(After Sebah, Die ottomanische Baukunst.)

Fig. 1, and 8. **Stalactite capitals,** after Sinan.
„ 2, and 4. **Pedestal of column,** after Sinan.
„ 3. **Stalactite capital and principal cornice.**
„ 5, 6, and 7. **Various capitals of piers.**

Plate 123.

(After Sebah, Die ottomanische Baukunst.)

Fig. 1. **Frontal with ornamental Cufic characters from the Yeshil-Jami mosqe in Brûsa.** This mosque was completed by the architect Ilias Aali in the year 827 Mahometan time, which in our time correspondends to the year 1424 A. D.
„ 2. **Border of a niche in the Yeshil-Jami mosque in Brûsa.**
„ 3, and 4. **Portal borders from the same mosque.**
„ 5. **Bronze trellis work in the Taouk Bazaar.**

Plate 124.

(After Sebah, Die ottomanische Baukunst.)

Fig. 1, and 2. **Finals of Ottoman cupolas.**
„ 3. **Stalactite mouldings on the large window of the Yeshil-Jami mosque in Brûsa.**
„ 4. **Glass window from the same mosque.**
„ 5. **Decoration on bars of window in the same mosque.**
„ 6. **Door panel from the same mosque.**

Plate 125.

(After Sebah, Die ottomanische Baukunst.)

Fig. 1. **Frieze with glazed brick from the Yeshil-Jami mosque in Brûsa.**
„ 2, 4, and 5. **Iron mountings.**
„ 3. **Shaft of column from the tomb of Sultan Suleiman.**
„ 6. **Bronze lattice work.**
„ 7. **Window with pierced work dating from the time of Sultan Selim.**
„ 8. **Ceiling from the Yeshil-Jami mosque in Brûsa.**
„ 9. **Paving-tile ornament.**

Plate 126.　　　MAHOMETAN ORNAMENT.　　　221

Plate 126.

Fig. 1, 2, and 4.   **Taken from a fountain in Pera, Constantinople** (Owen Jones).
„　　3.   **From a tomb in Constantinople** (Owen Jones).
„　　5, and 6.   **From the Yeni Jami mosque in Constantinople** (Owen Jones).
„　　7, and 8.   **Glazed clay ornaments from the tomb in Mouradieh** (Dolmetsch).
„　　9, 10, and 18.   **Glazed clay ornaments from the tomb of Mahomet I.** (Dolmetsch).
„　　11—13, 16, and 19.   **Glazed clay ornaments from the mosque of Yeshil-Jami at Brûsa** (Dolmetsch).
„　　14, and 15.   **From tomb of the Sultan Suleiman I., Constantinople** (Owen Jones).
„　　17.   **Decoration of the dome Sultan Suleiman I. in Constantinople** (Owen Jones).

Ornamental Pea-tendril.
Transition from naturalistic to Ottoman Ornament
(Sebah, Die ottomanische Baukunst).

Plate 127.   MAHOMETAN ORNAMENT.

223

Persian Ornament.

Although in its system of ornamentation Persian-Islamite art followed the fundamental principles of Mahometan art, still, its most marked characteristic feature consisted in the employment of richly coloured glazed tiles. The extreme loveliness and beauty of the architectural structures of the ancient Kaliphate under Haroun-al-Raschid in Bagdad and Ispahan are due to this method of ornamentation. Although the geometric Ornament in this style does not show such prolific combinations as that of the Saracens or the Moors, its vegetable Ornament, on the other hand, with its greater variety while keeping close to nature, more than makes up for it. Persian art reached its highest glory towards the end of the 19th century.

Plate 127.

From Ispahan.

(After Dolmetsch, Ornamentenschatz.)

Fig. 1, and 2. **Spandrels from the college or Medressé of Maderi-Chah-Sultan-Hussein.**
,, 3. **Openworked window-arch of stone.** The dotted background is stained glass.
., 4, and 6. **Finials.**
,, 5. **Faience tile,** 16th century.
,, 7. **Border of faience.**
,, 8. **Openworked window-case of stone** (belongs to Fig. 3).
,, 9, and 11. **Columns.**
,, 10. **Minaret of the mosque Mesdjid-i-Chah.**
., 12. **Wall border.**

Plate 128.

(After Friedrich Sarre, Denkmäler der persischen Baukunst.)

Fig. 1. **Tile paintings from a palace of Shah Abbas the Great.** In possession of F. Sarre.
,, 2. **Wainscot in the dome of the Medressé of the Kora Tai in Konia.**
,, 3, and 4. **Wainscot in the Liwan of the Court of Medressé Sirtscheh in Konia.**
,, 5. **Brickwork mosaic from the mausoleum of Mumine Chatun in Nakhichewan.**
,, 6. **Inscription from the same mausoleum.**

Plate 129.

(After Friedrich Sarre, Denkmäler der persischen Baukunst.)

Fig. 1. **Faience mosaic from the dome-chamber in the Blue Mosque at Tabriz.**
,, 2. **Brickwork mosaic in the mausoleum of Mumine Chatun at Nakhichewan.**
,, 3—5. **Mural decorations in the dome chamber of the Medressé of Kari Tai. in Konia.**

Plate 130.   MAHOMETAN ORNAMENT.   227

Plate 130.

Fig. 1. **Copper vessel from Kaschan** (Dolmetsch).

„   2, and 3. **Ornaments from the British Museum** (Owen Jones).

„   4. **Wall decoration of faience tiles** (Dolmetsch).

„   5, 11, and 12. **Ornamental work on metal vessels** (Dolmetsch).

„   6. **Glazed ball** (Dolmetsch).

„   7, and 8. **Old-Persian faience plate in the Cluny Museum, Paris** (Dolmetsch).

„   9, and 10. **Fragments of knives and forks** (Dolmetsch).

„   13. **Persian carpet,** 16th century (Dolmetsch).

„   14. **Manuscript painting from the Koran** (Dolmetsch).

Faience decoration from the mosque of Sheik Safi in Ardebil
(F. Sarre).

Plate 131.   MAHOMETAN ORNAMENT.   229

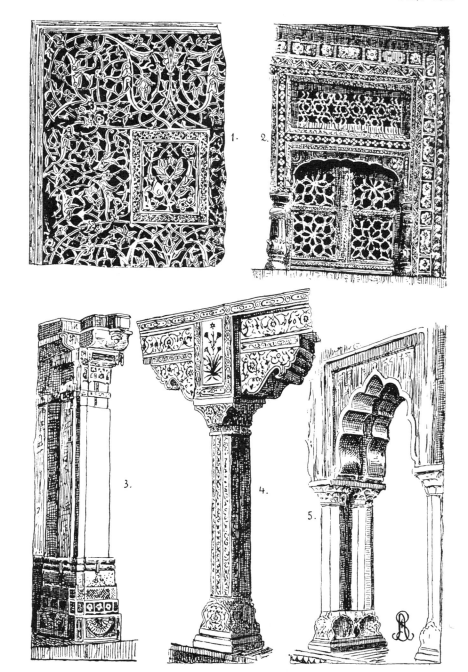

Indo-Saracenic Ornament.

When Islamism made is appearance in India in the 12th century, it found already there an ancient style of art which was characterised by great elaboration, a distinction which very naturally became also associated later on with Indo-Saracenic ornamentation. The buildings erected at this period display, however, a peculiar splendour entirely their own, a splendour which very often rises into the most luxurious beauty. This style of ornamentation, made up of ancient Indian elements and of Saracenic art, reached its highest glory in the 16th century, plants in natural style being preferred to the geometric ornament of the Moors. The Saracenic restriction laid down by the Koran that living animals should not be represented artistically was not regarded either in the Indo-saracenic or Persian art.

Plate 131.

Fig. 1. **From the temple at Vijayananagar,** Dravidian style, 1434 (Uhde).
  „   2, and 3. **From a minaret in Ahmedabad,** built in the years 1430—1450 (Uhde). Figure 2 is to be placed above fig. 3.
  „   4. **Principal entrance to the mosque at Jaunpur,** 1438—1448 (Uhde).
  „   5. **Wood Carving from Burma** (Dolmetsch).

Plate 132.

Fig. 1. **Pierced-panelling in sandstone, from Futtipore-Sikri** (Dolmetsch).
  „   2. **Window from a house in Amritza** (Indian Architecture and Ornament).
  „   3. **Piers from the mosque Ranee Sipre in Ahmedabad** (Indian Architecture and Ornament).
  „   4. **Column from the palace of the Shah Jehan in Agra** (Indian Architecture and Ornament).
  „   5. **Arch from the palace of Amber** (Indian Architecture and Ornament).

Plate 133.

Fig. 1. **Copper flagon in the Munich museum** (Libonis).
  „   2. **Dancer's costume from Ceylon** (Libonis).
  „   3. **Mahout's lance** (Libonis).
  „   4. **Embroidered quiver** (Libonis).
  „   5. **Powder-horn** (Libonis).
  „   6. **Faience plate** (Libonis).
  „   7. **Battle-axe with etched ornament** (Dolmetsch).
  „   8. **Vase of incrusted silver** (Libonis).
  „   9. **Faience jug** (Libonis).
  „ 10. **Damascened vase** (Libonis).

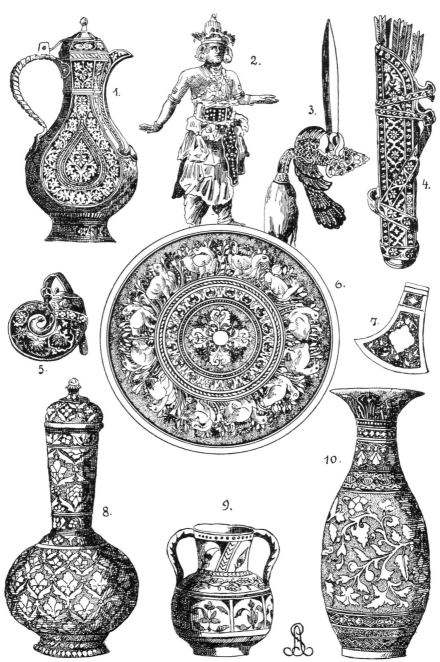

Plate 134.

Decorative work on a damascened shield, gold on steel, in the Ethnographical Museum of the Louvre (l'Art pour tous).

GOTHIC ORNAMENT.

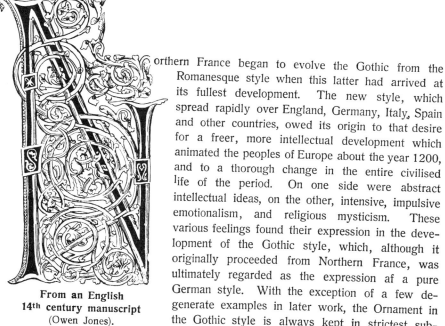

orthern France began to evolve the Gothic from the Romanesque style when this latter had arrived at its fullest development. The new style, which spread rapidly over England, Germany, Italy, Spain and other countries, owed its origin to that desire for a freer, more intellectual development which animated the peoples of Europe about the year 1200, and to a thorough change in the entire civilised life of the period. On one side were abstract intellectual ideas, on the other, intensive, impulsive emotionalism, and religious mysticism. These various feelings found their expression in the development of the Gothic style, which, although it originally proceeded from Northern France, was ultimately regarded as the expression af a pure German style. With the exception of a few degenerate examples in later work, the Ornament in the Gothic style is always kept in strictest subordination to the Form. It never overgrows or conceals the masonic substructure, but, on the contrary, is specially employed to supplement and complete the expression of the Form in a harmonious manner. The principal Ornament of Gothic is the leaf-moulding, the plants being always selected from native Flora, the manner in which they are worked being in nearly every case a pretty sure guide to the period in which they were produced. In Early Gothic, in the 13th century, the leaves were nearly always more or less conventionalized with a slight naturalistic leaning. Later on, the leaves were produced with more force and energy, becoming finally, in Late Gothic, much more naturalistic in their form. During this epoch they were thick set in appearance, and were also sometimes very much under cut, two circumstances which resulted, first in imparting stiffness and rigidity, and secondly, from the sharp contrasts of light and shade which the hollow leaves produced, in giving them constantly varying movement. In the selection of plants, symbolic allusions were also often taken into account. The figures of men and animals made use of in the Gothic were employed in very many cases in a humorous and exaggerated manner. The name Gothic has no connection whatever with the Goths.

Already in the Romanesque style will be found nearly all the essential principles of the Gothic style, so much so that it was at one time suggested to give the term of round arched Gothic to its complete development at the commencement of the 12th century; the title Romanesque is, however, that by which it is best known and therefore has been adhered to here.

The term, however, is generally applied to all its phases, which vary in different countries; thus in North Italy the term Lombard is generally followed. In central and south Italy it is known as Central and Southern Romanesque, in Sicily as Siculo-Norman. In North Germany it is called Rhenish; in North France, Norman, in the South, Provençal or Perigordian, and in England as Saxon and Norman. These various developments were all based on constructional requirements and the materials employed, but these elements form no part of the province of this work, dealing as it does with ornament only. At the same time it is impossible to dismiss some of the early Evolutions which took place, as they form the ground work both in the Romanesque and Gothic styles for the ornament applied to them. The variety of the ornament which is found on the doorways and windows of the Norman style, such as are illustrated on Plates 81, 88, 93, 95 and 99, and which eventually led to that of the great portals of the French, Spanish and English cathedrals, and of which an example at Beverley is shewn on plate 158, cannot be correctly understood without some reference to their construction. In order to emphasize and give importance to the entrance doorway, a series of concentric arches were thrown one above the other, some times called "orders", each one projecting further than the one beneath, to this characteristic Sir Gilbert Scott gave the title of "subordination of the arches". The Roman, Byzantine, and many of the Italian Romanesque arches were all in one plane. In France, Germany and England, and especially in the latter country, there are many planes formed by the concentric rings of masonry one on the other, and these are all moulded and sometimes carved with the designs shewn on plate 99, but the subordination of arches led to a subdivision of the piers carrying them and to the employment sometimes of shafts or columns as a means of decoration and accentuation. On Plate 81, Fig. 3 for instance, are two angle shafts, each of which has a differently ornamented capital, and the same on Plate 93, Fig. 3. In the Gothic style Fig. 1, 3, 11, Plate 136 are examples of the variety of design of the capitals on compound piers and in Fig. 1, Plate 158, are illustrated many slender shafts, each with its respective capital, which gives variety and change to the main design. There is in fact in the evolution of the Romanesque and Gothic styles that characteristic to which reference has already been made, viz, that the ornament is specially employed to supplement and complete the impression of the Form in a harmonious manner.

In the earlier Gothic style, the foliage has a certain conventional character, which will be seen in plates 135 and 146. About the middle of the 13th century it became more naturalistic, as shewn on plates 136 and 137, and this tendency increased in the 14th century, so that, as in Fig. 3, 4, and 9, Plate 162, the sculptor would seem to have imitated the natural leaves so far as the material would allow, this is specially the case in the porch of the Chapter House of Southwell Cathedral. At a later period, and especially in Germany, the ornament became very debased, and what were originally constructive features, such as the shafts of compound piers, were looked upon as decorative features, as, for instance, the columns of St. Blasius Cathedral in Brunswick, of the 15th century, Fig. 5, Plate 162, where they are carried spirally round the columns. The ribs of the tracery in panels were cut short, forming stumps as in Fig. 8, Plate 161, having no sense of fitness or beauty.

On the other hand, in her wrought metal work Germany takes the lead in the 15th century and it would be difficult to find more magnificent specimens than those which are illustrated on plate 173, where the decorative forms follow closely the nature of the material in wrought iron or bronze. The Gothic lettering engraved on the bronze plates of tombs, as illustrated on plate 175 shews how beautiful a surface or flat ornament inscription can become, having the additional value of being an historical record. In the German initial letters also represented on plate 174 there is a plethora of design of the most beautiful character.

From a German 15th century manuscript (Dolmetsch).

Gothic Ornament in France.

ery gradually from Northern France, where its origin is to be found, Gothic architecture spread over the whole of Christian Europe. After many constructive attempts made both at Autun and Vezelay, Abbot Suger finally erected in the years 1141—1144 the Abbey Church of St. Denis. Although this church shows very many traces of Romanesque influence, as do all Early Gothic buildings, and is a combination of old architectural habits with new ideas, it is still **From a** the first and most important example of Gothic architecture. **14th century** That great master-piece of Early Gothic, the cathedral of **Manuscript** Notre Dame in Paris, was erected in the years 1163—1182. **(Racinet).** Towards the beginning of the 13th century the complete, fully-developed and fully-ripened form of the Gothic was finally arrived at, from which time it began to flourish until it developed at last into the period of its highest glory. The after-growths of the Gothic in the 14th and 15th century were called, in Germany Late-Gotic, but were designated in France as the Flamboyant Style. The desire for greater lightness becoming now apparent, and the purity of design being neglected at the same time, it finally happened that the Ornament grew apace and masked the form, a fate which in the end overtook almost all styles of architecture.

Principal cornice from Notre Dame de Paris (Viollet le Duc).
Base from Paris Cathedral (Viollet le Duc).
Cornice from the Notre Dame at Chalons (Viollet le Duc).

Plate 135.

GOTHIC ORNAMENT.

Plate 135.

Plate 136.

Plate 137.

Gothic Flora.

(From Viollet le Duc, Dictionnaire Raisonné de l'architecture Française du XIe au XVIe siècle.)

Plate 136. GOTHIC ORNAMENT. 241

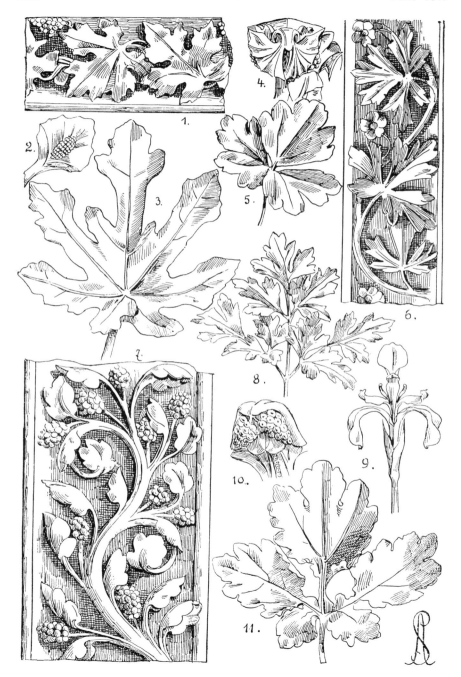

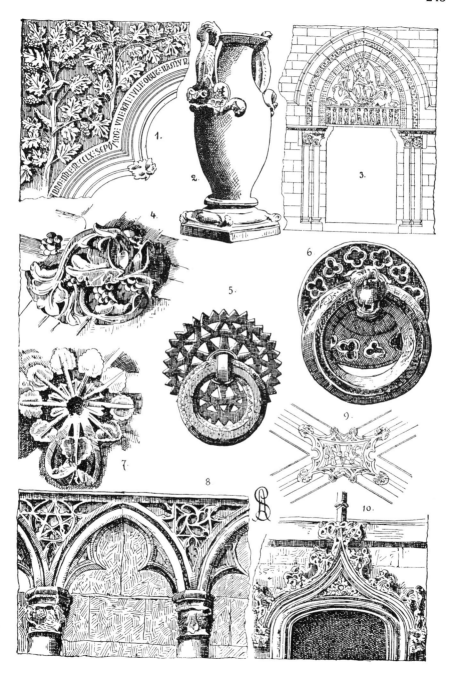

Plate 138.

Fig. 1. **Spandril from the church of St. Severin in Bordeaux,** 1247 (Viollet le Duc).

„ 2. **Stone vase,** 13th century; found in Aix, Provence Raguenet, Matériaux).

„ 3. **Doorway of the church of St. Genest at Nevers,** middle of the 12th century (Viollet le Duc).

„ 4. **Boss of vault from the priory of St. Martin des Champs, Paris,** 13th century (Raguenet).

„ 5. **Door-knocker from Cordes, Tarn** (Raguenet).

„ 6. **Door-knocker from Bayonne,** 13th century (Raguenet).

„ 7, and 9. **Boss of vault from the church of St. Severin, Paris** (Raguenet).

„ 8. **Arcade from St. Chapelle, Paris,** 15th century (Raguenet).

„ 10. **Doorway of the Episcopal palace at Beauvais, Oise,** 16th century.

Plate 139.

(Gothic mural painting after P. Gélis-Didot et H. Laffillée, La peinture décorative en France du XIe au XVIe siècle.)

Fig. 1. **Stencil painting from the church of Chateloy near Herisson, Allier.**

„ 2. **Frieze painting from Coney Castle** (Aisne).

„ 3. **From the roof of the church at Cunault,** Maine et Loire, beginning of the 14th century.

„ 4—6. **Textile paintings in the chancel of Amiens cathedral.** These patterns, which have had their origin, without any doubt, in the Orient, were also very frequently used in flat-painting.

„ 7. **From the chapel of St. Antony in the cloister of the Jacobines in Toulouse.**

„ 8. **From the church of the Jacobins in Agen.**

„ 9. **From the church at Romans** (Drôme).

„ 10. **From the chapel of Saint-Crépin in Evron** (Mayenne).

„ 11. **From the church of Saint-Ours in Loches** (Indre et Loire).

„ 12. **From the sacristy of the cathedral at Clermont.**

„ 13. **From the chapel at Pritz** (Mayenne). This represents the month of September, and is one of the 12 Panels which illustrate the twelve months of the year.

Plate 140.

Fig. 1, and 2. **Belt with knife,** 15th century (Viollet le Duc, Dictionnaire raisonné du mobilier française).

„ 3. **Reliquary, in the Cluny museum,** a crystal cylinder with gilt copper mountings (Viollet le Duc).

„ 4. **Coiffure of Queen Isabel of Bavaria,** 1395 (Viollet le Duc).

„ 5. **Buckle,** 14th century (Viollet le Duc).

„ 6. **Embroidered Prayer-book Bag,** 14th century (Viollet le Duc).

„ 7. **Purse,** 15th century (Racinet, Le costume historique).

„ 8. **Lock of coffer** Viollet le Duc).

„ 9. **Harness,** 15th century (Viollet le Duc).

Plate 139.   GOTHIC ORNAMENT.   245

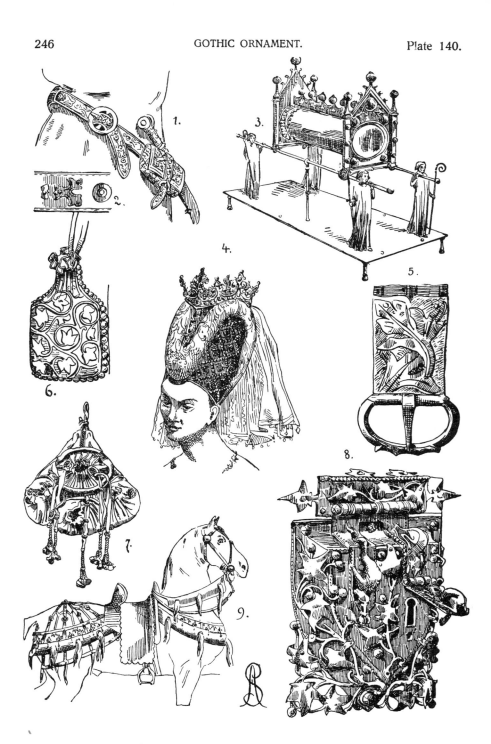

Plate 141.   GOTHIC ORNAMENT.   247

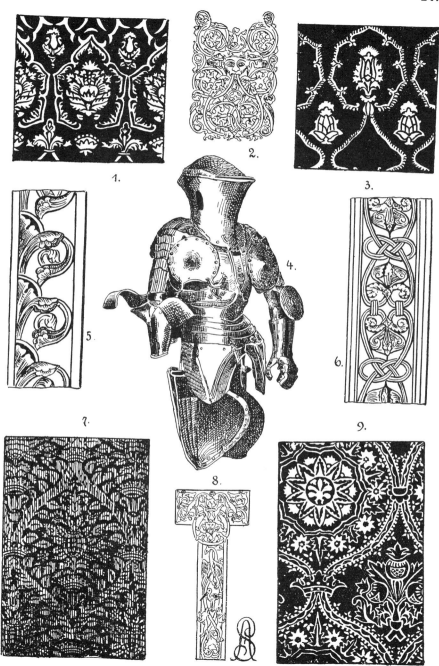

1.

2.

3.

4.

5.

6.

7.

8.

9.

Plate 141.

Fig. 1, and 3. **Textile pattern,** 15th century (Gélis-Didot et Laffillée).
„ 2, and 8. **Enamel-work on copper** (Roger-Milès).
„ 4. **Armour,** 14th century (Roger-Milès).
„ 5. **Glass painting from Bourges cathedral** (Owen Jones).
„ 6. **Glass painting from Angers cathedral** (Owen Jones).
„ 7, and 9. **Textile patterns,** 16th century (Gélis-Didot et Laffillée).

Plate 142.

Fig. 1. **Painting from a prayer-book in the National Library at Paris.** The Latin text dates from the year 1398, the painting, which has been ascribed to Israel of Mekenen is, however, of a later period.
„ 2. **Stall i Cluny museum,** 15th century (E. Bajot, Collection des Meubles anciens).
„ 3. **Credence table,** 15th century (Raguenet).
„ 4. **Stool from the bedroom of Louis XI.**
„ 5. **Lorraine wooden coffer in the museum at Cluny,** 14th century (Bajot).

Plate 143.

Fig. 1. **Napkin border,** 16th century (Raguenet).
„ 2. **Printed cloth,** 15th century Raguenet).
„ 3. **Goblet, with transparent enamel** (Havard).
„ 4. **Antique cameo, said to be portrait of King Charles V** (Havard).
„ 5. **Processional crucifix of beaten silver, chased and gilt** (Havard).
„ 6. **Silver cooling-tankard** (Havard).
„ 7. **Altar candlestick of chased silver** (Havard).
„ 8. **Prayer-book belonging to St. Louis** (Havard).
„ 9. **Bread-knife, in gilt silver filigree-worked sheath** (Havard).
„ 10. **Wine cup in Silver gilt,** in the cathedral at Reims (Havard).
„ 11. **Neck ornament and goblet of the Niveller rifle-corps** (Havard).
„ 12. **Ebony coffer in the Cluny museum** (L'art pour tous).

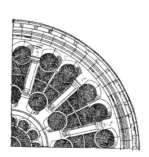 

Rose window from the Abbey at Braisne (Viollet le Duc).
Base from the Cathedral of Maux (Viollet le Duc).

Plate 142.   GOTHIC ORNAMENT.   249

1.

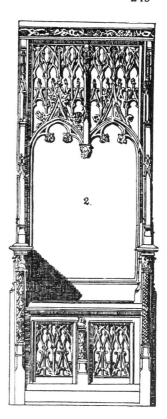

2.

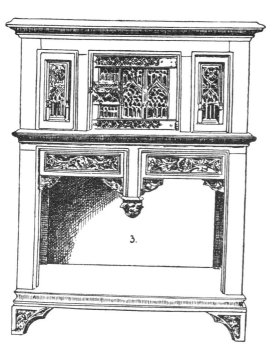

3.

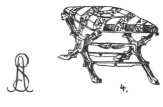

4.

5

Plate 144.

GOTHIC ORNAMENT.

1.

2.

3.

4.

GOTHIC ORNAMENT.

Gothic Ornament in the Netherlands.

Initial from Israel of Mekenen (Hirth).

nto the Netherlands, Gothic architecture soon made its way, a most natural circumstance considering how near that country lay to France, the land where the Gothic style had its origin. Varied specimens of Gothic architecture appeared all over Belgium, but in Holland, where this style was latter on very strongly influenced by Germany, and where, for obvious reasons, plain brick-work architecture had to predominate, the examples are far more simple and not so varied. One very remarkable and most peculiar feature of the Gothic style in Belgium consists in the extreme care with which the entire decorative-work, even the very minutest details, is carried out. The most important cathedral in Holland, Utrecht was built by Bishop Henry of Vianden in the years 1251—1267; the most important Gothic monument in Belgium being the celebrated cathedral of Antwerp, which was begun by Jean Amel of Appelmans from Boulogne in the year 1352. The finest examples of Gothic architecture, however, were the Town Hals, the most beautiful specimen being in Louvain.

Plate 144.

(After Ysendyck, Art dans les Pays-Bas.)

Fig. 1. **Embroidery-work from the frock of a king-at-arms, during the reign of Philip II.** The Spanish coat of arms are embroidered in coloured silk on a foundation of carmine-red velvet. Two robes similar to this are still preserved in the arsenal at Madrid.

„ 2. **Window from the cloister of St. Servais, Maestricht,** 15th century.

„ 3. **Chimney-piece in blue stone from the Pas-perdus Hall in Mons,** 15th century.

„ 4. **Balustrade of granite,** 16th century. This is employed at present plinth for a copper grating in the church of Walburg in Furnes.

Wrought iron hinge on the door of the treasury chamber in the cathedral of St. Paul, Liege (L'art pour tous).

Plate 145.　　　　GOTHIC ORNAMENT.　　　　253

Plate 145.

Fig. 1. **Flemish sculpture,** 15th century (Raguenet).
  „ 2. **Brass wine goblet,** 15th century (Ysendyck, Art dans les Pays-Bas).
  „ 3. **Tabernacle door of wrought iron,** 15th century (Ysendyck, Art dans les Pays-Bas).
  „ 4. **Wrought iron candlestick,** 15th century (Libonis).
  „ 5. **Lectern from the church at Tongres,** 15th century (Raguenet).
  „. 6. **Fountain from Quentin-Matsys, Antwerp,** 15th century (Raguenet).

Gothic Ornament in England.

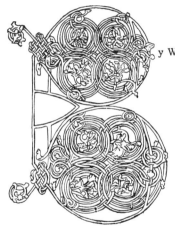

y William of Sens, an architect of French origin, Gothic was employed in the Cathedral of Canterbury which was begun in the year 1175. Even in Westminster Abbey, which was erected in the years 1245—1300, French influence is also plainly discernible. Notwithstanding this, however, the Gothic style in England soon learned to move along on independent lines of its own. The English Gothic Tudor arch and the Ogee arch, are specially peculiar of late English Gothic. There are three Gothic periods in England.

1. *Early Gothic* (Early English) in the 13th century, characterised by the Lancet Arch.
2. *The Decorated Style,* so-called on account of its rich decorative development.
3. *The Perpendicular Style* in the 15th century. In this style the Tudor and the Orgee Arch predominate, and the forms become gradually more and

From a 15th century manuscript (Owen Jones).

more fantastic. The vaulting is carried to its greatest elaboration, and therewith begins the decline of this style.

Plate 146.

Fig. 1. **From Stone church, Kent** (Owen Jones).
  „ 2, and 4. **From Wells cathedral, decorated style** (Owen Jones).
  „ 3. **Rosette from Oxford** (Pugin, Gothic Ornament).
  „ 5, and 6. **Capitals from Warmington church,** Northamptonshire (Owen Jones).
  „ 7. **Capital from Wells cathedral,** early English (Owen Jones).
  „ 8, and 9. **Leaf mouldings from Trinity Stratford-on-Avon** (Pugin).

Plate 146.　　　　GOTHIC ORNAMENT.　　　　255

Plate 148.   GOTHIC ORNAMENT.   257

Plate 147.

(After Pugin, Gothic Ornament.)

Fig. 1. **Crocket from Winchester cathedral.**
„ 2. **Finial to a stall in All Soul's College Chapel, Oxford.**
„ 3. **Portion of Stone canopy from York minster.**
„ 4. **Crocket from Trinity church, Stratford-on-Avon, Warwick.**
„ 5. **Finial of a stall in New Walsingham church, Norfolk.**
„ 6. **Capital from St. Saviour's church, Southwark.**
„ 7. **Stringcourse from Winchester cathedral.**

Plate 148.

(After Pugin, Examples of Gothic Architecture.)

Fig. 1. **Turret over entrance gateway, East Barsham manor house, Norfolk.**
„ 2. **Window from the Cloisters, New College, Oxford.**
„ 3. **Monument of Sir Richard Carew, Beddington church, Surrey.**
„ 4. **Oak Tracery at the back of stalls in All Soul's College chapel, Oxford.**
„ 5. **Canopy to one of the stalls in St. Catherine's church, Tower Hill, London.**

Plate 149.

(After Pugin, Examples of Gothic Architecture.)

Fig. 1—3. **Sin bracket, George Inn, Glastonbury.**
„ 4. **Window in gable of the Abbot's Barn, Glastonbury.**
„ 5, 6, and 8. **Details from the Abbot's Barn, Glastonbury.**
„ 7. **Window from Raglan Castle, Monmouthshire.**
„ 9. **Canopy on the west front of the chapel at Houghton-in-the-Dale, Norfolk.**

Plate 150.

(After Pugin, Examples of Gothic Architecture.)

Fig. 1. **Panel from the Common room of the Vicar's Close, Wells.**
„ 2, 3, 5, 6, and 8. **Details from the banqueting hall of the Manor House, Great Chalfield, Wilts.**
„ 4, 7, 9. **Details from the western doorway of Magdalen College, Oxford.**
„ 10. **Chimney-piece in the Bishop's palace, Wells.**

Plate 151.

(After Pugin, Examples of Gothic Architecture.)

Fig. 1. **Oriel window on the north side of the quadrangle of Balliol College, Oxford.**
„ 2. **Canopy in Falkenham church, Norfolk.**
„ 3. **Door handle, temp Henry VII.**
„ 4. **Doorway at the westend of Magdalen College chapel, Oxford,**
„ 5. **Small lock for a chest, temp Henry VII.**

Plate 149. GOTHIC ORNAMENT. 259

Plate 151. GOTHIC ORNAMENT. 261

Plate 153.   GOTHIC ORNAMENT.   263

Fig. 6. **Fan vault from All Souls' College, Oxford.**
„ 7, 8, and 9. **Moulded tiles from chimney stacks, East-Barsham Manorhouse. Norfolk.**
„ 10. **Oak ceiling, New Walsingham church, Norfolk.**

Plate 152.

(Talbot Bury, Remains of Ecclesiastical Woodwork.)

Fig. 1—4. **Roof of St. Mary's church, Bury St. Edmunds.**
„ 5, and 6. **Roof of Lavenham church, Suffolk.**
„ 7, 9, 11, and 12. **Roof of Burford church, Oxfordshire.**
„ 8, and 10. **Roof of Wantage church, Berkshire.**

Plate 153.

Fig. 1. **Finial from Exeter cathedral,** 14th century (Raguenet).
„ 2. **Solid springer from the same cathedral** (Raguenet).
„ 3. **Rosette from Chester cathedral,** 15th century (Raguenet).
„ 4. **Font from Bradfield church, Suffolk** (Raguenet.)
„ 5. **Pulpit in Bridgewater church, Somersethshire** (Talbot Bury).
„ 6. **Grotesque figure, Oxford** (Pugin).
„ 7. **Panel from the façade of Wells cathedral** (Raguenet).
„ 8—10. **Encaustic tiles,** 14th century (Owen Jones).

Plate 154.

Fig. 1. **From a stall in the church at Weston Zoyland, Somersetshire** (Talbot Bury, Remains of Ecclesiastical Woodwork).
„ 2. **Chandelier from church at Piddletown, Dorset.**
„ 3. **Goblet of silver gilt,** 15th century (Libonis).
„ 4, 7, and 8. **From a manuscript of the Middle Ages** (Owen Jones).
„ 5. **Coronation chair in Westminster Abbey** (Libonis).
„ 6. **Stall in Wantage church, Berkshire** (Talbot Bury).
„ 9. **Stained glass window in Merton College chapel, Oxford** (Pugin).
„ 10. **Stained glass window Southwell minster, Nottinghamshire** (Owen Jones).

Plate 155.

Fig. 1. **Middle Gothic glass-painting in Norbury, Derbyshire.**
„ 2. **Lead glazing in Brabourne church, Kent.**
„ 3. **Head of Queen of Sheba in window at Fairford.**
„ 4, 6, and 8. **Grisaille glass from Salisbury cathedral.**
„ 5. **Late Gothic glass-painting in Wells.**
„ 7. **Glass painting, with figure of Edward the Confessor, St. Mary's, Ross.**

Plate 154. GOTHIC ORNAMENT. 265

Plate 156.

GOTHIC ORNAMENT.

Plate 157.

Plate 156.

Fig. 1. Coffer in the sacristy in Louth church, Lincolnshire (Colling).
„ 2. Panel from the church at Trull, Somersetshire (Colling).
„ 3, and 4. Panels from the font in the church at Great Conerby, Lincolnshire (Colling).
„ 5. Gilt iron lock from the hall of Beddington Manor House, Surrey (Pugin).

Plate 157.

(Franklin A. Crallan, Gothic Woodwork.)

Fig. 1. Bench end, Breadsall church, Derbyshire, 15th century.
„ 2. Stall from St. Andrew Gatton, Surrey.
„ 3. Canopy over the tomb of Edward III. in Westminster Abbey, 1380.
„ 4. Door from the church of St. Laurence, Norwich.
„ 5. End of a seat from Witley, Surrey, 15th century.
„ 6. Panel in Tudor Style from the South Kensington Museum.

Plate 158.

Fig. 1. West doorway of St. Mary's church, Beverley (Colling).
„ 2. Gate of the Bishop's Chapel in Ely cathedral (Bailey Scott Murphy).
„ 3. Doorway of the Presbytery at North Petherton, Somersetshire (Colling).
„ 4. Door of the church at Bocking, Essex (Colling).

Plate 159.

(Henry Shaw, Mediaeval Alphabets and Devices.)

Fig. 1. Lettering from the monument of Henry III. in Westminster Abbey, 1272.
„ 2—4, 6, and 7. Letters from the monument of Richard II. in Westminster Abbey, 1400.
„ 5. Letters from a benedictional, 1480.
„ 8. Grotesque lettering from a printed book, 16th century.
„ 9. Signature of a wood-engraver, 15th century.
„ 10. Initial from a manuscript in the British Museum.

Plate 160.

Ornament on English Monuments.

(From C. A. Stothard, The monumental effigies of Great Britain.)

Fig. 1. From a tombstone in the Ingham church, Norfolk.
„ 2. Crown of the Earl of Arundel, died 1487.
„ 3. Ladies' coiffure, 15th century.
„ 4. Sheath of dagger belonging to Lord Hungerford, died 1459.
„ 5. Crown of Queen Berengaria, wife of Richard Cœur de Lion.
„ 6. Shoe of Henry III., died 1272, from a tomb in Edward the Confessor's chapel.
„ 7, and 8. Bag and brooch of Queen Berengaria.

Fig. 9. **Necklace,** 15th century.
„   10, and 11. **Heads of Sir Edmund de Thorpe and Lady in Ashwelthorpe church, Norfolk.**
„   12. **Spur of Sir Hugh Calvely, in Bunbury church, Cheshire.**
„   13. **Belt buckle of the Earl of Warwick.**
„   14. **Hilt of sword belonging to Sir John Peche,** from his tomb in the church at Lullingstone, Kent.
„   15, and 16. **Sword-hilt and sword-belt belonging to John de la Pole,** Duke of Suffolk.
„   17. **Shoe of Edward III.,** died in 1377, taken from his tomb in Westminster Abbey.
., 18. **End of sword-belt,** 14th century.
„   19. **Coiffure of the Countess of Westmoreland.**
„   20. **Glove of Ralph Neville, Earl of Westmoreland,** from his tomb in Staindrop church at Durham.

Head-dress of Beatrice, Countess of Arundel.
From a statue in Trinity church, Arundel, 13th century (Viollet le Duc).

Plate 158.

GOTHIC ORNAMENT.

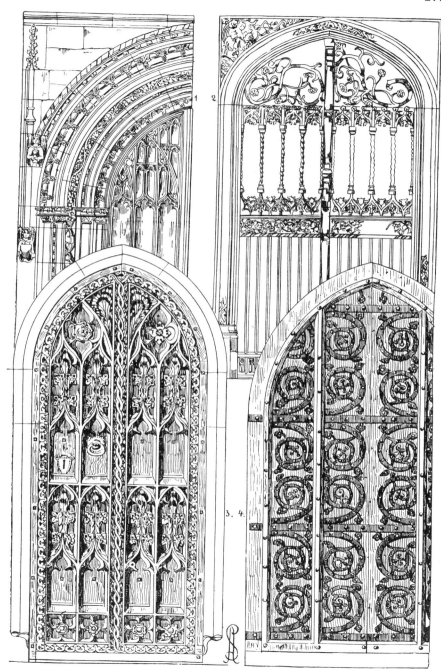

1.

2.

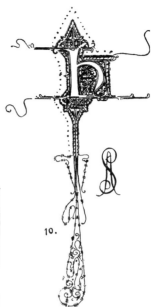

3.

4.

5.

10.

6.

7.

8.

9.

Plate 160.

GOTHIC ORNAMENT.

Gothic Ornament in Germany and Austria.

**From a 15th century Manuscript
(Dolmetsch).**

s soon as the Gothic Style had well entered on its victorious march throughout England, it began also to make its way gradually throughout Germany, where, on account of its French origin, it became generally known under the title of "OPUS FRANCI-GENUM". Although it had not completely won the victory over Romanesque Art until about the commence of the 14th century, it was nevertheless, at this time, fully perfect in all its forms. The Early Gothic continued up until the beginning of the 14th century. The oldest Gothic building in Germany is the Choir in the cathedral at Magdeburg which was consecrated in the year 1234. The most beautiful specimens of the Gothic are however to be found in the Rhineland where the Gothic Style reached its highest perfection, the Cathedral at Cologne, which was begun in the year 1248, being its noblest work.

**Coat of Arms from the
Town Hall at Lüneburg.**

**Rosette
from Neubrandenburg.**

Rosette from Stargard.

(Fritz Gottlob, Formenlehre der norddeutschen Backsteingotik.)

Plate 161. GOTHIC ORNAMENT. 275

Plate 161.

(After Heideloff, Ornamentik des Mittelalters.)

Fig. 1. **Frieze from the passage between the Nicholas Chapel and the cathedral-church at Aix-la-chapelle, 1480.**

„ 2. **Finial from the fountain in the market square at Rottenburg on the Neckar, late Gothic.**

„ 3. **Crocket from St. Kilian's church at Heilbronn.**

„ 4, and 8. **Balustrade, and inscription from the court-yard of the house Adler Str. L 308, Nüremberg.**

„ 5. **Capital from Cologne cathedral.**

„ 6. **Finial from a stone Tabernacle in the Hospital church, Esslingen,** the work of Matthäus von Böblingen.

„ 7. **Finial from the shrine of St. Sebald in Nüremberg,** wrought in bronze by Peter Vischer and his son (1508—1519).

„ 9. **Corbel of vault from the Lilienfeld Cloister near Vienna.**

„ 10. **Baptismal font in Münnerstadt on the Lauer.**

Plate 162.

Fig. 1, 3, and 6. **Capitals from the cathedral church of St. Peter at Wimpfen in the valley near Heilbronn** (Zeller, St. Peter zu Wimpfen i. T.).

„ 2. **Capital from the church of the Cistercian Cloister Lilienfeld near Vienna.**

„ 4. **Capital from the cathedral at Frankfurt on the Main,** 14th century (Raguenet).

„ 5. **Column from the St. Blasius cathedral, Brunswick,** 15th century (Hartung, Mittelalterliche Baukunst in Deutschland).

„ 7. **Capital and base from the princes' tomb in the Holy Cross church near Vienna** (Heideloff).

„ 8. **Capital from a window of the Saalburg on the Saale** (Franconia) (Heideloff).

„ 9. **Capital from the cathedral at Worms** (Raguenet).

Plate 163.

Fig. 1. **Door from Ober-Kranichfeld** (Heideloff).

„ 2. **Late Gothic door from Coburg fortress** (Heideloff).

„ 3. **Portal of the Elizabeth church in Marburg** (Hartung).

„ 4. **Bridal door on the north side of the choir in the church of St. Sebald, Nüremberg,** 14th century.

Plate 164.

(After Heideloff, Ornamentik des Mittelalters.)

Fig. 1—4. **Late Gothic ornaments in flat wood relief in the gallery balustrade of a house in the Hauptmarkt, Nüremberg.**

„ 5, and 8. **Wood-carving from a writing-desk in the rectory of St. Lorenz, Nüremberg.**

„ 6, and 7. **Panelling from stone gallery in the choir of the Cloister church in Blaubeuren.**

Plate 162. GOTHIC ORNAMENT. 277

1.

2.

3.

4.

5.

6.

7.

8.

9.

Plate 164. GOTHIC ORNAMENT. 279

Fig. 9. **From a stall in the Cloister church of St. Clara, Nüremberg.**
„ 10, and 11. **Wooden rosettes from the rose chamber in the Princes House, Coburg Castle.**
„ 12. **Window head in the St.** Lawrence rectory, Nüremberg, 1458.
„ 13. **Window head of a private house in Nördlingen.**
„ 14, and 15. **Window heads from the ruined Hospital in Esslingen.**

Plate 165.

Fig. 1, and 3. **Glass window from the church at Hundelshausen** (Ungewitter, Land- und Stadtkirchen).
„ 2. **Relief over the door of the chapel tower in the Parish church, Rottweil** (Heideloff).
„ 4. **Stained glass from the cathedral at Regensburg, now in the National Museum at Munich** (Dolmetsch).
„ 5. **Glass painting from the Frauenkirche, Esslingen** (Dolmetsch).
„ 6. **Pulpit from the church of the Ursuline Convent in Fritzlar** (Ungewitter).
„ 7, and 8. **From the Cathedral church of St. Peter in Wimpfen-im-Tal** (Zeller, St. Peter zu Wimpfen-im-Tal).

Window from the
Stargard Gate,
New Brandenburg.

Gable at the Market
side of the Town Hall
of Königsberg.

From the South Chapel
of the Katharinen
church, Brandenburg.

(Fritz Gottlob, Formenlehre der norddeutschen Backsteingotik.)

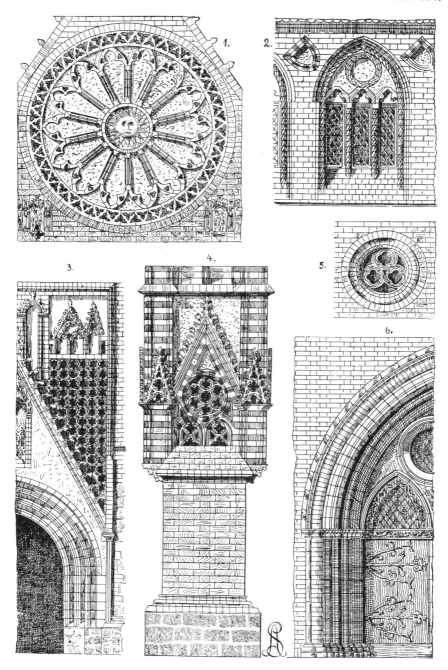

Plate 167.　　　　GOTHIC ORNAMENT.　　　　283

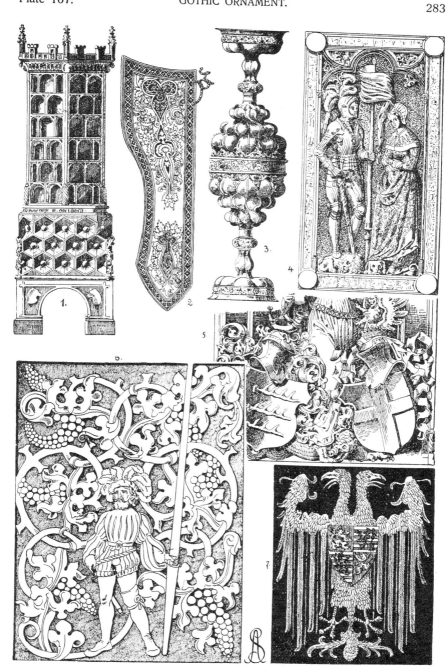

GOTHIC ORNAMENT.

Plate 166.

German Gothic Brickwork.

(After Fritz Gottlob, Formenlehre der norddeutschen Backsteingotik.)

The Romanesque Brickwork of North Germany, which had its origin in North Italy, became, naturally, when Gothic Architecture developed and became prevalent, gradually changed into the Gothic style. The marked differences between the two were due, to the different materials used, and to the manner in which these materials, stone and brick, had to be treated. The Brickwork was very probably prior to the Stone Gothic, and in the level plains of North Germany, where sandstone is scarce, there gradually arose a special style of Gothic Brickwork quite in keeping with the peculiarity of the building material and the character of the people.

Fig. 1. **Window from the Nikolai church in Wismar.**
  „ 2. **Window from the Town Hall of Lübeck.**
  „ 3. **North doorway of the church of St. Mary, Königsberg, Prussia.**
  „ 4. **Buttress in the same church.**
  „ 5. **Rose window from the church at Prenzlau.**
  „ 6. **Principal doorway in the Cloister church, Berlin.**

Plate 167.

(After Heideloff, Ornamentik des Mittelalters.)

Fig. 1. **Glazed heating stove in Burg Füssen on the Lech.** The stove contains the following inscription „Dieser Ofen Wol-gestalt ward gemacht do man zallt 1514 jar bey Hannsen Seltzmann Vogt zu Oberndorf". — This stove was made in 1514 by Hannsen Seltzmann, Steward at Oberndorf.
  „ 2. **Quiver, after a painting from Albrecht Dürer,** showing Hercules conquering the Harpies. At present in the Burg at Nüremberg.
  „ 3. **Late Gothic double goblet in silver gilt,** in possession of the family Knopf in Nüremberg.
  „ 4. **Monument to Graf von Henneberg,** done in bronze by Peter Vischer, from a sketch by Albrecht Dürer.
  „ 5. **Arms of Württemberg and Savoy,** from a tomb in the Stifts church in Stuttgart.
  „ 6. **Late Gothic ornament from the bridal-carriage of Agnes of Hesse,** wife of Duke John Frederick of Saxe-Coburg (1555), in flat relief, carved in wood and gilt.
  „ 7. **Eagle from panelling of the door of the Emperor's room in Scheurlis House,** Nüremberg.

Plate 168.

(After F. Paukert, Tiroler Zimmergotik.)

Fig. 1. **Wood ceiling in Jochlsturm, Sterzing.**
  „ 2. **Tiles from the Burg in Meran.**
  „ 3. **Marquetry from a table.**
  „ 4—7. **From a wood ceiling in Freienstein.**
  „ 8—11. **Tie-beams of a wood ceiling in St. Martin, Ahrntal.**

Plate 168. GOTHIC ORNAMENT. 285

Plate 170.   GOTHIC ORNAMENT.   287

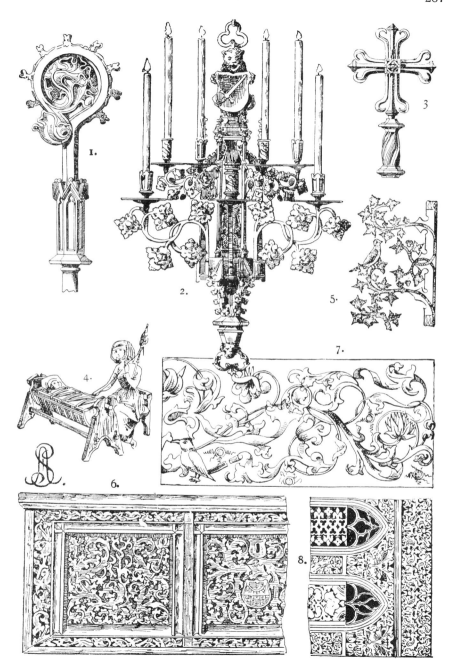

1.

2.

3

4.

5.

6.

7.

8.

Plate 169.

Gothic ornamental Iron-work from Nüremberg Museum.

Fig. 1, 4, 7, 9, 11, 13, and 16. **Door handles.**
„ 2, 8, and 10. **Lock mountings.**
„ 3, 5, 12, 14, and 15. **Door mountings.**
„ 6. **Wood door with iron mountings.**

Plate 170.

Fig. 1. **Late Gothic crozier,** from a tombstone in the cathedral at Regensburg (Heideloff).
„ 2. **Late Gothic candelabrum of bronze from the church of Kraftshof near Nüremberg** (Heideloff).
„ 3. **Gilt wooden cross,** from an altar in the church of St. Mary at Hersbruck (Heideloff).
„ 4. **Gothic cradle** (Heideloff).
„ 5, and 7. **Manuscript painting, 15th century** (Dolmetsch).
„ 6. **Coffer from Bozen** (Paukert, Zimmergotik).
„ 8. **Late Gothic balcony soffit from St. Michael's church, Hildesheim** (Ebe, Die Schmuckformen der Monumentalbauten).

Gothic Wood Carving.

Plate 171. GOTHIC ORNAMENT. 289

Plate 173.   GOTHIC ORNAMENT.   291

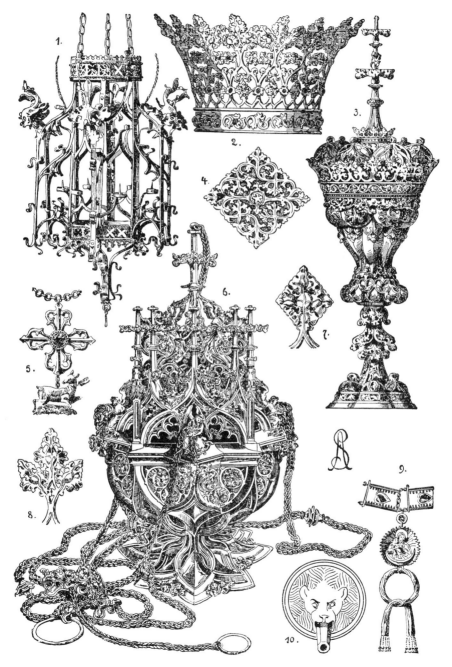

Plate 171.

Fig. 1. **Late Gothic arm-chair from the ancient armoury in Nüremberg.**

„   2. **Arm-chair from Tyrol,** 15th century.

„   3. **Door from Kunkelstein Castle** (Paukert).

„   4. **Late Gothic lectern from the Stifts church at Herrieden, near Ansbach** (Heideloff).

„   5. **Stall from the Elizabeth church, Marburg** (E. Wasmuth, Alte und neue Kirchenmöbel).

„   6. **Table from the Rhineland,** 15th century (Falke, Mittelalterliches Hausmobiliar).

„   7. **Church stall in oak.** In all probability this belonged to the rival Kaiser Wilhelm of Holland, and is therefore from the 13th century; it is now in the Wartburg

Plate 172.

Gothic Flat Ornament.

(After E. Paukert, Tyroler Zimmergotik.

Fig. 1, and 3. **Ornament from Kunkelstein Castle.**

„   2, 4, and 6. **Stuff patterns after paintings in the castle of Trotzburg.**

„   5. **Ornament from Neustift.**

„   7, and 8. **Wall-paper,** printed on linen.

Plate 173.

Fig. 1. **Wrought-iron candelabrum,** end of the 15th century, in the National Museum at Munich (Hirth).

„   2, 7, and 8. **Crown and details in a picture of the Blessed Virgin in the church of St. Martha, Nüremberg** (Heideloff).

„   3. **Late Gothic goblet in silver gilt** (Heideloff).

„   4. **Rosette of sheet-iron on the knocker of the sacristy door in the church of St. Lawrence, Nüremberg** (Heideloff).

„   5. **Badge of the confraternity of the "Holy Mount",** with the symbol of St. Aegidius (Heideloff).

„   6. **Late Gothic censer,** from a copperplate by Martin Schongauer (Heideloff).

„   9. **Chain of the order of the Swan** (Heideloff).

„   10. **Spout of a water barrel** (Heideloff).

Plate 174.

Fig. 1—8. **Late Gothic initals,** from different parchment manuscripts (Hirth, Formenschatz).

„   9—13. **Early Gothic letters,** from Rhenish manuscripts (Dr. Karl Lamprecht, Initial-Ornamentik).

Plate 174. GOTHIC ORNAMENT. 293

Plate 175.

(After Wilhelm Weimar, Monumental-Schriften.)

Fig. 1. **From a bronze plate in the Monastic church at Baden-Baden, 1497.**

„ 2. **From the bronze tomb of Bishop Tilo of Trotha in the cathedral at Merseburg, died 1514.**

„ 3. **Inscription, engraved in bronze, from the tombstone of Anna von Wiershausen (died 1484) in the church of St. Elizabeth, Marburg.**

„ 4. **From the engraved bronze tomb-plate of the Scholt in Nüremberg, who died in 1469. In the church at Langenzenn near Fürth.**

„ 5. **Bronze tomb-plate of Jakob von Gulpen (died 1455) in the St. Gumbertus church, Ansbach.**

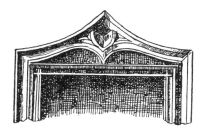

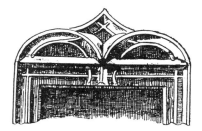

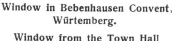

Window in Bebenhausen Convent, Würtemberg.	**Window in the Reichenbach Cloister, Ulm, Würtemberg.**
Window from the Town Hall at Nüremberg.	**Window from the gable of the now ruined Preacher's church in Nüremberg.**

(Heideloff, Ornamentik des Mittelalters.)

Plate 176.

Gothic Ornament in Hungary.

(After Dr. Béla von Czobor and Emmerich von Szaley, Die historischen Denkmäler Ungarns.)

Fig. 1. **Helmet of Banus from Croatia and Helden, by Szigetvar Nikolaus Zrinyi** (died 1566), in the Court Armoury Collection, Vienna.

„ 2. **Helmet of Georg Castriota Skanderbeg, Duke of Albania** (1403—1467), in the Court Armoury Collection, Vienna.

„ 3. **Goblet of silver gilt,** 15th century, was presented in 1640 to the Protestant church in Miskolcz by Gregor von Miskolcz.

„ 4. **Horn vessel for holding oil,** silver gilt mountings, property of the Eszertom cathedral.

„ 5. **Reliquary Hermes of St. Ladislaus,** of silver gilt, ornamented with chain mail. Hungarian 15th century work. In the cathedral church at Györer.

Bronze Baptismal Font, made in 1484 for Menardt church
by Johannes von Novavilla.

Gothic Ornament in Italy.

From a 14th century Manuscript (Racinet).

nto Italy Gothic art made its way at about the same time as it did into Germany. This style of an first received the title of Gothic in Italy, a word which was used by the Italians at that time to signify barbarian, or anything coming from the north. In Italy more importance was placed on the horizontal than in either Germany or France, and it was only very seldom that the vertical predominated in that country. The Italians did not pay much attention to the development of the tower, which very often stands quite apart from the church altogether. The Franciscan and Dominican Orders played a very important part in the spread of the Gothic throughout Italy. The Italian Gothic, however, could never free itself from Classic, Romanesque and Byzantine reminiscences, and Italian Late-Gothic is mixed with noumerous Renaissance motifs. Classic art had taken too strong a hold on the Italians, it was so much a part of their life, they had become so imbued with its spirit that they really found it impossible to become true lovers of the Gothic. As a consequence, Gothic art rapidly declined, and, in the 13th century, a decided movement to break away altogether from the style of the period, and to turn back again to the old Classic Art began to make itself evident.

Plate 177.

(From Rohault de Fleury, La Toscane au Moyen Age.)

Fig. 1, and 5. **Arch of the Loggia of the Palace of the Signoria, Florence.**
„ 2. **Painting by Piero di Guido (1386) representing Charity, in the Loggia of the Palace of the Signoria, Florence.**
„ 3. **Lion from the city wall in Pisa.**
„ 4. **Pillar from the corn-market in Florence.**
„ 6. **Mural painting from the city hall, Florence.**

Plate 178.

Fig. 1. **Window from a house in the Synagogue Street in Trani,** 13th century (Raguenet).
„ 2. **Crest of the church of Santa Maria del Fiore in Florence,** 14th century (Raguenet).
„ 3. **Bronze knocker from Florence,** 14th century (Raguenet).
„ 4. **Window from the Convent of St. Theresa in Trani** (Raguenet).
„ 5. **Mosaic floor from Florence cathedral** (D'Espouy, Fragments d'architecture du Moyen-age).
„ 6, and 7. **Mural painting and pillar from the Castle of Pandino,** 14th century (Camillo Boito, Arte Italiana).

Plate 177.   GOTHIC ORNAMENT.

299

1.

2

3.

4.

5.

6.

7.

Plate 179.

GOTHIC ORNAMENT.

1.

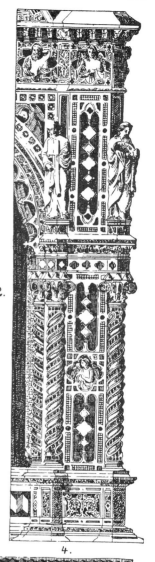

2.

3.

4.

Plate 179.

Fig. 1, and 2. Altar in the church of Or San Michele (D'Espouy).
„   3. Band-pattern, 15th century (Raguenet).
„   4. Door border from Florence, 15th century (Raguenet).

Plate 180.

Fig. 1—4. Locks and keys from the National Museum, Florence (Boito).
„   5. Credence from the Villa Reale del Poggio near Florence, 15th century (Raguenet).
„   6. Fragment of a fresco-painting by Jacopo Avanzi in the Oratorium of the St. Giorgio church in Padua (Boito).
„   7. From a monument by Bonjacopo Sanoita in the choir of the St. Antonio Convent, Padua (Boito).

Plate 181.

Fig. 1. Tunic from the Museo Civico in Turin, made of carmine-red velvet on a gold ground, 15th century (Boito).
„   2. Carpet pattern from a tempera painting by Niccolo Alunno (1466) in the Pinakotheca at Perugia (Dolmetsch).
„   3. From a tomb in Fano (D'Espouy).
„   4. Mural painting from the Castle of Pandino, end of the 14th century (Boito).
„   5. Table-cloth border, 15th century, the pattern is blue (Raguenet).
„   6. Railing round the Scaliger monument in Verona (D'Espouy).
„   7. Reliquary in the treasury of the Pitti palace, Florence, end of the 14th century (Boito).

Plate 182.

The Venetian Gothic.

(After Cicognara, Monumenti di Venezia.)

Fig. 1. Capital and base from the court-yard of the Cà d'oro palace.
„   2. Balustrade in the first story of the same palace.
„   3. Window Ornament, capital and base, in the first story of the same palace.
„   4. Capital and base from the second story of the same palace.
„   5. Capital and base in the first story of the Doges palace.
„   6. Ground plan of No. 5.

Plate 180. GOTHIC ORNAMENT. 303

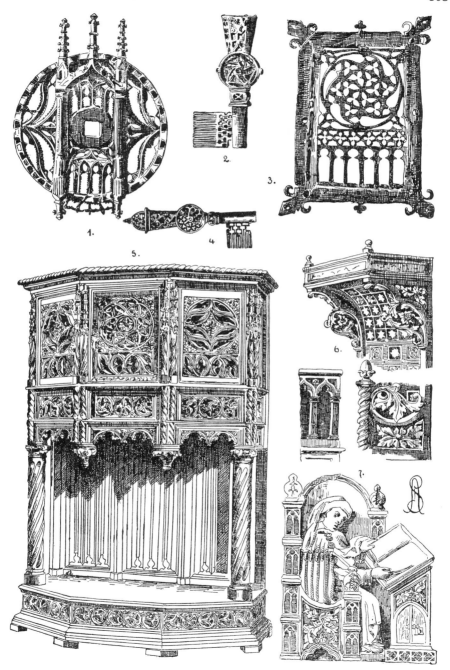

Plate 182.   GOTHIC ORNAMENT.

305

Plate 183.

Fig. 1—8. Manuscript paintings from the 14th and 15th centuries (Racinet, L'Ornement polychrome).

Stuff pattern from an altar in Milan, with the badge of the Duchess Bonne of Savoy. At present in the Museum Poldi Pezzole, Milan (L'art pour tous).

Plate 185. GOTHIC ORNAMENT. 309

1.

2.

3.

4.

5.

6.

Gothic Ornament in Spain.

From a 15th century Manuscript
(Monumentos de España).

ery soon after it had begun to reach its highest development in France, that is, in the first half of the 13th century, and about the year 1225, Gothic was introduced from France into Spain. It did not, however, undergo here that change in accordance with the national ideas of the people which it underwent in Germany and Italy, the very extensive number of Moorish remains still existing in the country having made their influence felt. One of the oldest Gothic monuments in the Peninsula is the cathedral of Burgos which was built under Northern French influence in the 13th century. The Western tower of this cathedral was completed in the years 1442—1456 by Meister Johann of Cologne.

Plate 184.

Transition Style (estilo mudelar).

(After Monumentos arquitectónicos de España.)

Fig. 1, and 3. **Door and window heads from the Palace de los Ayalas in Toledo.**
  ,,   2. **Door head from the chapel of Santiago of Santa Maria in Alcala de Henares.**
  ,,   4. **Details from the house called de Mesa in Toledo.**
  ,,   5. **Decoration over the door in No. 2.**
  ,,   6. **Crest of the church of St. Mark, Seville.**

Plate 185.

(After Monumentos arquitectónicos de España.)

Fig. 1, and 2. **Window from the house Lonja in Valencia.**
  ,,   3. **Window from the cloister of St. Juan de los Reyes in Toledo.**
  ,,   4. **Middle column of a double window from the tower of the Lonja house in Valencia.**
  ,,   5. **Stair newel from the Hospital de la Latina in Madrid.**
  ,,   6. **Tombstone of King Don Alphonso VIII and his Consort Donna Leonor,** in the choir of the church of Santa Maria La Real de Huelgas in Burgos.

Plate 186.   GOTHIC ORNAMENT.   311

Plate 186.

Fig. 1—3. Details from the cloister of St. Juan de los Reyes in Toledo (Monumentos de España).

„   4. Balcony from the court-yard of St. Gregorio in Valladolid (Raguenet).

Plate 187.

Fig. 1. Finial from transept of the church of St. Juan de los Reyes in Toledo (Monumentos de España).

„   2. Linen hanging, 16th century, blue pattern on a red ground (Raguenet).

„   3. Wrought iron chandelier from Tarrasa, province of Barcelona, 13th century (Mira Leroy).

„   4. Window panel from the cloister of St. Juan de los Reyes in Toledo (Monumentos de España).

„   5. Back of a stall seat in the cathedral of Leon, 15th century (Mira Leroy).

„   6. Ceiling of the cloister of St. Juan de los Reyes in Toledo (Mira Leroy).

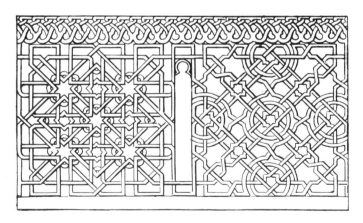

Painted balustrade in the interior of the tower of Santo Domingo,
called the Hercules Tower in Segovia
(Monumentos de España).

Plate 187.   GOTHIC ORNAMENT.   313

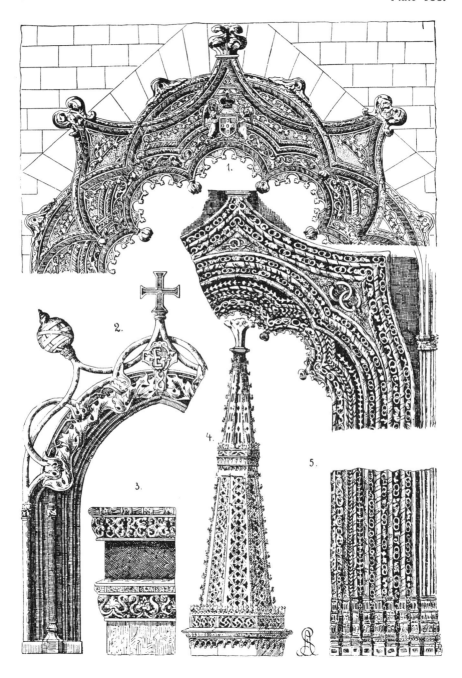

Plate 188.

The *Manoel Style in Portugal.*

(After Frei Luis de Souza, Church of Batalha.)

An extremely peculiar Gothic, influenced by Moorish, and other foreign forms, developed in Portugal, its most beautiful example being the church at Batalha with its monument erected to the memory of king Manoel. On the 14th august 1385 Dom João, King of Portugal at the time, found himself opposed to a very powerful Spanish army, far superior to his own in numbers, under the command of Don Juan, King of Spain. Dom João turned to the Virgin for help in this critical situation, and promised, if She would give him the victory, that he would erect a building in her honour which would far outshine in size and beauty any similar structure throughout Christendom. As the Portuguese did actually beat the Spanish, and gained an overwhelming victory over them, Dom João immediately proceeded to carry out his promise. He called together the foremost architects and artists from all parts of Europe, and in the very same year, 1385, in which he won his great victory, close to the scene of battle, laid the foundations of the famous and beautiful church at Batalha. The mausoleum erected to king Manoel, who reigned later, is the most beautiful item in this structure. It was, however, never finished and is still incomplete.

Fig. 1. **Arch over the door of the mausoleum to King Dom Manoel.**
„   2. **Arch of one of the chapels in the same.**
„   3. **Principal cornice of the same.**
„   4. **Spire of the tower in the north façade of the church at Batalha.**
„   5. **Entrance door to the mausoleum.**

Shaft and band on the South front of the church of Santa Maria in Belém
(Haupt, Baukunst der Renaissance in Portugal).

CHINESE ORNAMENT.

**Chinese
Ornamental Frame**
(Racinet.)

Although the earliest record of Chinese architecture dates back to the 23 century B. C., when
the Baku tribes emigrated east from Elam and Babylonia, and introduced their systems of building, there
are no examples of their architectural ornament
existing earlier than the 13th century A. D., owing
to the ruthless destruction which has taken place at
all periods of her history. In their temples and halls
they would appear to have adhered to one universal
type of design, the earliest example still existing of
which, is that which was first built in Japan in 607
A. D. by Koreans. It was then a completely developed style, consisting of wood columns, carrying
open timber roofs covered with tiles, and the principal ornaments were those
found in the groups of brackets which carried the overhanging eaves and the
ridge and hip rolls of their roofs: all in glazed terracotta of bright colouring.
Owing to the peculiar nature of the construction of their roofs (of which an
example is shewn in Plate 159, Fig. 2), the horizontal beams, instead of being
carried on the tops of the columns are tenoned into them. There are therefore
no capitals so that the Chinese and Japanese are the only nations in the world
to whom the capital—the principal ornamental feature of all styles—is unknown.
At an early period also the Chinese discarded in their pagodas the timber construction which they introduced into Japan and built them in brick, covering them
sometimes with porcelain and glazed terracotta plaques of the greatest beauty,
and it is in this branch of art and in their ceramics that they excel, and in
the plates devoted to Chinese ornament are represented some of the finest works
of this kind. In bronzes also they are very great masters, as also in gold
and silver embroideries.

Plate 189.   CHINESE ORNAMENT.   317

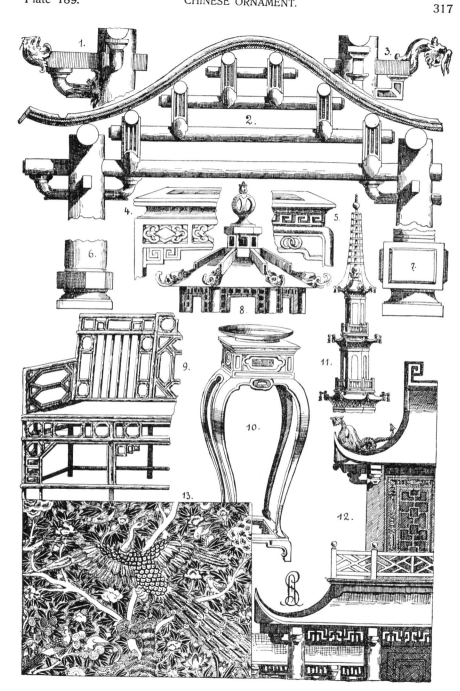

Plate 189.

Fig. 1. **Pillar crest of the Pagoda of Ho-nan.** The Chinese column has no capital, the beams and brackets being tenoned in at the sides (Chambers, Designs of Chinese Buildings).

„ 2. **From the colonnade in the court-yard of the Pagoda of Cochin-China** (Chambers).

„ 3. **Corbel of a Pagoda in the eastern suburb of Canton** (Chambers).

„ 4, 5, 9, and 10. **Chinese 17th century furniture** (Chambers).

„ 6, and 7. **Bases of the colums in No. 2.**

„ 8. **Roof crest of a small temple in the western suburb of Canton** (Chambers).

„ 11. **Spire of a Pagoda on the Ta-Ho,** between Canton and Hoang-Pou (Chambers).

„ 12. **Upper part of a Pagoda in Cochin-China** (Chambers).

„ 13. **Part of a curtain of a canopy bed,** embroidered in gold and silk, 15th century (Dolmetsch).

Chinese Ceramics.

In his history of Chinese Ceramics, Ernest Grandidier divides the products of Chinese Ceramics, chronologically, into five epochs:

1. Under the dynasty of Sung (960—1260) and the dynasty of Yonen (120—1368).
2. Under the dynasty of Ming (1368—1620).
3. From the end of the latter dynasty to the death of K'ang Hsi (1620—1722).
4. Under the reign of Yung-Chêng and Kien-Long (1722—1796).
5. The modern epoch.

Plate 190.

Fig. 1. **Censer,** used by the Emporer Fon-Hi when making offering to the spirits of Heaven and Earth, dates from beginning of the 18th century.

„ 2. **Vase with the mythological dragon,** from the Yung-Tsching epoch (1723—1736).

„ 3. **Vase with the goddes Si-wang-mow, Goddess of a long life,** from the same period.

„ 4, and 5. **Tea-pots,** from the Ming epoch, 1368—1620.

„ 6. **Vase,** from the K'ang Hsi epoch, 1662—1723.

„ 7. **Statue of Konan-inn, goddess of Charity.**

„ 8. **Antique vase in the Museum Adrien Dubouchet, Limoges.**

Plate 191.

Fig. 1, and 2. **Vases from the Yung-Chêng epoch.**

„ 3. **Vase from the K'ang Hsi epoch.**

„ 4. **Wine-can from the K'ang Hsi epoch.**

„ 5. **Vase from the Sung epoch** 960—1260.

Plate 190.　　　　　CHINESE ORNAMENT.　　　　　319

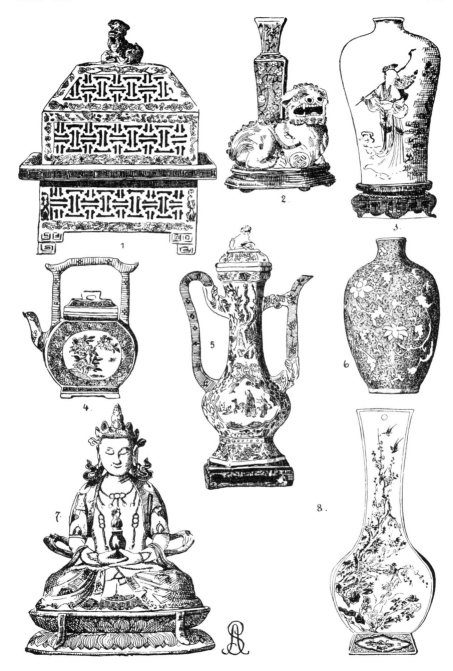

Plate 192. CHINESE ORNAMENT. 321

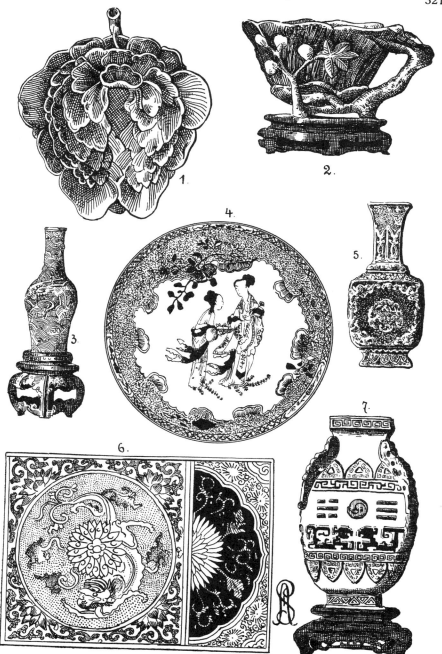

Plate 192.

Fig. 1. Escutcheon from the K'ang Hsi epoch.
„ 2. Cup from the same epoch.
„ 3. Vase from the Sung epoch.
„ 4. Plate from the Kien-Long epoch.
„ 5. Vase from the same epoch.
„ 6. Fragment of table plate from the K'ang Hsi epoch.
„ 7. Vase from the Yung-Ching epoch, with raised gold meander, which, it is more probable to suppose, was discovered by the Chinese themselves, rather than an imitation from the Greek. The other patterns on the vase relate to Buddhist Mythology.

Plate 193.

(After L'art pour tous.)

Fig. 1—3, and 8. Ornamental butterfly from an antique porcelain plate, in the Gasnault collection.
„ 4. Antique gold censer, in the possession of Admiral Coupvent des Bois.
„ 5. Antique tea-pot, from the Gasnault collection, now in the Museum at Limoges.
„ 6. Antique bronze vase from M. Desaye's collection.
„ 7, and 9. Bronze vases from the period of the Ming dynasty, in the Bing collection.
„ 10. Antique bronze candle-stick.

Ornament for laquer painting (Racinet).

Cambodian Ornament.

In the countries lying between India and China an extremely peculiar and very ancient art developed into existence, which may be regarded as a transition from Indian to Chinese art. It is but very little studied and was first made known in Europe on the formation of the Musée des antiquités cambodgiennes by M. Louis Delaporte, Lieutenant in the French Navy. Similar to Indian architecture, the Cambodian is overloaded with ornament, but this overloading is, however, made up for in the regularity and harmony which characterises it.

Plate 194.

(After L'art pour tous.)

Fig. 1. From the sanctuary of the Temple of Angkor Vat, 10th century.

„ 2. Upper portion of podium in the same sanctuary with mask of the God Rheon.

„ 3. Bas-relief carved on the exterior of the same sanctuary.

„ 4. Mural decoration in the same with the Brahma Gods.

Plate 195.

(After L'art pour tous.)

Fig. 1. Doorway of the temple of Loley, 11th or 12th century.

„ 2. Square pier and entablature with sculptured frieze representing the Apsaras (celestial dancing girls) from the Temple of Angkor Vat.

„ 3. Balustrade window of the Temple of Angkor Vat.

Plate 194. CAMBODIAN ORNAMENT. 325

JAPANESE ORNAMENT.

The actor Tomedjuro Nakamura in the role of the Kaishi. Painted by Tori-i-Kiyonobu 1750 (Bing).

espite the fact that Japanese art had its origin in China, it nevertheless represents a decided individuality peculiar to itself. This is due to the less strict manner in which they divided their work. The Japanese Ornamentation is not so conventional as the Chinese, as they took their models more from nature than the latter. It is perhaps remarkable and worthy of note that the Japanese have adhered to the original models introduced from China through Korea, whereas the Chinese in some cases have entirely departed from them. Thus the Japanese Pagoda represents the same type of design as that which was first built by Korean carpenters at Horiuji in 607 A. D. and is still carried out at the present day, whereas the Chinese gave up the timber structure a few centuries later, and introduced one built in brick, which in their country, at all events, was not liable to be overthrown by earthquakes, as it might have been in Japan. In both China and Japan the general tendency has been to over-elaborate the decoration, and in their temples the ornament applied to their columns and beams is very much the same in both countries. In their halls of state and domestic buildings the contrary is the case, those in China are overloaded with ornament, the great halls being painted and gilded in profusion and the residences of the Mandarins enriched with

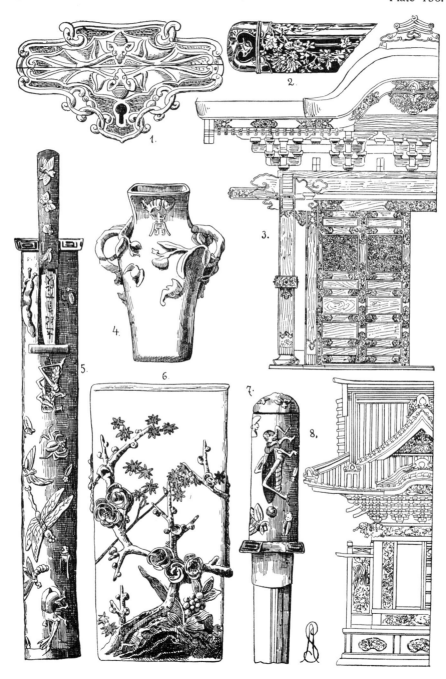

marbles of various kinds and elaborate carved woodwork whereas in Japan the greatest simplicity is observed, in the palaces of the Mikado and Shogun the woodwork is simply polished, shewing the grain of the wood, with mounts in gilt bronze.

The oldest Japanese Art report dates from the 6th century A. D., when the Buddhist religion was introduced into the country from China through Korea: shortly afterwards the Fujiwara family engrossed the power of the state for nearly four centuries, when they were displaced by the Taira and Minamoto clans. The former were overthrown at Danno-ura in 1185 A. D., when Yoritomo te chief of the Minamotos obtained from the Mikado and his court the title of Shogun (generalissimo). Later on, the Ashigawa family ruled as Shoguns from 1338 to 1590 A. D., and they were succeeded by the Tokûgawa family whose head Iyeyasu was a scion of the Minamoto family. They held power till 1868, when the Shogunate was abolished and the Mikado again recovered his power and position as ruling sovereign. In 1542 the Portuguese missionaries entered Japan and endeavoured to convert the people, but they had brought discord into the country, so that in 1624 Iyemitsu, the third Shogun of the Tokûgawa Dynasty expelled the missionaries and closed the country to all foreigners, the Dutch only being allowed to carry on trade which was confined to the Island of Deshima. During the two and a half centuries of exclusion, the Japanese made rapid advances in Art and their lacquer and metal-work reached a perfection unknown in any other country, whilst their painting and printing, greatly influenced by the Chinese school, are now recognised as the finest works of their kind.

Plate 196.

Fig. 1. **Lock mounting** (L'art pour tous).
„ 2. **Scabbard mounting** (L'art pour tous).
„ 3. **From the eastern door of the temple Shin-Shiu Sect in Kioto** (Uhde, Konstruktionen und Kunstformen der Architektur).
„ 4, and 6. **Ancient Japanese vases** (L'art pour tous).
„ 5, and 7. **Sword scabbard and hilt** (L'art pour tous).
„ 8. **Altar Shrine in the temple of Miyo-Jin-Akagi** (Uhde).

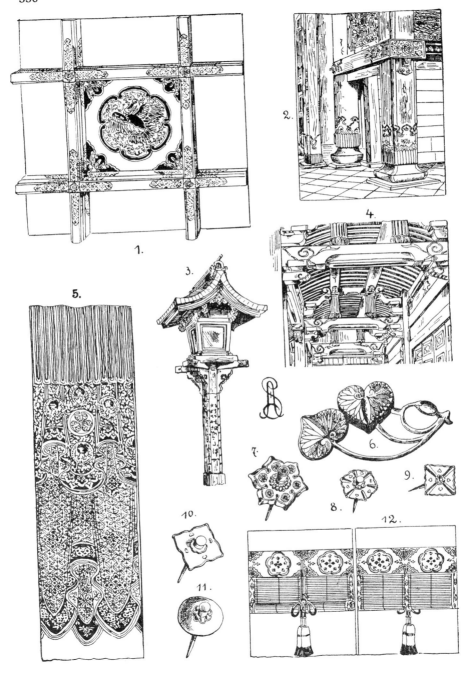

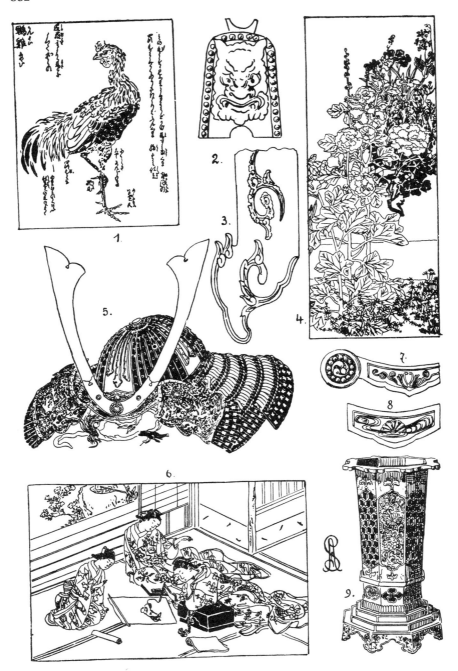

Plate 197.

(After Justus Brinkmann, Kunst und Handwerk in Japan.)

Fig. 1. **Wooden ceiling in the temple** of Shogun Tokugawa Iyemitsu at Uyeno near Tokio.

„ 2. **Posts at the entrance of the principal door of the temple Nishi-Hongwanji in Kioto.** The bases of the post and the cross bars are encased in bronze.

„ 3. **Roofed public lantern in the province Ise.**

„ 4. **Open timber roof of the Hondo from O-baku-san in Uji valley.**

„ 5. **Painted drapery on a wooden column of a Nikko temple.** Above, is the three-leaved Holly-hock of the Tokugawa-Shoguns.

„ 6. **Bronze nail-head from the castle of Himeiji.** Shows a branch of the Holly hock (Asdrum caulescens).

„ 7—11. **Nail-heads from an old temple and old castles.**

„ 12. **Rolled-up window-blind,** front and back views.

Plate 198.

Fig. 1. **Iron sword guard (Tsuba)** from the chaser Kinai, 18th century (Bing, Japanischer Formenschatz).

„ 2. **Painting on an ancient beaker-shaped vase** (Dolmetsch).

„ 3. **From an embroided silk robe,** 16th century (Bing).

„ 4. **Cloisonne inlay from a copper dish decorated on both sides** (Racinet, l'ornement polychrome).

„ 5—12. **Japanese lacquer painting.**

Plate 199.

Fig. 1. **Domestic cock,** from the book Yé-hon sha-hò-fu-Kuro, beginning of 18th century. The text gives the names of the different colours (Brinkmann).

„ 2. **Ridge-tile,** Oni-gawara from the temple of Horiuji, 7th century (Baltzer, Das japanische Haus).

„ 3. **Ornamental phoenix head as ending of a projecting timber** (Baltzer).

„ 4. **Leaf of screen,** from the designs of the artist Kôrin 1700 which were published by Ho-itsu (Brinkmann).

„ 5. **Helmet of Minamoto Yoshi-iye,** called also Hochinamen-Toro, conqueror of the Tairi, about the year 1180 A. D., at present in the temple treasury of Itsukushima. The rounded, turned-down sides of this helmet are of leather, on which is stencilled a picture of the God Indra who is surrounded with flames. Taken from the Itsukushima meisho published in the year 1842 (Brinkmann).

„ 6. **Young girl painting,** from a wood-cut in the Ehon Tama Kadzura by Nishigawa Sukenobu, 1736.

Fig. 7. **Border-tile ornamentation** (Baltzer, Das japanische Haus).
„ 8. **Border-tile ornamentation,** with chrysanthemum and water waves, the arms of the renowned hero Kusunoki (Baltzer).
„ 9. **Bronze vessel, chased, for storing the utensils used for smoking** (Brinkmann).

Plate 200.

Japanese Textile Designs.

(After L'art pour tous.)

Fig. 1, and 4. **Carpet patterns.**
„ 2, 3, 5, and 7. **Stuff patterns,** 17th century.
„ 6. **Pattern from the mantle of a Bonze, or priest.**

Sword and scabbard of a Daimio, from the Arima Family,
18th century (Bing).

Pier decoration from the temple of Angkor Vat
(L'art pour tous).

RENAISSANCE

AND

MODERN TIMES

Belgian Tea Urn in beaten Copper, Ghent.
(Ewerbeck und Neumeister, Die Renaissance in Belgien und Holland).

RENAISSANCE ORNAMENT.

From an Italian Manuscript
(Dolmetsch).

The Renaissance in Italy in the 15th century may be regarded to a certain extent as a revolution in art, a peaceful revolution, of which the seeds had already been germinating for many years in Painting and Sculpture, showing the tendency to revert to that earlier classic art, many of the masterpieces of which still existed and in greater profusion than at the present day. Whilst in other countries the Gothic style had always represented in its gradual development the true feelings of the people who produced it, in Italy its principles had never been understood or appreciated, and although in the 14th century in Florence, Venice, Verona, Pisa and in the towns further south magnificent examples of Gothic ornament were evolved, which hold their own in comparison with those in other countries, their beauty consisted chiefly in their exquisite detail as apart from the general desigin of the structures which they adorned and enriched.

On the revival of letters in the 15th century, the Italians began to recognise that they were the national descendants of those who had produced the master pieces in ancient Italy, the art practised by them was not a foreign importation like that of the Gothic style, but their own, an art which had been developed in their own country, which recalled the history of their own people, who were at one time the conquerors of the whole world. Beyond this there were other changes, among which the advance of civilisation, the Reformation in Religion, the printing press etc., all of which contributed to new requirements, whilst the patronage of men of letters, such as those of the Medici in Florence and later on that of the Papal court in Rome, all tending therefore and leading to the evolution of a new interpretation of Classic art. All these considerations, however, belong more to the History of the Renaissance style rather than to the actual results, the ornamentation which constitutes the principal object of this work.

It has already been pointed out that the Painters and Sculptors were the first who in their works showed a tendency towards the resuscitation of classic art and this is specially the case with the latter, who, not only in Italy but in France, Spain, England, Germany and in the Netherlands showed in tombs and other works of a decorative character how complete was the change in conception and execution. In architecture the construction forms of the Gothic style, the traditional craft of the mason could not be thrown aside at once, but for a tomb in which, as an ideal subject uninfluenced by questions of utility or construction, the artist was free to mould his design in accordance with his imaginative powers there was no restriction. Hence we find that not only in Italy, but in other countries the earliest examples of the Renaissance are to be found in tombs, as in those at Le Mans and Nantes in France and in England, in Torregiano's work at Westminster Abbey, 1516.

It was in the earlier Renaissance that ornament received its chief development both in design and beauty of execution, and this not only in Italy, but in France and Spain. The examples on plate 205 from the Miracoli church in Venice (1480—89) by Pietro Lombardo, those on plate 207 from the façade of the Certosa near Pavia (1473) by Burgognone and the pilasters of the Town hall at Brescia are among the more remarkable in Italy, whilst in France, in the choir stalls and screens of some of the cathedrals and churches and in the chateaux of Blois, Chambard, and Azay-le-Rideau on the Loire and in the South of France at Toulouse and Rodez (Fig. 3 Plate 216), and in Spain. in the University of Salamanca (Fig. 3 Plate 253) will be found a richness and variety of design which is characteristic of the period.

The Renaissance in Italy.

The Early Renaissance commenced in the first quarter of the 15th century in Florence, whence it spread to Milan, Venice and other towns in the North of Italy, and towards the end of the 15th century to Rome. The first architect who studied seriously the monuments of classic art and transmitted their spirit into his own work was Filippo Brunelleschi, an artist of powerful genius, who in the construction of the cupola of the Cathedral at Florencé (1220—34) and the churches of St. Lorenzo and St. Spirito in the same town showed his great qualities as an artist and builder. He was followed by Michelozzo, to whom we owe the Chapel of St. Peter (1460) in St. Eustorgio, Milan, and the Riccardi (1430) the first Renaissance example of a palace of which the second was the Strozzi palace 1489 by Majano (1442—97) and Cronaca (1454—1509). Then followed Alberti (1404—72), whose chief work was the front of the church at Rimini (1446—54) and the church of St. Andrea at Mantua (1472), Giovanni de San Gallo (1445—1516), Antonio de Sangallo (1455—1534), Bramante d'Urbino (1444—1514) the architect of the church at Todi but better known in connection with his work of St. Peter's, Rome, which he commenced in 1505 and the Cancellaria Palace in the same city. Peruzzi (1481—1531), the architect of the Massimi palace in Rome; the Lombardi family in Venice, Pietro Lombardo (1430—1515) the architect of the Miracoli church, Sante Lombardo (1504—1560) who designed the Vendramini Palace and Tullio Lombardo (1452—1537) the Cornaro-Spinelli Palace. To these must be added San Micheli (1494—1559) the architect of the Bevilacqua palace at Verona and the Grimani palace at Venice; Sansovino (1477—1570) who designed the Library and the Loggia at Venice, Vignola (1507—73) whose chief work was the castle of Caprarola, 40 miles from Rome, and Palladio (1519—81) the architect of the Basilica and other palaces at Vicenza.

Illustrations of the work of some of the architects above mentioned are given in the plates. Thus in plate 201 Michelozzo and San Gallo are represented, and in plate 203 San Gallo and Sansovino. In plate 204 illustrations from the Loggia of the Vatican are given which was painted by Raphael, who drew his inspiriation from the rich decoration in painting and stucco found in the Golden House of Nero, which had been buried beneath the Thermæ of Titus. To this type of decoration the title Raphaelesque is frequently given. Pietro Lombardos work is shown on Plate 205, end Burgognone's on Plate 207.

Plate 201.

Florence.

Florence was the principal centre of the Early Renaissance and developed a type of palace which become the standard for all Italy.

Fig. 1. **Window from the court-yard of the Palazzo Riccardi.** This palace was designed and begun in the year 1430 by Michelozzo Michelozzi. The court-yard was built by Bartolomeo Amanati. (Schütte, Ornamentale und architektonische Studienblätter aus Italien.)

„ 2. **Principal cornice of the façade of the Riccardi palace** (Schütte).

„ 3. **Octagonal column in stucco-work from the Palazzo Vecchio.** This palace was built in the year 1298 by Arnolfo di Cambio, but enlarged in 1434 by Michelozzi, and in 1550 by Vasari. The stucco-work of the column was done in the year 1565 by Marco da Faenzo on the occasion of the marriage of Francesco de Medici (Schütte).

„ 4. **Capital of column in the court-yard of the Palazzo Gondi.** The palace was commenced in 1481 by Giuliano de San Gallo (Schütte).

„ 5. **Sepulchral slab from Santa Croce, Florence** (Dolmetsch).

„ 6. **From a monument in the church of the Holy Apostles in Florence** (L'art pour tous).

Plate 202.

Florence.

Fig. 1. **Façade in sgraffito-work from the palace of Montalon** (D'Espouy, Renaissance).

„ 2. **Detail of a cornice from the Hall of the Two Hundred in Palazzo Vecchio** (Schütte).

„ 3. **Door border in the Hall dell'Orologio in the Palazzo Vecchio** (Schütte).

„ 4. **Sketch for a folding-door,** from a pen and ink drawing by Giovanni da Bologna. In the Florence (Hirth, Formenschatz).

„ 5. **Coat of arms curved in stone from the Palazzo Feroni** (L'art pour tous).

Plate 203.

Rome.

In the development of the Early Renaissance Rome played no part at first, the style being introduced from Florence.

Fig. 1. **From the tomb of a prelate in the church of Santa Maria del Popolo.** This tomb, which was built by Andrea Tatti called Sansovino, is, according to Burkhardt, the most perfect work which has ever been produced by the union of Decoration and Sculpture (Hirth).

„ 2. **Balustrade of a balcony in the Sixtine Chapel** (Holtzinger, Geschichte der Renaissance in Italien).

„ 3, and 4. **Details from the façade of the Palazzo Farnese,** built by San Gallo in the years 1470—1546 (Schütte).

„ 5, and 6. **Flat-reliefs from a tomb in the church of Santa Maria del Popolo** (Dolmetsch).

„ 7. **From a tomb of a prelate in the church of Santa Maria del Popolo.** This, the same as Fig. 1, was built by Andrea Tatti called Sansovino in the years 1460—1529. These tombs in the choir of the church are the tombs of the two Prelates Basso and Sforza Visconti (Hirth).

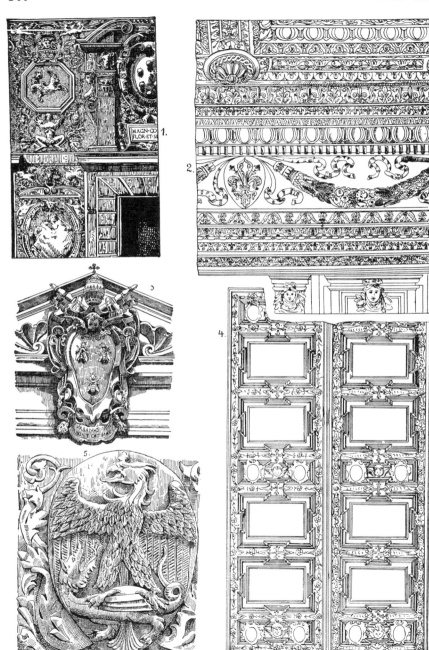

Plate 203. ITALIAN RENAISSANCE ORNAMENT. 345

Plate 205. ITALIAN RENAISSANCE ORNAMENT. 347

1.

2

Fig. 8. **Sgraffito-work from the house No. 82, Via Giulia** (Dolmetsch).
„ 9. **Sgraffito-work from the house No. 148, Via dei Coronari** (Dolmetsch).
„ 10. **Sgraffito-work from the house No. 4, Borgo al vicolo del Campanile** (Dolmetsch).

Plate 204.
Rome.

Fig. 1. **Marble frieze in the church of Santa Maria del Popolo** (Holtzinger).
„ 2. **Mural painting from the Raphael Loggia in the Vatican** (L'art pour tous).
„ 3. **Sgraffito-work from the house No. 82 Via Giulio** (Dolmetsch).
„ 4. **Mural painting by Annibale Caracci in the Palace Farnese** (Hirth).
„ 5. **Painting in the Raphael Loggia in the Vatican** (D'Espouy).

Plate 205.
Venice.

The Renaissance did not make its appearance in Venice until the year 1450, but in combination with the older architecture native to the city developed into a peculiar and characteristic style.
(After Cicognara, Monumenti di Venezia.)

Fig. 1, and 2. **Column and archivolt in the Presbytery of the church of Santa Maria dei Miracoli.**

Plate 206.
Venice.
(After Cicognara, Monumenti di Venezia.)

Fig. 1. **Monument of Generosa Orsina, erected by her husband in the church of Santa Maria Gloriosa dei Frari.**
„ 2. **Door border from the Royal Chapel in St. Marks.**
„ 3. **Equestrian statue by Bartolommeo Colleoni on the Piazza of San Gio and Paolo.**
„ 4. **Mantel piece in the Sala del Collegio in the Ducal Palace.**

Plate 207.
Certosa of Pavia.
(After Hirth, Formenschatz.)

Fig. 1. **Pillars from the niche with principal façade.** The material used is white marble. The principal sculptor was Ambrogio da Fossano, called Borgognone, but the work was begun in the year 1473. In this master work of the Italian Early Renaissance, however, which was completed at the end of the 15th century, other sculptors also took part, amongst them being Giov. Ant. Amadeo, Christoforo da Roma, Andrea Fusina, Christoforo Solari called il Gobbo and Agostin Busti called Bambaja.
„ 2. **Window in the principal façade,** Burkhardt calls it the Triumph of all Decoration Work.
„ 3. **Pilaster, frieze, and principal cornice.**

Plate 208.   ITALIAN RENAISSANCE ORNAMENT.   351

Plate 208.

Sicily.

(After J. J. Hittorff et L. Zanth, Architecture Moderne de la Sicile.)

Fig. 1. **Door from the Benedictine Cloister in Catania.**
„ 2, and 5. **Fountain in the cathedral Square at Messina.**
„ 3, and 6. **Reliefs from the large fountain on the cathedral Square, Messina.**
„ 4. **Window from the Benedictine Cloister in Catania.**
„ 7. **Statue of Neptune from the large fountain on the quay at Messina.**

Plate 209.

Fig. 1. **Doorway from the church of St. Andrea in Mantua** (Nicolai, Ornament der italienischen Kunst des 15. Jahrhunderts).
„ 2. **Glass painting in the Library at Florence,** painted by Giovanni da Udine (1494—1564), (Hirth).
„ 3. **Small column from the Palazzo Municipale in Perugia** (Raguenet).
„ 4. **Inlaid marble-work in the floor of the cathedral of Siena** (Dolmetsch).
„ 5. **Flat-relief from the Vendramini tomb in the church of San Giovanni e Paolo, Venice** (Dolmetsch).
„ 6. **Wrought-iron railing from Venice** (L'art pour tous).
„ 7. **Telamonic support from the Palazzo Durazzo in the Via Novissima, Genoa** (Raguenet).
„ 8. **Ceiling in the Ducal Palace in Mantua** (Nicolai).
„ 9. **Stairs of a Palace in Florence** (Raguenet).

Plate 210.

Fig. 1. **Intarsia work from a Stall in the church of Santa Maria Novella, Florence** (Teirich, Intarsien).
„ 2. **Coffer in the Parish Picture Gallery in Spoleto,** 10th century (Boito).
„ 3. **Table, Italian-work,** from the 16th century, at present in the Arts and Crafts Museum in Berlin (Boito).
„ 4. **Bronze knocker from the Strozzi Palace, Florence** (D'Espouy).
„ 5. **Wooden panel from the Castle of Salmes.** Piedmontese work of the 16th century.
„ 6. **Intarsia work from a Stall of the Certosa near Padua** (Teirich, Intarsien).

Plate 211.

Italian Majolica.

Fig. 1. **Faience dish from Urbino** (Roger-Milès).
„ 2. **Majolica dish by Maestro Giorgio da Gubbio,** in the South Kensington Museum. Dates from the year 1525. The Arabesques of this Master are generally executed in yellow and green (Jännicke, Keramik).

Plate 211.   ITALIAN RENAISSANCE ORNAMENT.   355

Fig. 3. **Apothecary's vase from Castel Durante.** In the British Museum (Jännicke).
„ 4. **Majolica can by Maestro Giorgio da Gubbio** (Jännicke).
„ 5. **Venetian dish.** In the South Kensington Museum (Jännicke).
„ 6. **Floor with marble mosaic in the cathedral of Siena.** The work of Beccafumi from the year 1372 (Raguenet).
„ 7. **Apothecary's pot from Siena.** In the South Kensington Museum (Jännicke).
„ 8. **Caffaggiolo.** In the South Kensington Museum (Jännicke).

Plate 212.

Fig. 1. **Sweetmeat tazza,** after a drawing ascribed to Benvenuto Cellini (Havard).
„ 2, and 4. **Venetian glasses from the Murano glass works,** 17th century (L'art pour tous).
„ 3, 10, and 11. **Venetian glasses** (Roger-Milès and Havard).
„ 5, and 6. **Ewer of enamelled gold,** at present in the Uffizien, Florence (Dolmetsch).
„ 7. **Goblet of beaten silver,** gilt and chased, said to be the work of Benvenuto Cellini.
„ 8, and 9. **Cut glass tazza with enamelled cover,** 16th century (Havard).

Plate 213.

Fig. 1. **Court mantle of embroidered silk** (Roger-Milès).
„ 2. **Crotchet-work,** 16th century (Roger-Milès).
„ 3. **Venetian embroidery with raised embroidered flowers** (Roger-Milès).
„ 4. **Application embroidery,** 16th century (Dupont and Auberville).
„ 5. **Silk damask,** 16th century (Dupont and Auberville).
„ 6. **Genoese velvet pattern** (Dupont and Auberville).

Plate 214.

Fig. 1. **Book-marker from the Milan Chronicles of Bernardino Corio.** Milan, Alexander Minutiano, 1503 (Hirth).
„ 2. **Alphabet for embroidery from the year 1529.** From the work "Esemplario di Lavori" by Nicolo Zoppino, a Venetian drawer and copper-engraver (Hirth).
„ 3. **Initial of Johannes Regiomontanus,** taken from his work "Epitoma in Almagestum Ptolemei", Venezia 1496 (Hirth).
„ 4. **Head-dress,** 16th century (Roger-Milès).
„ 5. **Initial of the printing-office of Ottavio Scoto.** Venice 1490—1510 (Hirth).
„ 6. **Leaf from the works of Nicolo Zoppino,** see Fig. 2 (Hirth).
„ 7. **Venetian embroidery pattern from the year 1543.** From the work "Esemplario di Lavori" by Giovanandrea Vavassore (Hirth).

Plate 214. ITALIAN RENAISSANCE ORNAMENT. 359

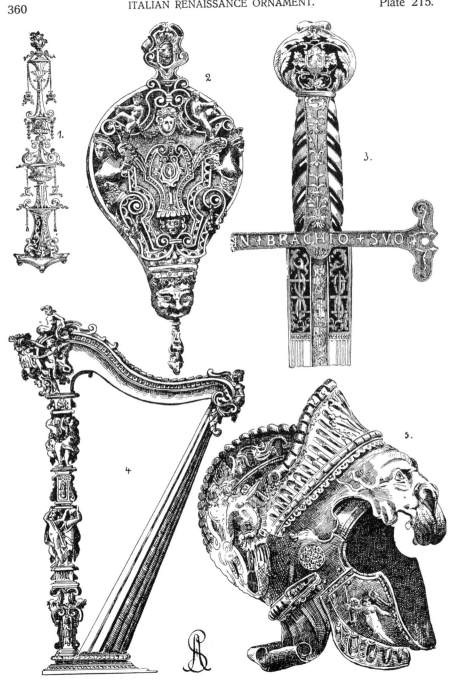

Plate 215.

(After Hirth, Formenschatz.)

Fig. 1. **Panel decoration** (Dolmetsch).
,, 2. **Venetian bellows,** 16th century.
,, 3. **Sword,** said to be given by Francis I to the Graf von Lannoy, Vice-Regent of Naples. It is, however, Italian work.
,, 4. **Design for a harp,** after a water-colour drawing in the Uffizi in Florence.
,, 5. **Helmet of the Archduke Ferdinand of Tyrol.** Italian gold-damascened ornamented work of the year 1550. In the Art Historical Collection of the Imperial House in Vienna.

Window from the Laurentian Library in Florence
(Dolmetsch).

The Renaissance in France.

Printing Initial
(Dolmetsch).

ext into France during the last quarter of the 15th century the influence of the Renaissance movement spread; but owing to the still lingering vitality of the Flamboyant Gothic Style, at first it was able only to modify the decorative details, forming that which is known as a transitional style, which lasted during the first quarter of the 16th century. On the accession of Francis Ist, the new art was devoted more to secular than to ecclesiastical architecture, and then arose the magnificent palaces and chateaux of the Loire at Chambord, Blois, Azay-le-Rideau, etc., which must be regarded as the masterpieces of the early French Renaissance; it was also gradually employed in domestic architecture throughout the towns of France. Here also, as in Italy, the individuality of the architect or master mason became a real factor and the work produced was connected with their names. Thus we have Hector Sohier, the architect of the chevet of the church of St. Peter's at Caen (1520); the Chambiges, uncle and nephew, Pierre Lescot (1510—1578), the architect of the Louvre. Robert Lerou, Pierre Fain, Philibert de l'Orme (1515—1570), who designed the Tuileries for Marie de Medicis, Jean Bullant (1520—1598), and others, bringing us down to the close of the 16th century. Shortly afterwards follow the periods of Louis XIII. and Louis XIV., whose work comes more under the range of the Later Renaissance. In the latter part of the reign of Louis XIV., when pomp and display were the fashion, the Renaissance ornament degenerated, leading the way to the last change, viz, that of the Rococo period.

Embroidery Pattern (Roger-Milès).

Plate 216.   FRENCH RENAISSANCE ORNAMENT.   363

1.

2.

3.

4.

Plate 216.

(After Raguenet, Matériaux.)

Fig. 1. **Door Head in Hotel Lallemand, Bourges,** 16th century.
" 2. **Window of a house in the Rue des Focques, Dijon,** 16th century.
" 3. **Decoration of pierced panel in the choir of the cathedral, Rodez** (Aveyron). From 16th century.
" 4. **Door of a private house in Langres,** Haute Marne, 16th century.

Plate 217.

Fig. 1. **Frieze ornamentation of a room in the Louvre** (Raguenet).
" 2. **Door at angle of house in the Rue de la Grosse Horloge in La Rochelle,** Charente Inférieur, 16th century.
" 3. **Capital from the Baptistery of Louis XIII. in the Palace at Fontainebleau** (Dolmetsch).
" 4. **Doric Renaissance Order after Philibert de l'Orme** (Mauch).
" 5. **Ceramic panel** (Raguenet).
" 6. **Fire-place in the Ducal Palace, Nancy,** Meurthe et Moselle, 16th century (Raguenet).
" 7. **Cresting of the stalls in the church of Arques near Dieppe,** 16th century (Raguenet).
" 8. **Hermes in the Hotel d'Assezat, Toulouse,** from the time of Henry II. (Dolmetsch).
" 9. **Bas relief in the Hotel Carnavalet, Paris,** 16th century (Raguenet).

Plate 218.

(Pfnor, Palais de Fontainebleau.)

Fig. 1. **Capital of marble in the Palace of Fontainebleau.**
" 2. **Exterior pilaster in the Chapel of St. Saturnin.**
" 3. **Pedestal from the Chapel of St. Saturnin.**
" 4. **Porte Dauphine.**
" 5. **Pilasters from the Baptistery of Louis XIII.**

Plate 219.

Fig. 1. **Ornament of the time of Francis I.** (Racinet).
" 2. **Ornament of the time of Henry II.** (Racinet).
" 3. **Ornament of the time of Charles IX.** (Racinet).
" 4. **Ornament of the time of Henry III.** (Racinet).
" 5. **Decorative motif by Jean Cousin,** from his book on Perspective (Racinet).
" 6. **Border from book** (Hirth, Formenschatz).
" 7. **Decorative panel in the Louvre,** time of Henry II. (Dolmetsch).
" 8. **Coffered ceiling from the ancient Grand Chamber of the Parliament of Normandy in the Law Courts at Rouen** (Racinet). This building, which was erected by order of Louis XII. and the Cardinal of Amboise, was begun in 1499 and completed in 1514. The ceiling is of oak.

Plate 219.   FRENCH RENAISSANCE ORNAMENT.   367

1.

5.

2.

3.

5.

8.

4.

6.

7.

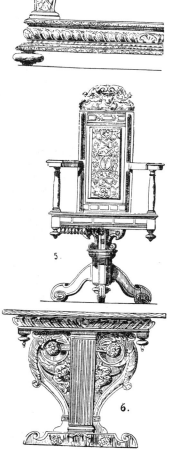

Plate 221. FRENCH RENAISSANCE ORNAMENT. 369

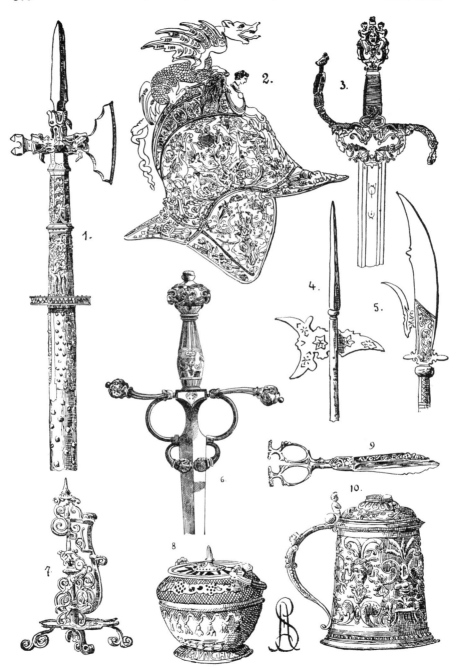

Plate 220.

Furniture.

(After Bajot, Musées de Louvre et de Cluny.)

Fig. 1, and 2. **Arm chair,** 16th century. In the Louvre.
„ 3. **Oak Buffet,** 16th century. In the Cluny Museum.
„ 4. **Cabinet in walnut,** from the time of Louis XIII. (L'art pour tous).
„ 5. **Arm chair,** 16th century. In the Cluny Museum.
„ 6. **Table,** 16th century. In the Cluny Museum.

Plate 221.

Fig. 1. **Mural decoration in glazed terra-cotta,** 16th century. In the Louvre (Havard, Dictionnaire de l'ameublement et de la décoration).
„ 2. **Faience dish,** by the celebrated potter Bernard Palissy, Agen (Jännicke).
„ 3. **Jug in Oiron faience.** In the South Kensington Museum (Jännicke, Grundriss der Keramik).
„ 4. **Terra-cotta figure.** In the Louvre (Jännicke).
„ 5. **Stoneware jug,** 16th century (Havard).
„ 6. **Small jug by Bernard Palissy, Agen** (Jännicke).
„ 7, and 9. **Inlaid floor-tiles after Viriot-Woeriot** (Roger-Milès).
„ 8. **Faience jug,** Bernard Palissy, Agen (Roger-Milès).

Plate 222.

Fig. 1, 4, and 5. **Halberds from the Early Renaissance** (1453—1515) with distinctly marked Gothic reminiscences (Roger-Milès).
„ 2, and 3. **Helmet and sword hilt,** probably owned by Francis I. (Roger-Milès).
„ 6. **Sword hilt,** from the 1st half of 16th century (L'art pour tous).
„ 7. **Wrought-iron candle-stick,** 16th century (Havard).
„ 8. **Silver warming-dish** (Havard).
„ 9. **Pair of scissors,** 16th century (Havard).
„ 10. **Tankard with cover,** 16th century (Havard).

Plate 223.

Fig. 1, 8, 10, and 14. **Silver knife, fork and spoon** (Havard, histoire de l'orfèverie française).
„ 2. **Neck pendant after Viriot-Woeriot** (Roger-Milès, Comment discerner les styles).
„ 3. **Enamelled crystal glass** (L'art pour tous).
„ 4. **Figures engraved glass** (L'art pour tous).
„ 5. **Wine decanter of rock-crystal,** ornamented with precious stones (Havard).
„ 6, and 9. **Fork and spoon, silver gilt** (Roger-Milès).
„ 7. **Enamelled plate,** ascribed to Meister Jean Pénicaud (Havard).
„ 11. **Helmet of Charles the Bold,** set with pearls and precious stones. From a drawing in the Arsenal Library (Havard).
„ 12. **Dagger-sheath** (Racinet).
„ 13. **Costume as emblem of the Jeweller's Art,** after Larmessin (Havard).

Plate 224.   FRENCH RENAISSANCE ORNAMENT.   373

Plate 226. FRENCH RENAISSANCE ORNAMENT. 375

Plate 224.

Fig. 1. **Valenciennes lace.** Mailles doubles. In the Dutuit Collection.

„ 2. **Valenciennes lace.** Mailles rondes. In the Dutuit Collection.

„ 3. **Silk pattern,** 16th century (Dupont-Auberville, Collection of Decorations).

„ 4. **Wall tapestry in the Palace of Fontainebleau,** 16th century (Dolmetsch).

„ 5. **Embroidery from the time of Catherine de Medicis,** Point coupé, that is, embroidery sewn on fine Cambric (Roger-Milès).

„ 6. **Embroidery from a bed.** Presented to the Trappists near Montague by Henry II. on his departure from the Monastery (Dupont-Auberville).

„ 7. **Velvet pattern,** 16th century (Dupont-Auberville).

„ 8. **Gold embroidered cushion,** 16th century (Havard).

Plate 225.

Fig. 1. **Ivory fan,** 17th century. In the Louvre (Hirth).

„ 2. **Hand mirror from a design by Etienne de Laune.** From a copper engraving from the year 1560 (Hirth).

„ 3. **Key by Mathurin Jousse de la Fleche,** of the year 1625 (Hirth).

„ 4. **Book cover with the arms of Henry II.** (Dolmetsch).

„ 5, 6, and 7. **Dagger hilts etc.** From designs by Antoine Jaequard, copper engraver and armourer in Poitiers, 1st half of the 17th century (Hirth).

Plate 226.

Fig. 1, 3—6, 9, and 10. **Painted ornament from the Castle of Cheverny near Blois** (Eugène Rouyer, L'art architectural en France).

„ 2, and 7. **Engraved frontispieces** from the Théâtre des bons Engins, published in Paris in 1539 by Guillaume de la Perrieire, and dedicated to Queen Margaret of Navarre.

„ 8, and 12. **Inlaid, gold in wood,** from the castle of Écouen (Eugène Rouyer, L'art architecturel en France).

„ 11. **Inlay from the Cardinal's Room in the Castle of Ancy-Le-Franc.**

Typographic ornamentation of the time of Louis XIII. (Dolmetsch).

Renaissance Ornament in Spain and Portugal.

Initial by Juan de Yciar (Hirth).

pain accustomed by Moorish Art to fantastic forms and configurations, worked the new italics, which came into the country from France and Italy towards the end of the 15th century, at first into the Plateresque or Goldsmith's Style in which form the Early Renaissance appeared in Spain. It was not until the time of Philip II., aïter Charles V. had a palace built by Malchuca in the Alhambra, that a pure Renaissance Style, called by the Spaniards, the Graeco-Roman, came to be established. The most magnificent structure of this period is the Escurial (1563—1581), which was built by Gian Baptista de Toledo, and his successor Juan de Herrera.

Plate 227.

(After Monumentos de España.)

Fig. 1. Head of a nail from the door of the University of Salamanca.
„ 2. Corner-piece from the tomb of Cardinal Ximenez or Cisneros as he is best known in Alcalá de Henares.
„ 3, and 9. Pilasters from the door of the University of Salamanca.
„ 4—8. Details of the façade of the University in Alcalá de Henares.

Plate 228.

(After Monumentos de España.)

Fig. 1. Figure from the façade of the University in Alcalá de Henares.
„ 2. Finial in the Court of the Archiepiscopal College, at present the Irish College, in Salamanca.
„ 3. Finial from the door of the vestibule of the ancient Hospitales Santa Cruz in Toledo.
„ 4. Doorway of a house in Palma, Majorca (Prentice).
„ 5. Pilaster capital from the gate of the University of Salamanca.
„ 6. Bracket capital of the gallery in the Archiepiscopal Palace in Alcalá de Henares.
„ 7. Cartouche from a house in Palma, Majorca (Prentice).

Plate 228.   SPANISH RENAISSANCE ORNAMENT.   379

Plate 230. SPANISH RENAISSANCE ORNAMENT. 381

Plate 232.   SPANISH RENAISSANCE ORNAMENT.   383

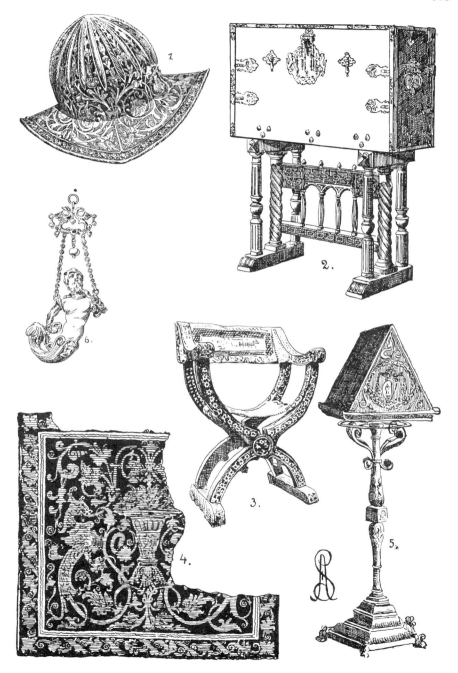

Plate 229.

Fig. 1, and 5. **Details of the north façade of the Royal Alcazar in Toledo** (Monumentos de España).

„ 2. **Order from the altar in the cloister of Poblet,** said to be the work of the Spanish Sculptor Berruguette, a pupil of Michael Angelos (Andrew Prentice, Renaissance Architecture in Spain).

Plate 230.

(After Andrew N. Prentice, Renaissance Architecture and Ornament in Spain.)

Fig. 1, 4, 7 and 8. **Ceilings in carved wood in the vestibule of the Archiepiscopal Palace in Alcalá de Henares.**

„ 2. **Column of a wrought-iron grating in the cathedral of Cuenca.**

„ 3. **Pillar from the Stairshouse in the cathedral of Burgos.**

„ 5. **Coronal of an iron trellis-work in the baptism-chapel of the cathedral of Toledo.**

„ 6. **Panel of a door in the palace of the Duke of Alba in Peñaranda.**

„ 9. **Cornice of the Consistory in Palma, Majorca.**

Plate 231.

(After Andrew N. Prentice, Renaissance Architecture and Ornament in Spain.)

Fig. 1. **Inner gallery of Polentina House in Avila.**

„ 2. **Gateway from Avila.**

„ 3. **Iron railing from Cuenca.**

„ 4. **Frieze from the stone door of the cathedral of Sigüenza.**

„ 5. **Iron railing from the cathedral of Sigüenza.**

„ 6. **Balcony from Palma, Majorca.**

Plate 232.

Fig. 1. **Helmet from the Armeria in Madrid** (L'art pour tous).

„ 2. **Secretaire,** 16th century. In the South-Kensington Museum. Transition period (Libonis).

„ 3. **Folding chair from the cathedral of Toledo.** Of black wood incrusted with ivory, 16th century (Raguenet).

„ 4. **Embroidered carpet,** end of 16th century. In Platersque style, from the Collection of Domingo Guerrero y Polo in Barcel (Mira Leroy).

„ 5. **Reading-desk of wrought chased iron,** end of 16th century (Mira Leroy).

„ 6. **Pendant ornament** (L'art pour tous).

Plate 233.

Fig. 1—5. **Lettering from designs by Juan de Yciar,** Painter and Writing Master, born 1525 in Durango, Biscaya: "Arte subtilissima por la qual se esenna a escrivir perfectamente, Saragossa, 1550" (Hirth, Formenschatz).

Plate 234.

(After Albert Haupt, Die Baukunst der Renaissance in Portugal.)

Fig. 1. Silver filigree cross from the Treasury in Belem.

,, 2, and 4. Balustrades from the chapel of the new Cathedral in Cimbra.

,, 3. Window column in transept of the cloister dos Jeronymos, Belem.

,, 5. Tile wainscotting in the chapel of St. Roque, Lisbon.

,, 6. Mosaic in a chapel in Penha Verde near Cintra.

,, 7. Court-yard in the Benedictine cloister in Porto.

,, 8. Wall tiles from the church of St. Maria da monte in Penha Verde near Cintra.

Application Embroidery, 16th century
(Dupont-Auberville).

The Renaissance in Germany, Austria and Switzerland.

(Dolmetsch.)

efore the new style of art, which was introduced from France into Germany, became firmly established in the latter country, a long period of time was necessary. Although at the period the new humanist movement carried on by Johannes Reuchlin, Erasmus of Rotterdam, and Ulrich von Hutten, was already in full activity in Germany, still it was more in a theological and philosophic rather than in an artistic direction. The foundation for the Renaissance of Art was far less favourable in Germany than in France. German architects were so tied to Gothic work that they strongly resisted the introduction of the Renaissance. The painters, however, Albrecht Dürer being the foremost amongst them were more amenable. Even though in his works one may notice the tendency not entirely to disregard the Gothic, still, on the other hand, his fine constructive sense and understanding for the new Italian Forms can also be clearly discernible. The first who really gave themselves up entirely to the Renaissance were Hans Burkmair and Hans Holbein. The engravings produced by these artists were circulated throughout the country, and even though they did not understand them, were the source from which builders and artistic handworkers took the elements of the new art. This fact explains the bizarre character which distinguished the Renaissance in Germany from that of Italy. It was only when an intimate connection was established between the German and Italian artists, when Italian artists came into Germany, and Italian works on architecture became known and read in that country, that the German artists first began to really understand what the Renaissance was. The Thirty Years War, however, which broke out at this time, put an end to all artistic activity throughout the greater part of Germany. Besides this, Protestantism, which also appeared, was an enemy to all kinds of decoration, and prevented the use of the Renaissance for monumental Ecclesiastical Buildings. The people therefore confined their work to the building of Castles and Town Halls. For this reason, the German Renaissance lacks monumental force of form, but shows instead of that, a picturesque grouping and decorative talent.

The most celebrated Masters of the German Renaissance were, Albrecht Dürer, Burkmair, the two Holbeins, Peter Fischer and his son, Manuel Deutsch, Joseph Graf, and Peter Flötner.

The German Renaissance did not succeed in developing into a homogenous Style or characteristic System, a circumstance due to ruling local conditions which rendered it impossible to do what was done in France, namely to unify the prevailing style of Architecture peculiar to the Middle Ages with the Antique forms. In all the numerous centres of art in Germany, the new Style developed in a different manner, according as it was influenced from France, Italy, or the Netherlands.

Plate 235.   GERMAN RENAISSANCE ORNAMENT.   389

The German Renaissance possesses no monumental aspect its chief power lying in the artistic grouping and ornamental treatment of details. It was only in a later period that a correct architectural tendency became apparent, which, however, was brought to a sudden termination by the Thirty Years War.

The German Renaissance dates its commencement from the year 1525, and it lasted up to 1620, the oldest German Renaissance Monument, however, the Entrance Gateway of the Castle of Mährisch-Trübau, dates from the year 1492, as do also some other Doorways.

In Germany as in Italy, three periods are distinguished, the Early, High, and Later Renaissance, or Rococo, the first dating from 1525 to 1570, and the second down to 1680.

Plate 235.

Fig. 1. **Column from Ensisheim** (Lambert & Stahl, Motive der deutschen Architektur).
„ 2. **Hermes from the Armoury in Brunswick** (Lambert & Stahl).
„ 3. **Wooden column from the Town Hall at Munden** (Ortwein). The construction of this building was begun in 1603.
„ 4. **Cartouche from the pulpit in St. George's church, Wismar** (Ortwein).
„ 5. **Fountain column from Berne** (Lambert & Stahl).
„ 6. **Capital from the fountain in the market-place at Berne** (Lambert & Stahl).
„ 7. **Portal from the Royal Mews in Berlin.** In the year 1665, the Royal Mews was burned, but afterwards rebuilt by Kurfürst Friedrich Wilhelm, who purchased the house of Herr von Ribbeck which lay next to the Mews, and whose façade remained uninjured. The doorway here given is found in this façade (Ortwein.)
„ 8. **Wooden pillar from church in Cologne** (Ortwein).
„ 9. **Plinth from the arcade of the church Buildings in the Castle at Baden-Baden** (Ortwein).

Plate 236.

Fig. 1. **Window from transept in the cathedral at Ratisbon** (Lambert & Stahl).
„ 2. **From the Organ Gallery in St. George's church, Wismar** (Ortwein).
„ 3. **Coat of Arms from the monument to Duke Johann in Oels** (Ortwein).
„ 4. **Inner gateway of the castle at Wismar,** built in the years 1553—1555 (Lambert & Stahl).
„ 5. **Gable of a house in Heilbronn** (Lambert & Stahl).
„ 6. **From an epitaph in St. George's church, Wismar** (Ortwein).
„ 7. **Font in the Parish church, Güstrow** (Ortwein).
„ 8. **Balustrade of the pulpit in the Jakob church, Goslar** (Ortwein).

Plate 237.

Fig. 1, and 2. **Console brackets from the ceiling of the Prince's Hall in the Town Hall at Augsburg** (Leybold, Rathaus von Augsburg).
„ 2. **Wall-paper in the Town Hall at Danzig** (Ortwein).
„ 4. **From the staircase of the Town Hall at Bremen** (Ortwein).
„ 5. **Finial from the Town Hall at Bremen** (Ortwein).
„ 6. **Portion of wood ceiling from the Town Hall at Görlitz** (Ortwein).

Plate 236.   GERMAN RENAISSANCE ORNAMENT.   391

Plate 238.   GERMAN RENAISSANCE ORNAMENT.   393

Plate 238.

(After Ortwein, Deutsche Renaissance.)

Fig. 1, and 2. **Chairs in the Historical Museum, Dresden.**

„ 3. **Cabinet with inlaid work.** This cabinet, which is in the Wallraf-Richartz-Museum, dates from the year 1599, and is made od seven woods, oak, sycamore, beech, and others each stained of a different colour.

„ 4. **Consol from the Kaiser House in Hildesheim.**

„ 5. **Ornament from wall-panelling in the Civil Service Office in Luneburg.**

„ 6. **Panel from a stall in the Ludgeri church at Münster.**

„ 7. **Door of the tabernacle in the church of St. Gereon, Cologne.**

„ 8. **Panel from a screen in Hildesheim.**

„ 9. **Cake mould in Luneburg Museum.**

Plate 239.

Fig. 1. **Stove in the Prince's Hall of the Town Hall at Augsburg** (Leybold).

„ 2. **Stone jug from Cologne.** The ornamentation is done in blue glaze (Ortwein).

„ 3, and 6. **Terra-cottas from the Castle in Schwerin** (Ortwein). Originally intended for the Furstenhof in Wismar.

„ 4. **Stone jug in the Museum at Munich,** from the beginning of the 17th century (Hirth).

„ 5. **Tin jug,** 17th century. In the Museum at Lubeck (Hirth).

„ 7. **Chimneypiece in the Town Hall at Münden** (Ortwein).

Plate 240.

Fig. 1. **Mural painting in the Golden Hall of the Town Hall at Augsburg** (Leybold). The Town Hall at Augsburg was begun in the year 1615, the architect being the Municipal Architect Elias Holl (1573—1646). It was completed, all except the interior fittings, in 1620. These latter were, however, not carried out in accordance with Holl's designs, but from designs by different masters, the most renowned of whom were the painter Peter de Witt, called the Candid, the Jesuit Matthäus Rader, and the Augsburg painter Matthias Kager.

„ 2. **Painting on ceiling in the Knights Hall of Trausnitz Castle near Landshut** (Ortwein). These paintings date from the years 1578—1580, the building itself being originally constructed in Gothic, and later on changed to the Renaissance style.

„ 3. **Glass painting from the cupola of the chapel in the Royal Residence in Munich.**

„ 4. **Book binding,** 17th century, gilt and painted. In the Nuremberg Museum (Hirth).

„ 5. **Pilaster panel from Wertheim Castle** (Ortwein).

Plate 239.   GERMAN RENAISSANCE ORNAMENT.

395

Plate 241.

GERMAN RENAISSANCE ORNAMENT.

Plate 241.

Fig. 1, and 2. **Bracket candle-sticks from the Upper Hall of the Town Hall at Augsburg** (Leybold).
„　3. **Silver spoon in the Luneburg Museum** (Ortwein).
„　4. **Key in the Munich Museum** (Hirth).
„　5. **Figure of a woman holding a candlestick in the Stertzing Town Hall, Tyrol.** The figure, which represents Lucretia dying, is carved in wood, and tastefully painted and gilt. It dates from the 1st half of the 16th century (Hirth).
„　6. **Chandelier in the church of St. Mary at Zwickau** (Ortwein).
„　7. **Iron cloth-shearing comb with etched design** (Hirth). Belongs to the Early Renaissance.

Plate 242.

Fig. 1. **Hinge on door of the Town Hall at Augsburg** (Leybold).
„　2. **Lock on the door of the Prince's Hall of the Town Hall at Augsburg** (Leybold).
„　3. **Door hinge from the principal doorway of the Town Hall at Augsburg** (Leybold).
„　4. **From the lock of a chest in the Munich Museum,** iron plate carved and engraved (Hirth).
„　5. **Finial from the Castle at Munden** (Ortwein).
„　6, and 7. **Wrought iron railings,** 16th century. In the Salzburg Museum (Hirth).
„　8. **Railing in the tower staircase, Castle Yard, Dresden** (Ortwein).
„　9. **Door knocker from Rostock** (Ortwein).

Plate 243.

(After Hirth, Formenschatz.)

Fig. 1. **Hunting spear,** 16th century. In the Imperial Collection in Vienna.
„　2, and 6. **Ornament of a halbard,** etched in iron, from the middle of the 16th century. In the Munich Museum.
„　3. **Ornament by Peter Flötner (1549).** In the Copper Engraving Cabinet, Munich.
„　4. **Black and white drawing by Albrecht Dürer.** Shows a cavalier an horse back in the triumphal procession of Emperor Maximilian. The original is in the Ambrose Collection in Vienna.
„　5. **Bridle-bit from Scutters "Bit Book",** Augsburg 1584.

Plate 244.

(After Hirth, Formenschatz).

Fig. 1. **Small book-cover** of engraved silver plate with velvet ground.
„　2, 6, and 9. **Sketches for gold ornaments.** Black and white drawings in watercolour from Hans Holbein in the British Museum.

Plate 242. GERMAN RENAISSANCE ORNAMENT. 399

Plate 244. GERMAN RENAISSANCE ORNAMENT. 401

Plate 246.   GERMAN RENAISSANCE ORNAMENT.   403

Fig. 3. **Gentlewoman of the 16th century,** after a drawing by Hans Holbein.
„ 4. **Gold chain with enamel-work.** Augsburg work of the 16th century.
„ 5. **Jewel of enamelled gold,** 17th century.
„ 7, and 8. **Samples of work of the goldsmith Jacob von der Heyden,** from the year 1620. Taken from the book "Suite de dessins d'ornements pour bijoutiers meilleurs et émailleurs sur fond noir", published in Strasburg.
„ 10, and 11. **Samples of lace-work from the book "Neues Modellbuch"** by Johann Sibmacher, Copper Engraver, who died in Nüremberg in the year 1611.
„ 12. **Ornament pendant** by Paul Birckenhultz.

Plate 245.
(After Hirth, Formenschatz.)

Fig. 1. **Bronze clock with engraved and chased ornamentation,** made by Benedict Fürstenfelder at about the middle of the 17th century.
„ 2. **Hock glass,** 17th century. In the National Museum, Munich.
„ 3. **Wedding goblet of gilt silver,** 16th century. The large goblet is formed by the hooped farthingale, the small one is moveable round its own axis. The bridegroom was obliged to drink from the large goblet and empty it without spilling any out of the small one. The bride drank from the small goblet.
„ 4. **Silver spoon and fork,** 16th century. In possession of the owner of the Possen Estate, Kurland.
„ 5. **Chalice** by Wenzel Janitzer.
„ 6. **Silver knives and forks from Nüremberg** (L'art pour tous).
„ 7. **Silver drinking-jug,** strongly gilt, Nüremburg work from the 16th or beginning of 17th century.

Plate 246.
(After Hirth, Formenschatz.)

Fig. 1. **Carpet pattern,** from an oil painting by George Pencz in the Royal Museum, Berlin. From the beginning of the 16th century. The colours, exclusive of the black outlines, are a dark and a light moss green.
„ 2. **Pattern of a gold brocade,** from a picture by Roger van den Weyden "Das Christkind erscheint den drei heiligen Königen" — The Christ Child appearing to the three Kings — in the Royal Museum at Berlin.
„ 3. **Gold brocade on black velvet,** from a picture of the Cologne School, in the Royal Picture Gallery, Munich.
„ 4. **Green velvet on a green silk ground,** 16th century. In the National Museum, Munich.
„ 5. **Black velvet on gold brocade,** from a picture by Dirk Bouts in the Royal Picture Gallery Munich.
„ 6. **Gold embroidery on black velvet,** from the mantle worn by the Pfalzgraf Wilhelm beim Rheyn on his marriage with Renata von Lothringen, on the 22nd February 1568. In the National Museum, Munich.

Plate 247. GERMAN RENAISSANCE ORNAMENT. 405

Plate 249.   GERMAN RENAISSANCE ORNAMENT.   407

Plate 247.

(After Hirth, Formenschatz.)

Fig. 1, and 3. **Initials by Lucas Kranach.**

„ 2, 4, and 5. **Letters from Caligraphic Work of Paulo Franken,** writing-master and arithmetician in Memmingen. From the year 1601.

„ 6. **The Hohenzollern Arms by Jost Amman.**

„ 7. **Ornaments from the work Imperatorum Romanorum Imagines,** published in Zurich in 1559 by Gessner, and drawn in all probability by Christoph Schweitzer.

„ 8, 9, 11, and 12. **Written text from the album of Wolfgang Fugger, Nüremberg,** 1553.

„ 10. **Letters for embroidery,** from the book: "Ein new getruckt model Buchli auf aussuchen und bartten wicken", 1529.

„ 13. **Initials of Lucas Kilian,** engraver at Augsburg.

Plate 248.

(After Wilhelm Weimar, Monumentalschriften.)

Fig. 1. **Engraved Solnhofer stone slab,** of the year 1636, formerly in the "Getreidekasten zum leeren Beutel", Ratisbon, at present in the Municipal Museum in the same city.

„ 2. **Engraved Solnhofer stone slab,** from the year 1592. In the Collection of the Historical Society of the Oberpfalz in Ratisbon.

Swiss Renaissance Wood Buildings.

Plate 249.

(After E. Gladbach, Holzbauten der Schweiz.)

Fig. 1. **Leaf-table from Filisur in the Engadine,** 1672.

„ 2. **Door of the hospital in Frutigen,** Canton Berne.

„ 3. **Wall panelling** in the drawing-room of the Baron von Reding-Biberegg in Schwyz.

„ 4. **View of the granary in Langnau,** Canton Berne, dated 1519.

Plate 250.

(After E. Gladbach, Holzbauten der Schweiz.)

Fig. 1. **Panelled ceiling** of the drawing-room of the Baron von Reding-Biberegg, Schwyz. (See also plate 249, Fig. 3.)

„ 2. **Detail** from the same room.

„ 3, 5, and 7. **Carving from Glion** in Canton Waadt.

„ 4, and 6. **Back of a child's chair in Rüti,** Meiringen.

„ 8. **Inn table** in Canton Schwyz.

Plate 250.   GERMAN RENAISSANNE ORNAMENT.   409

Fig. 9. **Corbel strut from Langnau,** Canton Berne.

„ 10. **Old House at Langnau.**

„ 11, and 15. **Sawn-out work from same.**

„ 12. **Back of chair from Canton Berne.**

„ 13. **Table from Rothenthums in Schwyz.**

„ 14. **Stool in Schwyz.**

Wood carving from the façade of Hütte's House in Höxter
(Ortwein).

Plate 251.   GERMAN RENAISSANCE ORNAMENT.   411

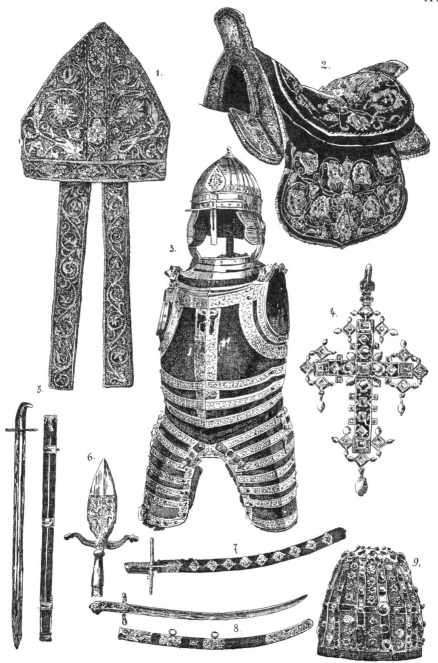

Renaissance Ornament in Hungary.

Plate 251.

(After Dr. Béla Czobor und Emmerich von Szaley, die historischen Denkmäler Ungarns.)

Fig. 1. **Bishop's mitre of red pearl-worked embroidery,** 15th century. In the Treasury of the Cathedral Church, Györ.

,, 2. **Saddle of red velvet with gold embroidery,** 17th century.

,, 3. **State armour of Stefan Báthory** (1533—1586). In the Art Historical Museum in Vienna.

,, 4. **Cross worn by the Cardinal Archbishop Peter Pázmány of Esztergom,** 16th century.

,, 5. **Cavalry broadsword,** 16th century.

,, 6. **Richly ornamented partisan,** 16th century.

,, 7. **Richly ornamented regal sword,** 16th century. In the Royal Collection of Arms, Vienna.

,, 8. **Richly ornamented sword from the Siebenbürger Museum.**

,, 9. **Tiara from Krusedole cloister,** 15th century.

Agraffe of gold and enamel, 17th century.
(L'art pour tous.)

Plate 252.   DUTCH RENAISSANCE ORNAMENT.   413

Renaissance Ornament in the Netherlands.

n Belgium, Renaissance Ornament did not develop to the same standard as Gothic Ornament. The earliest work of the Renaissance in Belgium is the palace of Margarete of Parma in Malines, built about the year 1520 by the French Architect Beauregard. The most renowned is, however, the Rathhaus, or Town Hall of Antwerp, built in the years 1561—1565 by Cornelius de Vriendt or Floris, a pupil of Giovanni da Bologna. The cities of Ghent, Ypres, Furnes, and others, possess also remarkable specimens of Town Halls in this style. The Renaissance appeared in Holland later than in Belgium, the most important buildings in Holland being also the Town Halls, that of the Hague (1564—1575), and Leyden (1597—1604). The most celebrated architects of this period were Hendrick de Kayzer (1567—1621), and his colleague, Cornelius Dankerts (1561—1634), who succeeded in Holland in directing Art along Italian lines, while in Belgium the Renaissance degenerated much sooner. There developed, therefore, in Holland, a specific, Dutch Style which spread also through North Germany and Scandinavia.

Door Handle from Ghent (Ewerbeck).   In consequence of the epoch-making introduction of the modern system of oil-painting by the brothers Hubert and Jean van Eyck, which rendered it possible to give true reproductions of nature, so absolutely necessary for the development of Realism, painting developed in a most magnificent manner in the Netherlands. Having its beginnings in Flanders it grew to be the ruling style and fashion.

Plate 252.

(After F. Ewerbeck und Neumeister, die Renaissance in Belgien und Holland.)

Fig. 1. **Glass painting of the year 1549.** In the Museum at Middelburg.
 „ 2. **Stone arm-chair from the year 1609.** In the Museum at Brüges, originally in the church at Damme near Brüges.
 „ 3. **Console from a fire-place in the Town Hall at Venlo.**
 „ 4. **Column of the pulpit in the cathedral at Hertogenbosch** (Bois-le-duc).
 „ 5. **Iron tee on a house in Zalt-Bommel.**
 „ 6. **Southern ornamental gable of the abattoir in Haarlem.** This is the most valuable monument of Renaissance Architecture in the Netherlands. It was completed 1603, but the name of the architect is unknown.
 „ 7. **Capital from a stall in the large church at Dortrecht.**

Plate 253.

Fig. 1. **Shaft of column after Vries,** 16th century (Libonis).
 „ 2. **Cartouche from the atlas of Abraham Ortelius,** Antwerp 1583 (Hirth, Formenschatz).
 „ 3. **Brüges guipure lace in the Grunthuze Museum.**
 „ 4. **Cartouche from the atlas of Waghenaer,** Amsterdam 1583 (Hirth).

IOECESIS TYPVS.

Plate 255.   DUTCH RENAISSANCE ORNAMENT.   417

Fig. 5. **Brussels lace.** Point de Bruxelles, "Drochel", foundation. From the Dutuit Collection.
„ 6. **Oak cabinet,** 16th century. In the Cluny Museum (Bajot).
„ 7. **Table,** 17th century. In the Cluny Museum (Bajot).

Plate 254.

(After Ewerbeck and Neumeister, Die Renaissance in Belgien und Holland.)

Fig. 1. **Balcony of the Town Hall at Furnes,** 17th century.
„ 2. **Wrought-iron door furniture,** in the Haller Tor Museum, Brussels.
„ 3. **Wrought-iron fire-dog, etc.,** in the Haller Tor Museum, Brussels.
„ 4. **Stalls in the Stadtor of Dortrecht.**

Plate 255.

(After Ewerbeck and Neumeister, Die Renaissance in Belgien und Holland.)

Fig. 1. **Wooden table in the Town Hall at Oudenarde** (L'art pour tous).
„ 2, 3, and 5. **Glazed wall tiles of Delft.**
„ 4. **Gold medallion** (L'art pour tous).
„ 6. **Gold pendant ornament** (L'art pour tous).
„ 7. **Delft plate** (L'art pour tous).
„ 8. **Brass fire dog** (L'art pour tous).

Table from the Salvator church in Brüges (Ewerbeck).

Ornament of the Northern Renaissance.

N the Scandinavian Lands the Renaissance style of art did not become properly prevalent until the 16th century, being introduced into Denmark from the Netherlands, and into Sweden from the Hansa Cities which were also, in a like manner, subject to Netherland influences. It did not, however, develop in any of these countries into a characteristic style. The Early Renaissance in Sweden extends up to the year 1630, and the Later Renaissance, which in consequence of the deeper study given by the artists, approached more the Italian forms of Art, from 1630 to 1720.

Book Ornament (Dahlerup).

The Renaissance did not begin to make itself felt in Norway until the beginning of the 17th century. Considering the lively commercial intercourse with Holland which obtained at this period, it is easy to understand that Norwegian Woodwork Architecture, besides being subject to Swedish, German, and Danish influences, was also especially influenced by Dutch Renaissance motifs, motifs which the skilled Norwegian peasants knew well how to handle independently, and to transform, by grafting them on the ancient native forms peculiar to the country.

Plate 256.

(After Dr. John Böttiger, Hedvig Eleonoras Drottingholm.)

Fig. 1. Door.
„ 2. Ceiling in drawing-room.
„ 3, and 4. Frieze of Chamber of state.
„ 5. Chimney-piece in the lower Retainer's Hall.
„ 6. Ceiling in the South Tower.
„ 7. Pilaster from the upper Retainer's Hall.

Plate 257.

Fig. 1—7. Norwegian wood ornaments of the 17th century (Dietrichson und Munthe Die Holzbaukunst Norwegens).
„ 8. Bronze chandelier with console of the year 1668.
„ 9. Fire-dog from Noergaard, Denmark, of the year 1588 (Dahlerup, Holm und Stork, Tegninger af ældre nordisk Architektur).

Plate 257.   NORTHERN RENAISSANCE ORNAMENT.   421

Slavonic Renaissance Ornament.

NTO Russia, and also into Poland, the Renaissance was introduced by Italian artists who had been invited into both countries. These artists, however, were unable to resist subordinating themselves to the Oriental influences already prevalent especially in Russia, the result being the development of a native, national Style, whose principal characteristics were the Imperial Roof and the Ogee Arch. The wood Architecture was also brought by the Renaissance to a high state of perfection, to which result Scandinavian and Lower Saxon influences very probably also contributed.

In Polish Art, where local influences were not so powerful, the evidences of Italian Renaissance influences are far more apparent than in Russia.

Baptismal Font in the Family Chapel of the Firlej near the Parish church in Bejsce, 1600 (Odrzywolsky).

Renaissance Ornament in Poland.

Plate 258.

(After Slawomir Odrzywolsky, Die Renaissance in Polen.)

Fig. 1. **Gold reliquary,** 16th century, in the Treasury of Cracow cathedral.

„ 2. **Silver candle-stick from the Sigismund chapel in Cracow cathedral,** dates from the year 1536.

„ 3. **Choir stalls in the King Stefan Bathorý chapel, Cracow cathedral.** In all probability the work of Santi Gucci.

„ 4. **Dutch-tile stove in the Castle of Podhorce.** Contains the arms of the Rzewuski Krzwada Family, very probably Danzig work.

Plate 258. SLAVONIC RENAISSANCE ORNAMENT. 423

Fig. 5, and 6. **Turret crest over the Sigismund chapel, Cracow cathedral.** The angels and the crown are cast in copper, the cross and ball of wrought copper, all are richly gilt.

Window of the Royal Castle in Cracow (Odrzywolsky).

Plate 259.   SLAVONIC RENAISSANCE ORNAMENT.   425

Renaissance Ornament in Russia.

Plate 259.

Fig. 1, and 2. **From a Croatian peasant-house in Progar near Semlin, Symrina** (Uhde, Die Konstruktionen und die Kunstformen der Architektur).

„ 3. **Gable of a peasant's house in Fataroff, Russia** (Uhde).

„ 4. **Window from the south side of the church at Tscherewkowo, Russia** (Sonslow, Ancienne Architecture Russe).

„ 5, 6, and 10. **Door wood-carvings,** 17th century (Sireitschikoff).

„ 7 to 9. **Table and ornaments from the Nicolo Mocky church** (Gagarin, Russische Ornamente).

Plate 260.

(After N. P. Sireitschikoff et D. K. Treneff, Ornements sur les monuments de l'ancien art Russe.)

Fig. 1. **Chased ornament from a chandelier,** 17th century.

„ 2, 3, and 5. **Enamel ornaments,** 17th century.

„ 4. **Painting from a holy picture,** end of 16th century.

„ 6. **Painting from a holy picture,** painted by Simon Ouchanoff in 1683.

„ 7. **Painting from a holy picture,** painted by Ninite Pauloff in 1677.

„ 8. **Decorative design,** of the year 1492.

„ 9. **Silver mounting from a holy picture,** end of 16th century.

„ 10. **Wood-carving from a door,** 16th century.

Mitre of a Patriarch, 17th century, in the Museum of the Kreml in Moscow. Shows marked Byzantine influence (L'art pour tous).

Ornament over the window in Winchester School.
(After Belcher and Macartney, Later Renaissance Architecture in England.

Renaissance Ornament in England.

Initial, 17th century
(Gotch).

s the Gothic style in England retained its vitality much later than in other countries, and in its last phase known as the Tudor Style, had already affected in Domestic Architecture the principal changes in plan and design which transformed the castle into the country mansion, the transitional period lasted for a much longer period. The first attempt to open the way for the introduction of the Renaissance in England was made by the Italian Pietro Torrigiano with the erection in the year 1519 of the beautiful monument to Henry VII. and his wife, and that to Margaret of Richmond, both in Westminster Abbey. The employment of the Renaissance in England was however for a long time confined to the enrichment of the principal entrance doorways of mansions. The artists Toto dell' Nunziata, Theodore Haveus and John of Padua also helped in bringing the new style into England.

The real, characteristic English Renaissance did not begin to develop itself until the reign of Queen Elizabeth (1558—1603) when it was known under the title of the Elizabethan Style, which was a transition style from the Tudor or Late Gothic to the Renaissance, similar to the transition in France of the style of Francis I. from the Gothic to the French Renaissance. The English style resembled the German and French Early Renaissance, in so far as it too, in a similar, way confined itself more to secular buildings, castles and country houses, than to ecclesiastical, while, on the other hand, the latter were of the very greatest importance to the Italian Renaissance. Even although the development of the Elizabethan Style was much influenced by Italian art, still it cannot be denied that it possesses a genuine, national character peculiar to itself. As Queen Elizabeth brought German and Flemish artists in the

Plate 261.   ENGLISH RENAISSANCE ORNAMENT.   429

country for the building of the castles of the period, it is clear that German and Flemish influences had also their effect upon the English Style. The architect John Shute, and the designer de Vries of authory contributed much to the development of the Elizabethan Style. Under the reign of Elizabeth's successor, James I. (1603—1625), the Renaissance took on a still more classic form, owing to the more intimate and deeper study of classic architecture, to the removal of all Gothic reminiscences, and to the labours of the architect John Thorpe.

The English Renaissance was rendered completely free of all Gothic elements by the two famous architects Inigo Jones and Christopher Wren, who may be considered as the founders of the pure Italian Style. Inigo Jones (1572—1652) studied in Italy, especially in Vicenza, under the personal supervision of Palladio, and when be returned to England after a second journey to Italy in the year 1612 he succeeded in introducing complete change in the architecture, and became the founder, in England of the pure classical School after Palladio. Sir Christopher Wren (1632—1723) was professor of astronomy and mathematics in Oxford, and, when London was almost destroyed by fire in the year 1666, designed a plan for its reconstruction which although it was not carried out led to his employment in the rebuilding of London. In consequence of his studies in Paris, there is more of French than Italian influence in Wren's work. At this period, when Vignola exercised great influence in France, and Palladio in England, Wren attempted to unite both styles. His principal work is St. Paul's cathedral, London, which with his numerous other works, is now included in the Later Renaissance Style.

Plate 261.

Fig. 1. **Detail of Tomb of Henry VII., Westminster Abbey** (H. O. Cresswell in Architectural Assoc. Sketch Book).

„ 2. **Balustrade Audley, End,** Essex (Richardson).

„ 3. **Garden Porch, Coombe Abbey,** (Richardson).

„ 4. **Carved Baluster, Blickling Hall,** Norfolk (Shaw).

„ 5. **Detail of Balustrade, Audley End,** Essex (Richardson).

„ 6. **Ceiling of great chamber in an old house formerly in Gravel Lane, Houndsditch,** London (Richardson).

Plate 262.

(After Gotch, Architecture of the Renaissance in England.)

Fig. 1. **Door of Dining-room in Gayton Manor House,** Northamptonshire.

„ 2. **Top of Bench end in Leeds church,** erected in the years 1631—1633.

„ 3—5. **Ceiling Decorations from the Manor House, South Wraxall,** Wiltshire.

„ 6. **Staircase Clare College,** Cambridge, erected after the year 1635.

„ 7. **Balustrade to terrace,** Claverton.

„ 8. **Chimney-piece in Bolsover Castle,** Derbyshire, 17th century.

„ 9. **Gable of Rushton Hall,** Northamptonshire, from the year 1636.

„ 10. **Balustrade to porch, Cold Ashton.**

„ 11. **Gatewey in Garden wall, Stibbington Hall,** Huntingdonshire, erected in 1625.

Plate 262. ENGLISH RENAISSANCE ORNAMENT. 431

Plate 263.

(After Gotch, Architecture of the Renaissance in England.)

Fig. 1. Panel from a pew in Leeds church.
,, 2. Part of Arcade of screen in Leeds church.
,, 3. Panel from a wood chimney-piece in Burton Agnes Hall, Yorkshire. Erected in 1610.
,, 4. Carved wood string from the Neptune Inn, Ipswich, 1620.
,, 5. Newel of Staircase, Aston Hall, Warwickshire.
,, 6. Wood work from Astbury church.
,, 7, and 8. Balustrade in the Library of Merton College, Oxford.

Plate 264.

Fig. 1—3. Carved wood strings from houses in Ipswich (Gotch).
,, 4. Arch at end of terrace Bramshill House (Gotch).
,, 5. Pillar and vaulting in Hall, Bolsover Castle, Derbyshire (Gotch).
,, 6. Wood panelling over a fire-place in Hull, 1550 (The Builder).
,, 7. Door to Library of St. John's College, Cambridge (Gotch).
,, 8. Boss to vaulting in Porch at Bolsover Castle, Derbyshire (Gotch).

Plate 265.

(Gotch, Architecture of the Renaissance in England.)

Fig. 1. Roof of the hall, Wollaton Hall, Nottinghamshire.
,, 2. Base to wood pilaster South Wraxhall Manor-House, Wiltshire.
,, 3. Balustrade from St. Catherine's Court House, Somersetshire.
,, 4. Panel from font cover in the church of St. Mary-the-less, Cambridge.
,, 5. Pew front Lanteglos church.
,, 6. Panelling from Burton Agnes Hall, Yorkshire.

Plate 266.

Fig. 1. Portion of Canopied Chair, Convocation House, Oxford (J. Gillespie in Architectural Assoc. Sketch Book).
,, 2. Carved Detail from Chimney-piece in old House formely in Lime Street, London (Spiers and Birch).
,, 3. Carved baluster pier, Claverton, Somersetshire.
,, 4. Staircase at Dorfold, Cheshire (Richardson).
,, 5. Portion of Ceiling, Sexton's House, St. James's, Bristol (Richardson).

Plate 265.   ENGLISH RENAISSANCE ORNAMENT.   435

Plate 267. ENGLISH RENAISSANCE ORNAMENT. 437

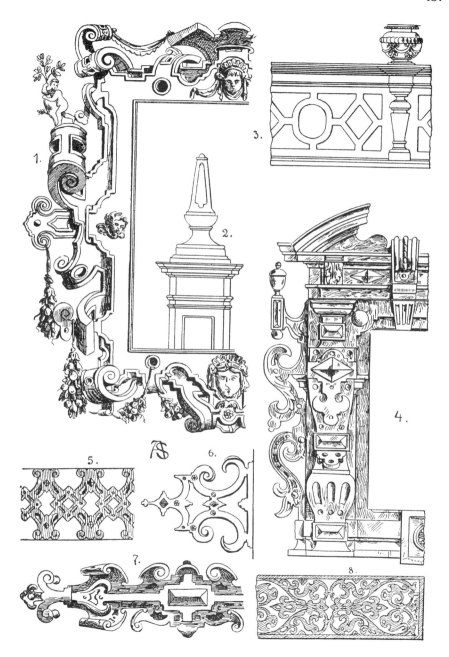

Plate 267.

Fig. 1. **Detail of Tomb, Westminster Abbey.**
„ 2. **Terminal to Gatepier, Claverton,** Somersetshire (Richardson).
„ 3. **Balustrade, with Vase, Duke's House, Bradford-on-Avon** (Richardson).
„ 4. **Carved Frame, Crewe Hall** (Richardson).
„ 5. **Balustrade Audley End,** Essex (Richardson).
„ 6. **Portion of Ceiling at Dorford,** Cheshire (Richardson).
„ 7. **Detail from Crewe Hall** (Richardson).
„ 8. **Detail from St. Lawrence church,** Kent.

Plate 268.

Fig. 1. **Toft plate.** From the Bateman Collection (Jännicke).
„ 2. **Fulham pottery (Stoneware).** From the Reynolds Collection (Jännicke).
„ 3. **Drinking-beaker.** From the Mayer Collection (Jännicke).
„ 4. **Stoneware jug.** In the Geological Museum, London.
„ 5. **Bed of Oliver Cromwell,** carved in oak (Bajot, Encyclopédie du meuble).
„ 6. **Red stoneware by Elers.** South Kensington Museum (Jännicke).

Plate 269.

Fig. 1. **Oak Cabinet at Wingfield Manor** (Sanders, Carved Oak Woodwork).
„ 2. **Chair 17th century** (A. E. Chancellor, Examples of Old Furniture).
„ 3. **Head of Oak cradle, 17th century** (Chancellor).
„ 4. **Armchair from Hampton Court,** 17th century (Chancellor).
„ 5. **Looking-glass in Elizabethan style** (Chancellor).
„ 6. **Oak chest,** 17th century (Sanders).
„ 7. **Table and scholar's seat from the Charterhouse,** 17th century (Chancellor).

Plate 270.

Fig. 1. **From a damask chair-cover at Knole Park, Kent.** From the time of James I. (Owen Jones).
„ 2—4, and 13. **Wood diapers,** from the time of James I. (Owen Jones).
„ 5, and 11. **Applique needlework,** from the time of James I. (Owen Jones).
„ 6. **Portrait of Jane Seymour, wife of Henry VIII., by Holbein.** In the Vienna Gallery (Hirth).

Plate 270. ENGLISH RENAISSANCE ORNAMENT. 441

Fig. 7, and 8. **Needlework tapestry from a tomb in Westminster.** From the time of Queen Elizabeth (Owen Jones).

„ 9, and 12. **Diapers from Burton Agnes, Yorkshire** (Owen Jones).

„ 10. **Plaster diaper from an old house near Tottenham.** From the time of Queen Elizabeth (Owen Jones).

Renaissance Chair (Bajot).

LATER RENAISSANCE ORNAMENT.

The term Later Renaissance is the title given to the second phase of the Renaissance and is applied to those buildings which were erected subsequent to the attempt made by Serlio, Vignola, and Palladio, to formulate principles which should govern the employment of the Classic Orders. In the earlier work of Brunelleschi, Michelozzo and Alberti, the architectural design was ruled more or less by an adherence to those principles which would seem to have guided the Roman architects, ornament was only sparingly introduced, and then only in such features as in the capitals of columns and friezes which required more decorative treatment. The tendency, however, in other work and more especially in those which were entrusted to sculptors, who paid but little attention either to the structural design of the building, to its setting out or to the principles of the classic models which they tried to reproduce, was to overload their structures with ornament. This would seem in the second half of the 16th century, to have led a reaction in art by the theorists, who attempted to formulate the tradition of classic art on fixed principles and to establish rules for the employment of purer architectural forms. This movement was probably influenced by the example set by Vitruvius, who in his manuscript, "de re aedificiatione", written about 25 B. C. laid down rules for the employment of the Orders of architecture. At all events it led to the publication of similar works, of which the first would appear to have been by Serlio (1475—1582), who in 1542 published a work on the Orders, followed by Vignola in 1563 and by Palladio in 1570. Vitruvius's manuscript, discovered about the middle of the 15th century, was accompanied by illustrations which have never been found; to supplement this loss these Italian authors introduced Orders of their own, based on the monuments of the first three centuries of our era, instead of those of Greece, which Vitruvius had described, as in his time the monuments of Imperial Rome had scarcely been commenced. Vitruvius had described three Orders only, the Doric, Ionic and Corinthian, to which he had added a primitive form of the Doric Order, which he called Tuscan. The Italians included that as a definite Order, and added a fifth, called the Composite Order. These publications henceforth constituted a copy book which became a standard universally adopted throughout France, Spain, England, and Germany and led to what used to be called the Italian revival, but which is now generally known in England as the Later Renaissance, and in Germany as the Barocco or Barock; as this latter term is unknown in England, that of the Later Renaissance has been adhered to in this work. Although in France the earliest influence in the Louvre and at Fontainebleau was that which must be attributed to Serlio, in later times Vignola became the chief authority, notwithstanding the fact that one of the greatest architects of the French Renaissance, Philibert de l'Orme had published a similar standard work in 1567. In England Palladio was generally recognised as the chief authority, owing probably to the influence of Lord Burlington, until Sir William Chambers in 1759 brought out his work on "Civil Architecture", which has since been regarded as the chief standard. As on the whole the five orders of Vignola are looked upon as better authorities not only in France but in America, they have been here reproduced.

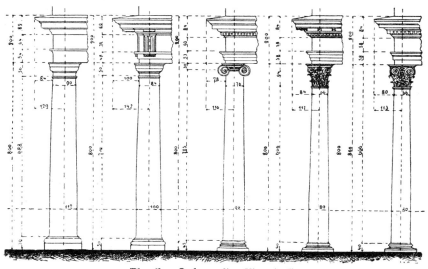

The five Orders after Vignola. *)

*) This numbers given in the drawing are millimetres on the supposition that the total height is a normal height of one metre, divided into 1000 millimetres. To find the dimensions in centimetres which correspond to this number simply multiply such with the height. For details see, "Speltz, Säulenformen der ägyptischen, griechischen und römischen Baukunst".

Later Renaissance Ornament in Italy.

As with the Earlier Renaissance, the names of the architects were always associated with the buildings they designed, so that the individuality to which reference has already been made existed in all their works. The chief followers of this school were Dominico Fontana (1543—1607) the architect of the lateral facade of St. John Lateran, Scamozzi (1552—1616) who continued Sansovino's work along the South side of the Piazza de San Marco and published a work on the Orders in 1615, Carlo Maderno (1556—1629), Bernini (1598—1680) the architect of the peristyles in front of St. Peter's, Rome, Borromini (1599—1661 and Pietro da Cortona (1596—1699).

Coat of Arms in the church
Sainte Agnèse by Borromini Rome,
16th century.

Plate 271.

Fig. 1. **Door in the entrance-hall of the Palazzo Cornaro della Cà grande in Venice** (Gurlitt, Geschichte des Barockstils in Italien).

„ 2. **Corner pilaster-capital from the Palazzo Nonfinito in Florence,** commenced by Briontolenti and continued by Scamozzi (Gurlitt).

„ 3. **Canopy over an altar in Rome,** 18th century (Raguenet).

„ 4. **Balcony support from the portal of the Palazzo Fenzi in Florence,** by Raffaele Curradi, of the year 1580 (Hirth).

„ 5. **Garden gate at Frascati** near Rome (Raguenet).

„ 6. **Window finial of a palace in Genoa** in the Via Loncellini, 17th century (Raguenet).

„ 7. **Gate pier from the Villa Lodovisi** near Rome, 18th century (Raguenet).

Plate 272.

(After Raguenet, Matériaux.)

Fig. 1. **Balcony and door-head from St. Domenico Square in Nice,** 18th century.
„ 2. **Shield from the Palazzo Riccardi in Florence.**
„ 3. **Balustrade in the interior of the St. Martino Cloister in Naples,** built by Fansaga.
„ 4. **Stair balustrade from St. Domenico and Sixto in Rome,** built by Bernini.
„ 5. **Door-knocker in Florence** (L'art pour tous).
„ 6. **Fountain in front of Brescia cathedral,** 17th century.

Plate 273.

Fig. 1. **Coat of arms from a palace in the Via Ponta Rossa in Florence.** Marigno sculpture from the end of the 17th century (Hirth).
„ 2, and 4. **Lace work in the Musée des Arts décoratif, Paris** (L'art pour tous).
„ 3. **Faience Vase by Savona,** from the Gasnault Collection, Paris (L'art pour tous).
„ 5, and 6. **Furniture from the Mansi Palace at Segromigno** near Lucca (L'art pour tous).

Plate 274.

Fig. 1. **Arm chair from the Cloister of St. Martino in Naples,** in the Museum at Naples, 18th century (Raguenet).
„ 2. **Hanging lamp from Bologna,** 17th century. Made of painted iron-plate, in the form of a 30 sided polygon. At present in the Arts and Crafts Museum in Berlin. (J. Lessing, Vorbilderhefte aus dem kgl. Kunstgewerbemuseum.)
„ 3. **Hanging lamp,** beginning of the 18th century. Made of gilt iron. At present in the Arts and Crafts Museum in Berlin (Lessing).
„ 4. **Cresting of a cupboard in the Parma Museum,** 17th century (Raguenet).
„ 5. **State carriage,** 18th century. In possession of Senator Davia in Bologna (Hirth).
„ 6. **From a bronze mantel-piece figure,** 16th century. From Giovanni da Bologna School. At present in the National Museum in Florence (Hirth).

Plate 275. ITALIAN LATER RENAISSANCE ORNAMENT. 451

Plate 275.

(After L'art pour tous.)

Fig. 1, 2, and 4.　Venetian lace collars, 17th century.
  ,,   3.　Gold embroidery table cover, 17th century.
  „   5.　Embossed Genoese velvet, 17th century.
  „   6.　Genoese work, silk on gold ground, 17th century.

Wheel of a State Carriage
by Filippe Passarini, born in Rome, 1638 (Hirth).

Later Renaissance Ornament in France.

(Louis XIV. Style.)

Initial Louis XIV. (Petzendorfer, Schriftenatlas.)

nder the influence of Debrosse (c. 1580—1641) and his pupil Lemercier (1585—1634), the former the architect of the Luxembourg palace (1611—16) and the latter of the Sorbonne, a new development began at the commencement of the 17th century, to which the title of the Later Renaissance has been given. The germs of the movement may really be traced in the Louvre (where Pierre Lescot would seem to have been influenced by Serlio), but it took a more decided form in the Luxembourg palace, and in the palace of Versailles and the Chateau of Maisons-sur-Seine by François Mansard (1599—1660). Then followed Perrault the architect of the East facade of the Louvre which marks a return to classic principles, Lemaire (1670 to 1745) the architect of the Hotel Soubise, Marot (1630—1679) who designed the Hotel de Noailles, and Jules Hardouin Mansard (1645—1708), the nephew of François Mansard, who may be said to have been the creator of the Louis XIV. style, a style better fitted for rich internal decoration than for the exterior of a mansion.

Plate 276.

(After César Daly, Motifs Historiques d'architecture et de sculpture d'ornement.)

Fig. 1, and 2. **Balcony and doorhead from the house No. 27 Rue St. André des Arts, Paris.**

„ 3, and 5. **Small consoles from Versailles.**

„ 4. **Mask from the Place Vendôme in Paris.**

„ 6. **Balustrade from Versailles.**

„ 7. **Console bracket in Paris.**

Plate 277.

(After César Daly, Motifs Historiques d'architecture et de sculpture d'ornement.)

Fig. 1. **Side door of the church of St. Nicolas-du-Chardonnet, Paris.**

„ 2. **Door of the Hotel Beauvais, Rue St. Antoine No. 62, Paris.**

Plate 277.   FRENCH LATER RENAISSANCE ORNAMENT.   455

Fig. 3. **Balustrade parapet and dormer window Rue St. Guillaume No. 22, Paris.**
„ 4. **Attic window from the Marble Court of the palace of Versailles.**

Plate 278.

Fig. 1, 2, and 3. **Console brackets from a hotel in the Rue St. Louis en l'île, No. 51, Paris** (Daly).
„ 4. **War trophy in the Park at Versailles** by François Girardon, born 1627 or 1630 in Troyes, died 1715 in Paris (Hirth).
„ 5. **Ornament in wrought-iron,** by Hugues Brisville, Paris (Hirth).
„ 6. **Door of a Confessional** from the church of St. Nicolas-du-Chardonnet, Paris (Raguenet).
„ 7, and 8. **Vases from the park at Versailles.** Cast in Bronze by Claude Ballin (1615—1678) (Raguenet).

Plate 279.

Fig. 1. **Handle of an vase,** by Coyzevox, born in Spain, but worked in Paris from 1640 to 1720 (Hirth).
„ 2. **Acanthus of the later Renaissance** (Raguenet).
„ 3. **Mural decoration,** after Johann Berain, born at St. Mihiel, Lorraine, in 1639, died in Paris, 1711. Taken from his work on ornamant (Hirth).
„ 4. **Ceiling decoration,** from an engraving by Daniel Marot, 1650—1712, Architect and Designer in Paris (Hirth).

Plate 280.

Fig. 1. **Door-knocker from Bordeaux,** Cours de l'Intendance No. 19, 18th century (Raguenet).
„ 2, 3, and 5. **Ornaments for rifle mountings,** from an engraving by Jean Berain (Hirth).
„ 4, 6, and 7. **Locksmith's handiwork by Hugh Brisville,** from an engraving by Jean Berain. Brisville was a locksmith in Paris about the year 1663 (Hirth).

Plate 281.

(After Hirth, Formenschatz.)

Fig. 1. **Mural decoration by Jean Berain.**
„ 2. **Design for ceiling,** from an engraving by Nicolas Loir, Painter and Engraver in Paris, 1624—1679.
„ 3. **Design for mural decoration** by Gilles Marie Oppenort. Period of the Regency.
„ 4. **Design for mural decoration** by Daniel Marot.

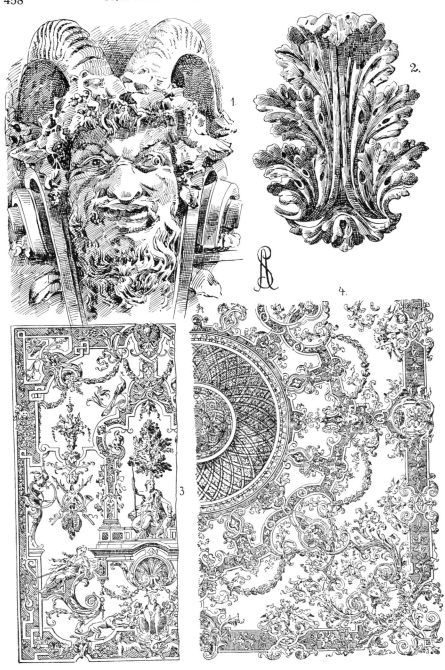

Plate 280.   FRENCH LATER RENAISSANCE ORNAMENT.

459

Plate 282. FRENCH LATER RENAISSANCE ORNAMENT. 461

Plate 282.

Fig. 1. **Door-knocker** (L'art pour tous).
„ 2. **Reading-desk of wrought-iron,** from the Le Secq Collection of the Tournelle (Champeaux).
„ 3. **Candelabrum of gilt wood,** 17th century. From the Collection of the Duke de la Tremouille (Champeaux).
„ 4. **Console** for a mantel-piece in chased, gilt bronze, from the period of the Regency. From the Collection of the Museum of Decorative Art, Paris (Champeaux).
„ 5. **Sedan chair** (Havard).

Plate 283.

Fig. 1. **Chest of drawers after Jean Berain** (Hirth).
„ 2. **Bracket-candlestick from the palace of Versailles,** probably after Berain (L'art pour tours).
„ 3. **Cupboard** of ebony with copper open-work. Meuble de Boule from the 18th century (Bajot, Encyclopédie du Meuble).
„ 4. **Chair of carved wood** in the Mobilier national, Paris (Champeaux, Portefeuille des Arts décoratifs).

Plate 284.

Fig. 1. **Window mantle by Daniel Marot,** Architect, Paris, 1650—1712 (Hirth).
„ 2. **Canopy bed by the same artist** (Hirth).
„ 3. **Design of a Candelabrum by Gilles Maria Oppenort** (Hirth).
„ 4. **Console table, Jean Berain** (Hirth).
„ 5, and 6. **Spinet with double keyboard,** 18th century (Bajot).
„ 7. **Emblem by Gilles Maria Oppenort** from the period of the Regency (Hirth).

Plate 285.

Fig. 1. **Beaten and chased silver ewer,** by Daniel Marot, from the year 1700 (Hirth).
„ 2. **Faience jar of the apothecary of the Duke of Orleans,** beginning of 18th century. In the Gasnault Collection (Jännicke).
„ 3. **Faience dish from Moustiers.** In the Gasnault Collection (Jännicke).
„ 4. **Faience jug from Rouen** (Jännicke).
„ 5. **Dish of beaten and chased silver,** from a drawing in the Robert Colle Album in the Cabinet des Estampes, Paris (Havard).

Plate 286.

Fig. 1. **Embossed velvet** (Havard).
„ 2, and 3. **Stuff patterns** by Daniel Marot (Hirth).
„ 4. **Curtain** by Daniel Marot (Hirth).

1.   2.   3.

4.   5.

6.

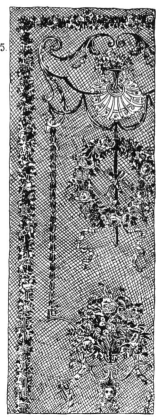

Fig. 5. **Curtain with ornament appliqué** (Champeaux).

„ 6. **Carpet pattern,** designed by Robert de Cotte for the Manufacture de la Savonnerie at the beginning of the 18th century. The drawing is now in the Cabinet des Estampes, of the National Library, Paris (Champeaux).

Vase in the Park at Versailles (Daly).

Later Renaissance Ornament in Germany, Austria, and Switzerland.

Vase before the Bridge in Kuppenberg (Ohmann).

ne of the greatest enemies to the development of Art is War. As soon as the horrors of the Thirty Years War were to a certain extent overcome, Art began again to bestir itself in Germany. The Palladian Classic Style which ruled in Holland established itself in North and South Germany, on the Rhine, and in Austria. Dutch Classic was introduced into Germany by Johann Arnold Nering, who died in 1605, in his famous building the Berlin Armoury, whose architectural reputation is only excelled by the work of his successor Andreas Schlüter. Schlüter, born in Hamburg 1664, died in St. Petersburg 1714, is the real founder of the Rococo style in Berlin. In Dresden, the foundation of the same was laid by George Baehr, 1666—1738, in the church known as the Frauenkirche which was commenced in the year 1726, and by Matthaus Daniel Pöppelmann, 1662—1735, in his building of the Zwinger Palace. The Court church in the same city was built by Gaetano Chiaveri of Rome, 1689—1770.

The Later Renaissance dominated Catholic South Germany, where it was introduced by Gaspare Luccali, 1629—1680, in his building of the church called the Theatinerkirche in Munich. In Austria it was specially influenced by the architects Dientzenhofer, and their pupil Johann Bernhard Fischer from Erlach, 1650—1723. But in consequence of the powerful position held by France at the period, the influence of the French Louis XIV style became felt in Austria also.

Plate 287.

Fig. 1. **Carved wood door from the Armoury in Berlin,** about the year 1700 (Cornelius Gurlitt, Das Barock- und Rokoko-Ornament).

„ 2, and 5. **Bracket and cresting from Archiepiscopal Palace in Salzburg** (Ohmann, Barock).

„ 3. **Pilaster and entablature in the Imperial Belvedère in Vienna** (Ohmann).

, 4. **Mask of a warrior from the Berlin Armoury.** By Andreas Schlüter, 1662—1714 (Hirth).

Plate 287. GERMAN LATER RENAISSANCE ORNAMENT. 469

Plate 289.   GERMAN LATER RENAISSANCE ORNAMENT.   471

Plate 288.

(After Ohmann, Barock.)

Fig. 1. **Window of a dwelling-house in Stein on the Danube.**
„ 2. **Balcony in the Court Library in Vienna.**
„ 3. **Window-head from Wendish Seminary in Prague.**
„ 4. **Window and door of a dwelling-house in Prague.**
„ 5. **Wrought-iron candelabrum from Elsgrab, Austria.**
„ 6. **Window from a house in Krems on the Danube.**

Plate 289.

Fig. 1. **Wrought iron grille in the Serviten church in Vienna** (Dr. A. Ilg and Dr. Heinrich Kábdebo, Wiener Schmiedewerke des 17. und 18. Jahrhunderts).
„ 2. **Lock of the principal door in the church of St. Charles Borromeo in Prague** (Ohmann).
„ 3. **Fan-light from the church of St. Clementine in Prague** (Ohmann).
„ 4. **Wrought iron gate of the Guild-hall at Meise in Zürich,** from the 18th century (Oberhäusli, Aufnahmen alter schweizerischer Kunstschmiedearbeiten).
„ 5. **Hinge of door in the church of St. Charles Borromeo in Prague** (Ohmann).
„ 6. **Door handle of the same** (Ohmann).

Plate 290.

Fig. 1. **Grandfather's clock from the Klosterneuburg Monastery on the Danube** (Ohmann).
„ 2. **Chandelier of wrought iron,** 18th century. In the Arts and Crafts Museum in Berlin (Lessing).
„ 3. **Reliquary from the church in Heiligenkreuz,** Lower Austria (Ohmann).

Plate 291.

(After Fr. Ohmann, Barock.)

Fig. 1, and 2. **Gilt console tables from the Imperial Palace in Vienna.**
„ 3. **Armchair from the Emperoᴵ's room in the Klosterneuburg Monastery on the Danube.**
„ 4. **Stool in private collection.**
„ 5. **Brass lock mount in the Imperial Court Library in Vienna.**
„ 6. **Upper part of fire screen from the Emperor's Room in the Klosterneuburg Monastery on the Danube.**

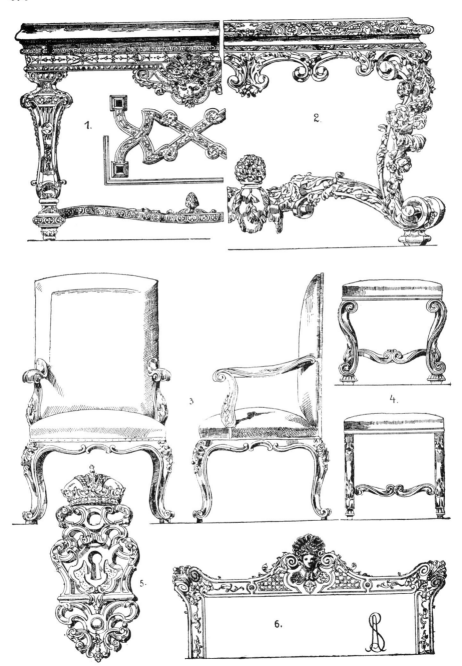

Plate 292. GERMAN LATER RENAISSANCE ORNAMENT.

475

Plate 292.

Fig. 1—4, and 6. **Goldsmith's work** designed by Friedrich Jacob Morisson, Draughtsman and Goldsmith in Vienna and Augsburg, 1693—1697 (Hirth).

,, 5. **Silver gilt jug,** the work of the Augsburg goldsmith Johann Heinrich Mannlich, who died in 1718. In the Imperial Palace at Laxenburg (Dr. Albert Ilg, Sammlung kunstindustrieller Gegenstände des Allerhöchsten Kaiserhauses).

,, 7. **Sword hilt.** From the work "Neu inventiöse Degengefäß" by Georg Heumann, Cutler in Nüremberg, who died in 1691 (J. E. Wessely, Das Ornament und die Kunstindustrie).

,, 8, and 10. **Goldsmith's work** from "Neues Groteskenwerk", engraved by L. Beyer (Wessely).

,, 9. **Plant ornament** by J. Honervogt, Draughtsman and Copper Engraver who lived towards the end of the 17th century (Wessely).

,, 11. **Door handle** by J. C. Reiff, Copper Engraver in Nüremberg in the 18th century (Wessely).

,, 12. **Goldsmith's work,** acanthus leaf work in the form of a goat by Wolfgang Hieronymus v. Bemmel, Goldsmith, end of 17th century (Wessely).

Plate 293.

Fig. 1. **Monstrance,** end of 17th century. In the Cathedral Treasury in Limburg on the Lahn (Hirth).

,, 2. **Carved relief on door in the Rochus church,** Vienna (Ohmann).

,, 3. **Church candlestick.** In the Deanery church in Klattau (Ohmann).

,, 4. **Nautilus goblet,** end of 17th century. In the Grunen Gewölbe in Dresden (Hirth).

,, 5. **Carved mirror frame** in the Glankirchen in Upper Austria.

Plate 294.

Fig. 1. **Embroidered vestment** in the Collection of Vaterlandischer Altertumer, Stuttgart (Dolmetsch).

,, 2. **Pattern of material dating from the end of the 17th century.** In the Pfalz Arts and Crafts Museum in Kaiserslautern (Hirth).

,, 3, and 5. **Wrought-iron candlesticks,** 1660—1680. In the Nüremberg Museum (Hirth).

,, 4. **Watch.** In the Munich Museum. Nüremberg work, beginning of the 18th century (Hirth).

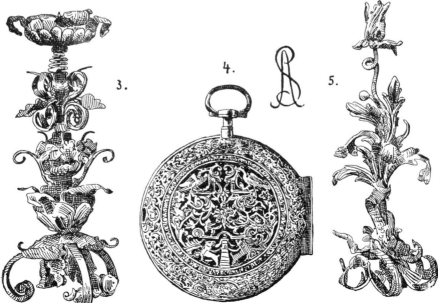

Plate 295. GERMAN LATER RENAISSANCE ORNAMENT.

479

Plate 295.

Fig. 1. **Initial letter after Lucas Kilian** (1627) (Petzendorfer).

„　2. **Initial letter** (Petzendorfer).

„　3. **From an etched Solnhofer stone plate,** in the "Getreidekasten zum leeren Beutel"'
Regensburg, 1718 (Weimar).

„　4. **Engraving on bronze by Franz Christoph von Rosenbach,** † 1687. In Würzburg
cathedral (Weimar).

„　5. **Etched on stone tomb of Thomas von Pirnitz,** † 1691. In the Jesuist church
at Straubing (Weimar).

Lantern in wrought iron
(L'art pour tous)

Later Renaissance Ornament in the Netherlands.

Initial from the Printing Works of J. Covens and C. Mortier, Amsterdam (Ysendyck).

arly in the 17th century began the great Art Epoch called into existence by Peter Paul Rubens. This development favoured the introduction of the Later Renaissance Style into the Netherlands. Cardinal Granvella, who introduced Italian artists into Belgium, was most active, and succeeded in erecting a most important series of architectural constructions. The Jesuits erected also a number of most magnificent buildings in the Rococo Style; in Holland, however, where rigid theology ruled, there was a tendency to more classical work, for which reason the former style never took root in the country. The chief exponent of the purer Italian style in Holland was Philip Vuyboons (1608—1675).

Plate 296.

(After Ysendyck, Art dans les Pays-Bas.)

Fig. 1. **Cartouche, c. 1639, engraved by Peter de Jode for the portrait of the Holland painter G. Flinck.**

„ 2. **Wall-paper from a sample book of the factory in Malines.** In the Royal Antiquarian Museum, Brussels.

„ 3—5. **Carriage of the Duke of Ossuna used when entering Utrecht 1713 as Extraordinary Ambassador from Philip V. of Spain.** From an engraving by Picart, Amsterdam 1714.

Plate 297.

(After Ysendyck, Art dans les Pays-Bas.)

Fig. 1. **Lace from the 18th century.** Is called "Point de Buiche", and is made with the spindle alone in one piece without any relief.

„ 2. **Arm-chair from the book by Crispin van den Passe,** printed in Amsterdam in the year 1642 under the title of "Boutique Menuiserie" by M. W. Silvius, Antwerp.

„ 3. **Chimney-piece.** From the work "Cheminées hollandaises" by G. de Gaendel, drawer, born in Middelburg. From the year 1730, published by Martin Gottfried Crosphius.

„ 4. **Wrought iron door knocker.**

Plate 297.   DUTCH LATER RENAISSANCE ORNAMENT.   483

Plate 298.

(After L'art pour tous.)

Fig. 1—3. **Sign of the old Inn "A l'Etrille" in the Market Place at Brüges.** From the 17th century.

" 4—8. **Wall tiles of Delft from the Inn "Le Diable au corps" in Brussels.** From the 17th century.

Delft Faience goblet in the Collection Gasnault (Jaenicke).

Later Renaissance Ornament in England.

Initial Letter
17th century (Belcher).

As already stated in the introduction to English Renaissance Ornament (page 429) the Later Renaissance, which used to be known as the pure Italian style, was introduced into England by Inigo Jones (1573—1652). The first building of importance erected in that style being the Banqueting House in Whitehall (1620). The style was further developed by Sir Christopher Wren (1632—1723), Sir John Vanburgh (1666—1726), Nicholas Hawksmoor (1666—1736), James Gibbs (1674—1754), William Kent (1684—1742), G. Leoni (1686—1746), John James of Greenwich (? 1687—1746), Thomas Archer (? 1690—1743); Colin Campbell (? 1690—1734); George Dance (1695—1768), Henry Flitcroft (1697—1769), John Wood of Bath (1704—1754), Sir Robert Taylor (1714—1788), John Carr of York (1723—1807), James Paine (1725—1789), Sir William Chambers (1726—1796), Robert Adam (1728—1792), Henry Holland (1746—1806), James Wyatt (1746—1813) and John Nash (1752—1835).

Plate 299.

(From John Belcher and Mervyn E. Macartney, Later Renaissance Architecture in England.)

Fig. 1. Capital and cornice of the Bastards' House, Blandford.
,, 2 Details of stalls, Trinity College chapel, Cambridge.
,, 3. Capital and cornice of the "Red Lion", Blandford.
,, 4. Details of window, Town Hall, Blandford.
,, 5. Gate pier, from a house in West Street, Chichester.
,, 6. Lead rainwater head from the Great Hall of Winchester College.

Plate 300.

Fig. 1. Detail of overdoor in Carved oak and cedar, Clifford's Inn, London (Henry Thomson in "Building News").
,, 2. Detail of Entablature of Reredos, St. Stephen's, Walbrook, London (E. H. Sedding).
,, 3. Detail of Pulpit Shaft, St. Stephen's, Walbrook (E. H. Sedding).
,, 4. Detail of Altar Rail, St. Stephen's, Walbrook (E. H. Sedding).
,, 5, and 6. Carved Panel, S. Margaret's church Lothbury, London (H. Inigo Triggs in Archl. Assoc. Sketch Book).
,, 7. Detail of chimney-piece, Clifford's Inn (John Barbour in "the Builder").
,, 8. Detail of Frieze, North Porch, St. Pauls Cathedral, London (R. W. Schultz in Archl. Assoc. Sketch Book).
,, 9. Carved panel in Chancel screen St. James's church, Piccadilly, London, 1683 (C. L. Gill in the Archl. Assoc. Sketch Book).

Plate 301.   ENGLISH LATER RENAISSANCE ORNAMENT.

489

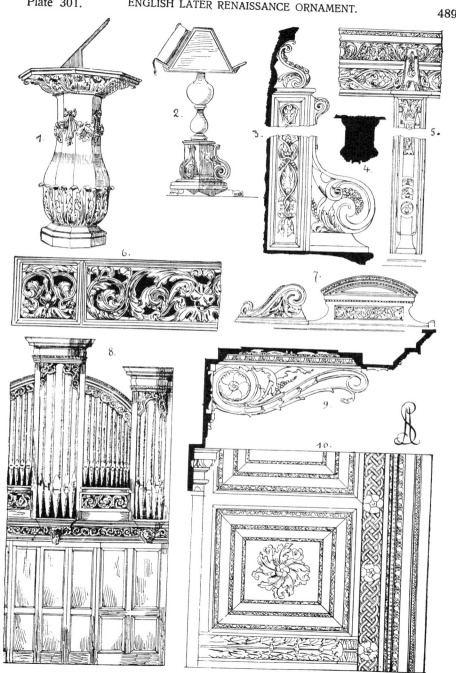

Plate 301.

Fig. 1. **Sundial from Wrest**, Bedfordshire (Belcher and Macartney).
„   2. **Hexagonal revolving lectern in Pembroke College chapel, Cambridge** (Belcher and Macartney).
„   3—5, and 7. **Details of stall Ends in St. Paul's Cathedral, London** (George H. Birch, London churches of the 17th and 18th centuries).
„   6. **Carved open-worked wooden panel from St. Mary Abchurch, London** (George H. Birch).
„   8. **Organ in St. Mary, Woolnoth, London** (George H. Birch).
„   9, and 10. **Details of soffit of the Gallery of the Senate House, Cambridge** (Belcher and Macartney).

Plate 302.

(From James Gibbs, A Book of Architecture 1728.)

Fig. 1, and 3. **Pedestals for busts.**
„   2. **Cartouche in the pediment of St. Martin's church, London.**
„   4, 6 and 7. **Designs for Vases.**
„   5. **Cartouche for monumental inscription.**
„   8. **Pedestal of sundial.**
„   9. **Cartouche for wall tomb.**

Plate 303.

(From John Belcher and Mervyn E. Macartney, Later Renaissance Architecture in England.)

Fig. 1. **Wrought iron gate, Fenton House, Hampstead.**
„   2. **Details of staircase from a house in the Close, Salisbury.**
„   3. **Clock of the Town Hall, Guildford.**
„   4. **Balusters of staircase from a house in Great Queen Street, London.**
„   5. **Chimney-piece in a house at Epsom, Surrey.**
„   6. **Section of panelling in the Chapel of Farnham Castle, Surrey.**
„   7. **Shield of arms over doorway in the same chapel.**

Plate 304.

Fig. 1. **Carved oak Desk, Pembroke college, Cambridge,** 1665 (R. S. Dods in Archl. Assoc. Sketch Book).
„   2. **Detail from chimney-piece, Northgate Club, Ipswich** (Henry Tanner, jun.).
„   3. **Upper portion of panelling Brewers Hall, London,** c. 1670 (A. Stratton in Archl. Assoc. Sketch Book).
„   4. **Terminal vase, North porch, St. Paul's cathedral, London** (R. W. Schultz in Arch. Assoc. Sketch Book).

Plate 304.   ENGLISH LATER RENAISSANCE ORNAMENT.   493

Plate 306.　ENGLISH LATER RENAISSANCE ORNAMENT.　495

Fig. 5. **Detail of wrought iron gate, Hampton Court Palace** (Hugh P. G. Maule in Archl. Assoc. Sketch Book).

„ 6. **Side of Canopy of Pulpit, St. Stephen's, Walbrook, London** (E. H. Sedding).

„ 7. **Side of bracket under doorway, Hampton Court Palace** (P. J. Turner in Archl. Assoc. Sketch Book).

Plate 305.

Fig. 1. **Wall cupboard** in the Hall of the Haberdasher's Company, Gresham Street, London, 1668 (Chancellor).

„ 2. **Mahogany table,** beginning of 18th century (Chancellor).

„ 3. **China cabinet,** middle of 18th century (Chancellor).

„ 4. **Cushioned chair** (Bajot).

„ 5. **Vase of English porcelain, Chelsea.** In the British Museum (Jännicke).

„ 6. **Georgian settee of the time of Chippendale** (Chancellor).

„ 7. **Toilet chest** of the time of Queen Anne (Chancellor).

Plate 306.

(From Bailey Scott Murphy, English and Scottish Wrought Ironwork.)

Fig. 1, and 3. **Wrought iron stair rail of the King's Great Staircase, Hampton-Court Palace.** End of the 17th century.

„ 2. **Wrought iron Staircase in Caroline Park House, Granton NB.** Erected by Viscount Tarbat in 1685.

„ 4, and 8. **Wrought iron Balusters in South Kensington Museum.**

„ 5, 6, 9, and 10. **Details of the Staircase in Caroline Park House, Granton.**

„ 7. **Wrought iron Staircase in Caroline Park House.**

Plate 307.

(From Bailey Scott Murphy, English and Scottish Wrought Ironwork.)

Fig. 1. **Sign of the "Bell" Inn at Melksham,** Wilts.

„ 2. **Wrought iron bracket in South Kensington Museum.**

„ 3. **Leg of a console table in South Kensington Museum.**

„ 4. **Lamp bracket in Micklegate Hill House,** York.

„ 5. **Entrance gateway to a house in Abbey Street, Carlisle.**

„ 6. **Sign of the "White Hart" Inn at Gretton,** Northants.

„ 7. **Lamp holder at the "White Hart" Hotel Salisbury.**

Plate 309.   ENGLISH LATER RENAISSANCE ORNAMENT.   499

Plate 308.

(From H. Inigo Triggs and Henry Tanner jun., Some Architectural Works of Inigo Jones.)

Fig. 1. **Details of upper order and cornice of the Banqueting House, Whitehall.** Built by Inigo Jones in 1619—1622.

,, 2, and 5. **Details of window of the same.**

,, 3. **Details of lower order and cornice of the same.**

,, 4. **Detail of lower window in the same.**

,, 6. **Carved frieze from chimney-piece in the Ambassador's Room, Knole Park, Kent.**

Plate 309.

Fig. 1. **Fire-place in the Salon at Forde Abbey, Dorset** (Inigo Triggs and H. Tanner).

,, 2. **Rain water shoot in Courtyard of Wilton House** (Inigo Triggs and H. Tanner).

,, 3, and 7. **Keystone in the church of St. Catherine Cree, Leadenhall Street, London** (George H. Birch, London Churches of the 17th and 18th centuries).

,, 4, 5, and 6. **Sections of mouldings from Wilton House** (Inigo Triggs and H. Tanner).

Plate 310.

Fig 1. **Door with balustrade at Coleshill House, Berkshire** (Inigo Triggs and H. Tanner).

,, 2, 3, and 5. **Cornices to fig. 4.**

,, 4. **The Spencer Monument in the church of St. Catherine Cree, Leadenhall Street, London** (George H. Birch).

,, 6. **Belvedere at Coleshill House** (Inigo Triggs and H. Tanner).

,, 7. **Door from Raynham Hall, Norfolk** (Inigo Triggs and H. Tanner).

Plate 311.

Fig. 1. **Detail of Internal Doorway** (Henry Tanner).

,, 2, and 3. **Ceiling at Kirby Hall Northants** (Inigo Triggs and Henry Tanner).

,, 4. **Ionic capital, St. Magnus church, London Bridge** (E. H. Sedding in Archl. Assoc. Sketch Book).

,, 5. **Carving in the Vestry, Chesterton church, Oxon.**

,, 6. **Font with cover, Christ's church Newgate Street, London** (Birch's London Churches).

ROCOCO ORNAMENT.

Border by Charles Eisen (Hirth).

Letter after Laurent (Hirth).

ococo is the term applied to the decadent forms of the Later Renaissance. The rivalry which existed in the 17th century between the free style of Michael Angelo and that based on the principles laid down by Palladio and Vignola was continued into the 18th century until about the year 1715 with the more or less complete adoption of the former. This resulted in a development which held sway until about 1760 and was known in France as the Louis XV. style, and in other countries as the Rococo. In this style the ornament is entirely seperated from constructional requirements and the lines run in free curves, symmetry being avoided. Consequently, as a rule, it is more generally employed for interiors and for decorative and industrial art.

The style flourished in France for about thirty-five years. It was rarely employed in either Italy or the Netherlands, but remained in Germany and England up to the end of the 18th century. In the latter country its chief exponent was Chippendale whose name is generally attached to the style. Shortly, however,

after its introduction a reaction took place in which classic work commenced again to predominate in the somewhat pedantic style of Louis XVI. This again became influenced by a new phase in which for the first time Greek art commenced to show itself, resulting in the development of what later-on became generally known as the Empire Style.

Rococo Forms.

Plate 312.

Fig. 1. **After Thomas Chippendale** (Gentleman and Cabinet makers Director).
„ 2. **After Meissonier** (Raguenet).
„ 3. **After Moudon** (Raguenet).
„ 4. **After Thomas Johnson.**
„ 5. **After Habermann.**
„ 6. **After F. de Cuvilliés** (Raguenet).
„ 7. **After Josef Klauber,** Augsburg (Raguenet).
„ 8. **From a clock in the Art Industrial Museum in Milan** (Raguenet).

Rococo Ornament in Italy.

Although the origin of the Rococo style is to be found in the works of Michael Angelo, Bernini, and Borromeo in Italy, it made very little progress so far as interiors are concerned, and in the place of Louis XV. and XVI. Ornament, the Italians adhered to their cold and formal classic style.

Plate 313.

Fig. 1. **Richly carved frame,** 18th century (Raguenet).
  „   2. **Console table in wood gilt** (L'art pour tous).
  „   3. **Bracket candlestick of bronze gilt,** 18th century. In the Arts and Crafts Museum in Milan (Raguenet).
  „   4. **Processional crucifix in the church of Pieve di Budrio,** 18th century (Hirth).

Ink-stand of gilt bronze (L'art pour tous).

Rococo Ornament in France
(Louis XV. Style).

Plate 314.

Fig. 1. Console bracket in the house No. 36, Rue Casette, Paris (Daly).
„ 2, and 3. From the Fontaine de l'Abbaye, Rue Childebert, Paris. View and vertical section (Daly).
„ 4. Terminal vase in Vic-sur-Cère, Lorraine (Raguenet).
„ 5. Gateway of the Porcelain Factory in Sèvres (Daly).

Plate 315.
(After Champeaux, Portefeuille des arts décoratifs.)

Fig. 1. Bracket clock, made of chased and gilt copper, belonging to A. M. Seligmann, Paris.
„ 2. Bracket candlestick from a drawing by René Michel Slootz in the Bibliothèque Nationale, Paris.
„ 3. Clock in case with chased bronze, by Duhamel. In the Collection of the Conservatoire National des arts et métiers, Paris.
„ 4. Chimney back of cast iron. From tinted drawing in Louis Fordrin's Style at beginning of the 18th century.
„ 5. Candelabrum of chased and gilt silver. In the Winter Palace, St. Petersburg, probably French work of the 18th century.

Plate 316.
(After Hirth, Formenschatz.)

Fig. 1. Scissors in case, by Meissonier.
„ 2. Chandelier in the Grand Ducal Palace in Karlsruhe. French work from the beginning of the year 1740. Drawing by A. Stuchi.
„ 3. Louis XV. vase (L'Art pour tous).
„ 4. Head of stick in metal chased, by Meissonier.
„ 5. Silver table centre-piece, by Meissonier.

Plate 317.

Fig. 1. Commode in rosewood marquetry (Bajot, Encyclopédie du Meuble).
„ 2. Chair with cane seat and back (Bajot).
„ 3. Key, by François de Cuvilliés père (Hirth).
„ 4. Design for an ambassador's carriage by Vaneroe, sculptor in Paris. From a drawing in the Bibliothèque Nationale, Paris (Champeaux).

Plate 316.   FRENCH ROCOCO ORNAMENT.   511

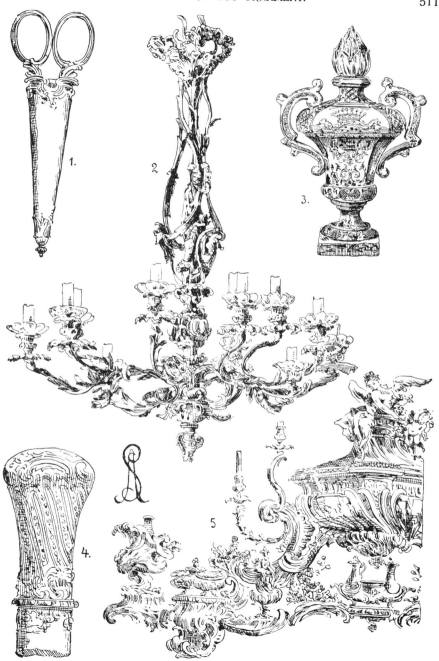

Plate 318.   FRENCH ROCOCO ORNAMENT.   513

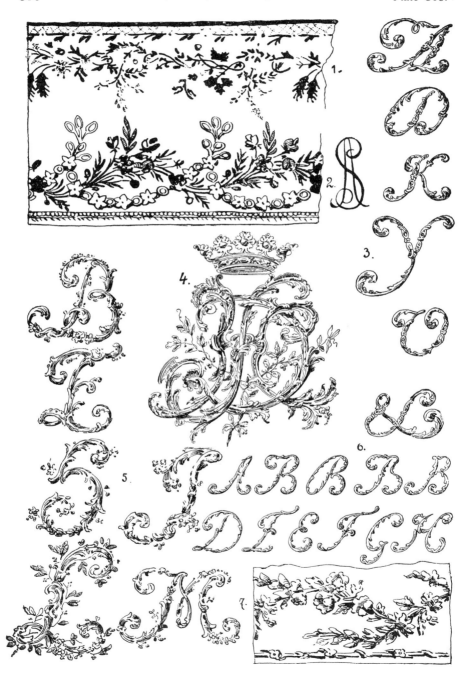

Plate 318.

Fig. 1. **Leaf from a book on ornament** by Juste Aurèle Meissonier, born in Turin in 1695, died at Paris 1750 (Hirth).

„ 2. **Mural decoration** (Hirth).

„ 3. **Design for a throne for Louis XV.** by René Michel Slootz. From a drawing in the Bibliothèque Nationale, Paris (Champeaux).

„ 4. **Top of gold frame** by Meissonier (Hirth).

„ 5. **Console table of carved and gilt wood,** from the Regency (Bajot).

Plate 319.

Fig. 1, 2, and 7. **Samples of embroidery from coloured drawings** by Charles Germain de St. Aubin, 1721—1786. In the Bibliothèque de l'Institut National (Champeaux).

„ 3, 5, and 6. **Letters by Laurent from a copybook by Schénau:** "L'alphabet de l'amour, ou recueil de chiffres à l'usage des amants et des artists". Paris 1766 (Hirth).

„ 4. **Monogram with ducal coronet,** ascribed to St. Aubin (Champeaux).

Plate 320.

(After Champeaux, Portefeuille des arts décoratifs.)

Fig. 1. **Back of sofa from a coloured drawing** by François Peyrotte. In the Bérard Collection.

„ 2. **Under mantle after a drawing** by St. Aubin.

„ 3. **Arm-chair of wood gilt the seat and back of Beauvais tapestry.**

„ 4. **Chair covering of embroidered silk,** from the end of the reign of Louis XV.

Plate 321.

(After Roger-Milès, Comment discerner les styles.)

Fig. 1, 4, 5, and 6. **Embroideries of court dress.**

„ 2, 3, 7, 8, and 9. **Ornaments.**

„ 10. **Sleigh carved in wood gilt.**

„ 11, and 12. **Spoon and fork** by Thomas Germain, Goldsmith in Paris.

Plate 322.

Fig. 1. **Design for interior decoration** by Meissonier.

1

2.

3.

4.

Plate 321.   FRENCH ROCOCO ORNAMENT.   517

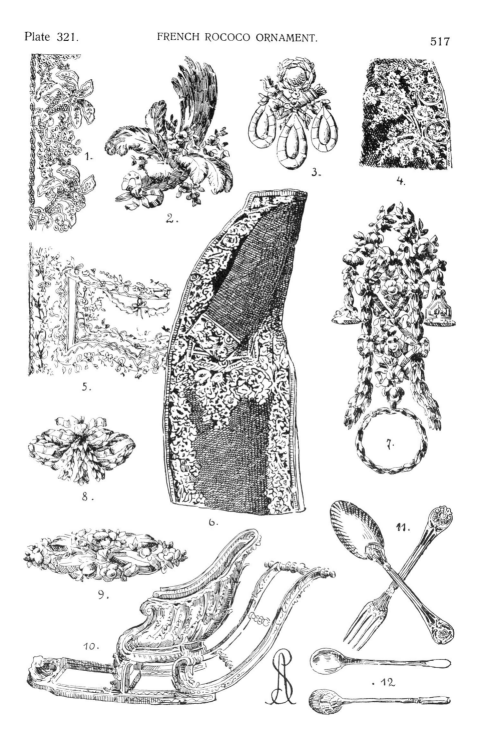

Rococo Ornament in Germany and Austria.

From the year 1725 onwards the Rococo held sway in South Germany with more strongly marked peculiarities than in France, being more fantastic and more varied in form but not, however, so elegant as the French Rococo. The first architects of this style were: Johann Balthazar Neumann (1678—1753), and François de Cuvilliés père (1678—1768) in South Germany, and Georg Wenzel von Knobelsdorff (1607—1753), architect of Frederick he Great, and Carl von Gontard (1738—1802) in Berlin.

Plate 323.

The Royal Castle in Dresden.

(After Carl Schmidt and Schildbach, der Königliche Zwinger in Dresden.)

This structure was begun by Daniel Mathäus Pöppelmann in the year 1711, but upon completion of the south front in 1722, had to be postponed for want of funds. This building is without doubt the most debased of the Rococo period, but it evinces a creative fancy whose equal it would be difficult to find

Fig. 1. **Corner cartouche in the south front of the wall pavilion.**
,, 2. **Pilaster decoration of the wall pavilion.**
,, 3. **Figure supports from the arch gallery.**
,, 4. **Acanthus spray on the wall pavilion.**

Plate 324.

(After P. Halm, Ornament und Motive des Rokokostiles.)

Fig. 1. **City arms on the Town Hall at Bamberg** by Meister Bonaventura Mutschell, 1750.
,, 2, and 3. **Details from the pulpit of St. Michaels church in Bamberg,** of the year 1750.
,, 4. **Garden figure from the Cardinal's Palace of Seehof near Bamberg,** of the year 1730.
,, 5. **Coat of arms on tomb in Bamberg,** of the year 1770.
,, 6. **Wrought iron cresting of a gate in Würzburg Castle.**

Plate 325.

Fig. 1. **Arm-chair of German work** (Champeaux).
,, 2. **Carved mirror frame** (Champeaux).
,, 3. **Frame of fire screen** (Champeaux).

Plate 324.   GERMAN ROCOCO ORNAMENT.

521

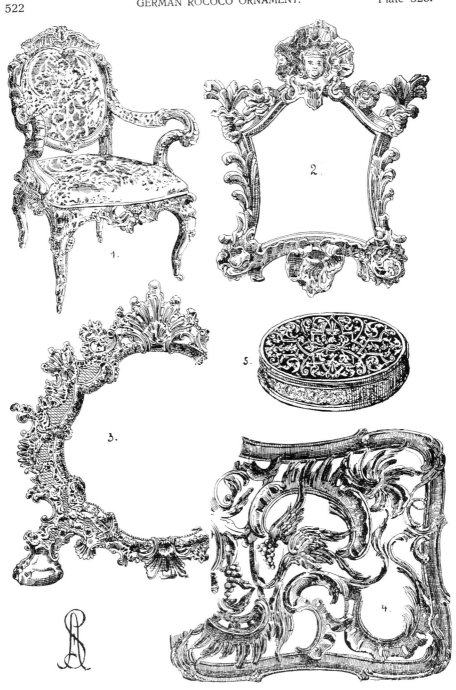

Fig. 4. **Balcony of carved wood,** middle of 18th century. In George Hirth's Collection.
„ 5. **Box by Joh.** Leonard Wüst, Engraver and Goldsmith in Augsburg in the year 1730 (Wessely).

Plate 326.

Design for Interior decoration by Habermann.

Plate 327.

Fig. 1. **Pulpit in the church at Naumburg** (Raguenet).
„ 2, and 3. **Shoe-buckle** by Jeremias Wachsmuth, Painter and Engraver, born in Augsburg in 1712, died 1779 (Wessely).
„ 4, and 6. **Sword hilt** by the same (Wessely).
„ 5. **Handle of a key** after Gottfried Forschter, Mastersmith in Brunn about the year 1750 (Wessely).
„ 7. **Stove from the Castle of Bruchsal** by Albert Stucki (Hirth).
„ 8. **Rosette from a ceiling in the Castle of Bruchsal** by Albert Stucki (Hirth).

Plate 328.

Fig. 1—5, and 7. **Meissener porcelain** (Dresden Cluna) (Champeaux).
„ 6. **Meissener (Dresden) Vase** from J. Double's Collection (Jännicke).
„ 8. **Meissener plate** from the year 1730 (Havard).

Plate 329.

(After Dr. Albert Ilg, Sammlung kunstindustrieller Gegenstände des Allerhöchsten Kaiserhauses.)

Fig. 1—5. **Articles belonging to the Empress Maria Theresa.** These consisted originally of 53 articles in beaten gold for the toilet and breakfast table and were manufactured by the sculptor and goldsmith Anton Mathias Joseph Domanek, born in Vienna 1713, died 1779.
„ 6, and 7. **Gold boxes,** presented by the Empress Maria Theresa to Duke Charles of Lorraine. After having been in the possession of Prince Kaunitz and later on of various private people these boxes were bought for the Crown Treasury by Francis II. They are the work of the Court Jeweller Franz Mack, born in Tyrol 1730, died 1805, the portraits are from the artist Antonio Bencini, who became Court Painter in 1753.
„ 8. **Grotesque figures,** appear to have been the work of the Dresden Goldsmith Melchior Dinglinger, died 1731. The bodies and legs are made of large pearls.
„ 9. **Sugar-tongs,** after Martin Engelbrecht, Engraver, died 1756 (Wessely).

Plate 327.   GERMAN ROCOCO ORNAMENT.   525

Plate 329. GERMAN ROCOCO ORNAMENT. 527

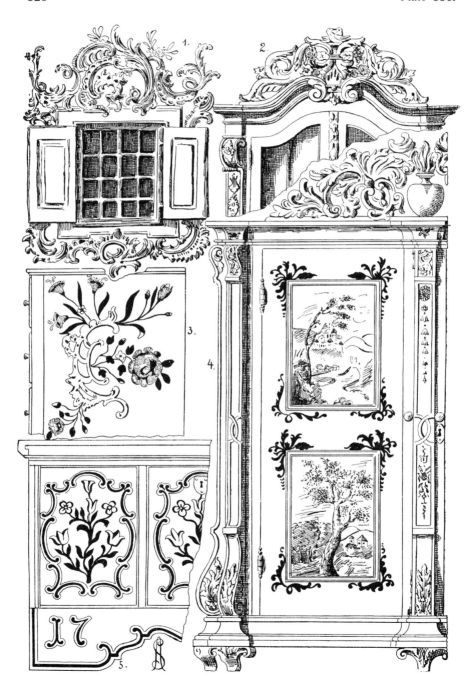

Plate 330.

(Village Rococo in Upper Bavaria.)

Fig. 1. **Window in Durchholzen near Walchsee** (Otto Aufleger, Bauernhäuser aus Oberbayern).

„ 2. **Top of wardrobe** from the Aiblinger District, dating from the year 1765 (Zell, Bauernmöbel).

„ 3. **Side of a chest of drawers in Rottach near Tegernsee** (Franz Zell, Bauernmöbel aus dem Bayrischen Hochland).

„ 4. **Cupboard from the Grafing District,** from the year 1770 (Zell).

„ 5. **Chest from Rinning near Ebersberg,** from the year 1756 (Zell).

Lady's Shoe (Hefner-Alteneck).

1.

2.

3.

4.

5.

6.

7.

8.

Rococo Ornament in England
(Chippendale Style).

In the 18th century Art in England was influenced more by Italy than by France and consequently the Rococo Style did not take much hold in the country.

Plate 331.

(From Chippendale, Gentleman and Cabinet Maker's Director, 1762.)

Fig. 1. **Ribband-back chair.**
„ 2. **Oval glass frame.**
„ 3. **Design for a chair.**
„ 4. „ **for a frame.**
„ 5. „ **for a chimney-piece.**
„ 6, 7, and 8. **Schemes for frets.**

Plate 332.

Fig. 1. **Mahogany bookcase of Chippendale period** (Chancellor).
„ 2. **Design for a bed, by Chippendale.**
„ 3. **Chair of the Chippendale period** (Chancellor).
„ 4. **Design for lantern, by Chippendale.**
„ 5. **Chair with cabriole legs of the Chippendale period** (Chancellor).

Plate 333.

(From Chippendale, Gentleman and Cabinet Maker's Director, 1762.)

Fig. 1. **Cabinet designed by Chippendale.**
„ 2. **Mouldings of a Cabinet designed, by Chippendale.**
„ 3. **Design for cabinet, by Chippendale.**
„ 4. „ **for brass handle.**
„ 5. „ **for brass escutcheon.**
„ 6, and 7, 12, and 13. **Glass doors.**
„ 8, and 11. **Design for lamp stands, by Chippendale.**
„ 9. **Design for Pedestal, by Chippendale.**
„ 10. „ **for upperpart of chimney-piece, by Chippendale.**

COLONIAL STYLE ORNAMENT
IN THE UNITED STATES.

It is evident that the Art of a new country like the United States must be in most intimate connection with the style of Art which predominates in the original country of the artist. This is the reason why Styles of almost all the European States were originally represented in America. After a time, however, all these different styles became united with one another forming themselves into the so-called Colonial Style. The buildings erected in America from 1725 to 1775 correspond somewhat to the Queen Anne and Georgian Styles in England, a typical example of the symmetrical construction of this epoch being Craigie House, Cambridge which dates from the year 1775. Churches and Meeting Houses were constructed after examples by Sir Christopher Wren. The best country houses were those found in Virginia and Maryland, while in Florida and California, on the other hand, the Spanish Renaissance style predominated.

From the declaration of Independence onwards, the Style in America became of a more monumental description but, after the fall of Napoleon, all the various historical styles in fashion in Europe were also included.

Notwithstanding the European reminiscences which they contain, the artistic creations of the 18th century in the United States possess undoubtedly certain characteristic national traits of their own.

Plate 334.   AMERICAN COLONIAL STYLE ORNAMENT.   535

Plate 334.

(After Goforth and Max Aulay, Details of American Colonial Style.)

Fig. 1. Mantel piece from Upsal Mansion in Germantown.
,, 2. Bookcase door.
,, 3. Medallion from principal cornice of a gateway in Philadelphia.
,, 4. Mantel piece from Wisterhouse in Germantown.
,, 5. Baluster from Fisher Mansion in Germantown.
,, 6. Mantel piece of wrought iron from Hamilton Mansion.
,, 7, and 8. Doorways in Philadelphia.
,. 8. Base of column illustrated in fig. 8.

Plate 335.

(After Goforth and Mac Aulay, Details of American Colonial Style.)

Fig. 1. Gate pier.
,, 2, and 5. Mantel pieces from Philadelphia.
,, 3. Dor head in Main Corridor of Independence Hall in Philadelphia, of the year 1729.
,, 4. Vase from the same Hall.
,, 6. From a doorway in Philadelphia.
,, 7, and 8. Details of a frame in the Independence Hall in Philadelphia.
,, 9. Side of the Corridor of Independence Hall in Philadelphia, 1729.

Plate 336.

Fig. 1. Sideboard (Alvan Croker Nye, Colonial Furniture).
,, 2. Chest of drawers (Nye).
,, 3. Hall clock from Hudson (Nye).
,, 4. Arm-chair from Brewton House in Charleston (A. Crane and E. E. Soderholtz).
,, 5. Bureau (Ware, The Georgian Period).
,, 6. Chair from the rooms of the American Society in Worcester (Nye).
,, 7. Oak chest (Ware, The Georgian Period).

Plate 337.

Fig. 1, and 2. Windows of Entrance Hall in Arnold Mansion, Mount Pleasant (Goforth and Mac Aulay).
,, 3. Hepplewhite chair (Nye).
,, 4, and 6. Sofa (Nye).
,, 5, and 7. Backs of chairs (Nye).
,, 8. Sofa (Nye).
,, 9. Door in Arnold Mansion, Mount Pleasant, 1761 (Goforth and Mac Auley).
,, 10. Chair in the rooms of the Connecticut Historical Society, Hartford (Nye).
., 11. Chair in Brewton House, Charleston (Crane and Soderholtz).

1.

2.

3.

4.

5.

6.

7.

Plate 337.   AMERICAN COLONIAL STYLE ORNAMENT.   539

1.

2

3.　　4

Plate 339.   AMERICAN COLONIAL STYLE ORNAMENT.   541

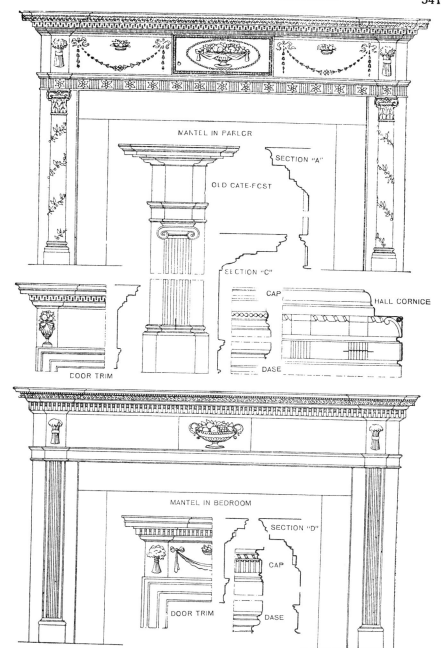

MANTEL IN PARLOR

SECTION "A"

OLD CATE-POST

SECTION "C"

CAP

HALL CORNICE

BASE

DOOR TRIM

MANTEL IN BEDROOM

SECTION "D"

CAP

DOOR TRIM

BASE

Measured by Claude Fayette Bragdon 92

Plate 338.

(After Edward A. Crane and E. E. Soderholtz, Examples of Colonial Architecture in South Carolina and Georgia.)

Fig. 1. Mantel piece in Corn House in Charleston, from the year 1790.
„ 2. Iron gate from S. Michael's Churchyard in Charleston.
„ 3. Ceiling in Gordon House, Savannah, Georgia, built in 1800.
„ 4. Stair balusters in Brewton House in Charleston, built in 1760.

Plate 339.

(After William Rotch Ware, The Georgian Period.)

Mantel pieces from the Pincre House, Salem, Mass.

Door (Goforth and Mac Auley).

ORNAMENT OF THE
CLASSICAL REVIVAL
OF THE 18TH CENTURY.

Frontispiece by Carlo Lasinio, draughtsman and engraver, 1789 (Hirth).

The Classical Revival of the 18th century.

The excavations in Herculaneum and Pompeii commenced in 1738, but at first very slowly proceeded with, resulted in discoveries which stirred up the interest in ancient classic art and brought new life to it. This was accentuated by the publication of Piranesi's engravings in Italy and in England by those of Wood on the ruins of Palmyra aud Baalbek (1757—59) and by Robert Adam on the palace of Spalato in 1764. These two latter revealed the existence of the remains of Imperial Rome, other than those in the Eternal City, and led to a further revival of classic art not so much in Italy as in foreign countries, and more especially in England where the works were published. Accustomed only to the copybooks of the Italian theorists, the architects found a new field and although the buildings discovered belonged to a decadent period, they were at all events purer in style and much more magnificent than the phases of the Later Renaissance and the Rococo. In England under the direction of Robert and James Adam and of Sir William Chambers, the new revival superseded that which is generally known as the Queen Anne Style, the quiet and unpretentious architecture of the commencement of the 18th century. In France it influenced the architecture and industrial art during the reign of Louis XVI. creating a style to which that monarch's name is attached and this style introduced then into Germany, led to what is known as the Zopfstil period of which the Palace at Potsdam, sometimes called the German Versailles, which was built in 1763—69, by the architect Carl von Gothard (1738—1802) is the best exponent. Of this style the examples from Freising and Schönbrunn (plate 352), show a return to classic forms differing widely from the Rococo style which existed in the first half of the 18th century throughout Germany and the Netherlands.

Fan in the Carnavalet Museum, Paris. Made at the death of Mirabeau (L'art pour tous)

18ᵗʰ century Ornament in Italy.

Although the Rococo style originated in Italy, the tendency in that country was towards the further development of the Later Renaissance, which in the Palace at Caserta (1752—70) by Vanvitelli (1700—78) was reduced to its lowest ebb as it would be difficult to find a more monotonous design than that immense structure. In the decoration of their interiors, and in furniture, however, owing to the genius of Piranesi (1704—84) and followed by Simonetti (1715—85), Piermarini (1734—1808) and Guiseppe Soli (1745—1822), a classic revival took place, not altogether however without some rococo influence as may be noticed in the mantelpiece on plate 340.

Plate 340.

Mural decoration from the work "Diverse maniere d'adornare i cammini" by Giovanni Battista, Piranesi, architect draughtsman and etcher.

Plate 341.

Fig. 1. Table by Guiseppe Soli, architect and painter. From the work "Ornamentale Entwürfe für Möbel im Stile Louis' XVI." (Hirth).
„ 2. Panel from a ceiling by Albertolli (Schoy, L'art de l'époque Louis XVI.).
„ 3. Bracket candlestick by Albertolli (Schoy).
„ 4. Design for wall decoration with table and clock, by Piranesi (Hirth).
„ 5. Chest of drawers by Soli (Hirth).

Plate 342.

(Designs by Giocondo Albertolli after Schoy, L'art de l'époque Louis XVI.)

Fig. 1. Ceiling in the palace of Prince Belgioso d'Este in Milan.
„ 2. Corner ornament of the same.
„ 3. Candlestick.
„ 4. Interior decoration.
„ 5. Study for centrepiece.

Plate 341. ITALIAN 18TH CENTURY ORNAMENT. 547

18th century Ornament in France.
(Louis XVI. Style.)

The principal supporters and patrons of this style, amongst others, were Constant d'Yvri, and Jacques Germain Soufflot. The art of the cabinet maker flourished in a specially unexpected manner under this style, as did also the Goldsmith's art and porcelain manufacture.

Plate 343.
(After César Daly, Motifs historiques d'architecture et de sculpture.)

Fig. 1, and 2. **Keystone of an entrance porch in Paris.**
 „ 3, 4, and 7. **Console brackets in Paris.**
 „ 5, and 6. **Detail of part of the façade of the Palais Royal, Paris; towards the garden.**

Plate 344.
(After César Daly, Motifs historiques.)

Fig. 1. **Over door of an hotel in the Rue de Francs-Bourgeois No. 10, Paris.**
 „ 2. **Decorated door of an hotel, Rue de Varenne No. 89, Paris.**
 „ 3. **Part of door of a house, Route de Chatillon No. 17, Paris.**
 „ 4. **Entrance door in the Hotel des Monnaies, Paris.**
 „ 5. **Door crest from Paris.**

Plate 345.
(After César Daly, Motifs historiques.)

Fig. 1. **Mantel piece from a country house in Blanquefort, Gironde.**
 „ 2. **Drawing-room decoration of an hotel in the Rue St. Charles, Bordeaux.**

Plate 346.
Fig. 1. **Balcony in the Rue Royale, Versailles** (Daly).
 „ 2. **Balcony from Paris** (Daly).
 „ 3. **Door and frame in wrought steel from Palais de Justice, Paris** (Daly).
 „ 4. **Vase from an engraving by Lalonde,** draughtsman and designer in Paris (Hirth).
 „ 5. **Pommel of stick by the same** (Hirth).
 „ 6. **Candlestick by J. F. Forty,** brass-founder and chaser in Paris, 1775—1790 (Hirth).

Plate 347.
Fig. 1. **Sofa of painted wood covered with embroidered silk** (Bajot).
 „ 2. **Small table of mahogany with gilt chased, copper mountings** (Bajot).
 „ 3. **Cabinet** (Havard).
 „ 4. **Tripod of bronze gilt** (Havard).
 „ 5. **Design for drawing-room decoration,** made for the Marquis de Sillery after a drawing by Rousseau de la Rottière. In the South Kensington Museum (Champeaux).
 „ 6. **Design for chased door lock, by Lalonde** (Hirth).

Plate 344. FRENCH 18TH CENTURY ORNAMENT. 551

Plate 346.   FRENCH 18TH CENTURY ORNAMENT.   553

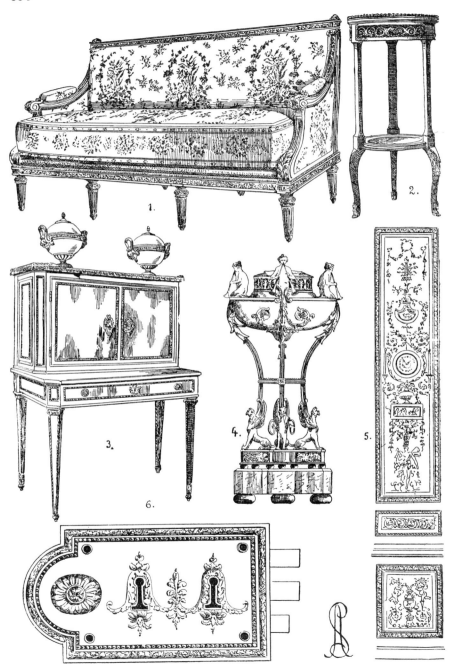

Plate 348. FRENCH 18TH CENTURY ORNAMENT. 555

Plate 350.   FRENCH 18TH CENTURY ORNAMENT.   557

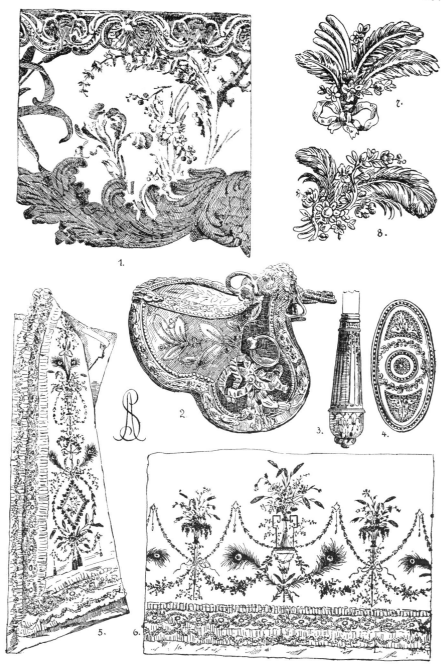

Plate 348.

Fig. 1. Fire screen of embroidered silk in a frame made of carved and gilt wood (Bajot).
„   2. Console table in wood gilt (Bajot).
„   3. Salon decoration of the Hotel d'Hallwill, in carved wood. Drawn by Architect Ledoux (Champeaux).
„   4. Hanging lamp (L'art pour tous).
„   5. Chair, showing transition to the Empire Style (L'art pour tous).
„   6. Chased door bolt by Lalonde (Hirth).
„   7. Bronze door mantle (Champeaux).

Plate 349.
(After Schoy, Art Louis XVI.)

Fig. 1, and 2. Stand and table by Jean François de Neufforge.
„   3, 4, 9, and 10. Doors by Antoine Joseph Rouvo.
„   5, and 12. Arm chair and sofa by Bouché Le Jeune.
„   6, and 7. Furniture feet by Neufforge.
„   8. Mirror frame by P. Ranson.
„   11. Candelabrum by Neufforge.

Plate 350.

Fig. 1. Window Valence of embroidered silk in the Musee des Arts décoratifs (Champeaux).
„   2. Driving saddle of leather with bronze gilt ornaments (Hirth).
„   3, and 4. Knife handle and lid of box after Lalonde (Hirth).
„   5, and 6. Dress of embroidered silk (Champeaux).
„   7, and 8. Aigrettes from the work "Nouveau recueil de parures et joaillerie", Paris 1764, by Poujet fils, engraver and goldsmith in Paris.

Monogram in precious stones, by Ranson (Schoy).

18th century Ornament in the Netherlands.

Plate 351.

(Designs for precious stones by L. van der Cruycen, after Schoy, L'art Louis XVI.)

Fig. 1. Designs for corsage.
  ,, 2, and 7. Brooches.
  ,, 3. Necklace.
  ,, 4, and 6. Ear-rings.
  ,, 5, and 8. Pendants.

18th century Ornament in Germany.

(Zopfstil Ornament.)

About the year 1771 the Rococo style in Germany gave way before the newly awakened Classicism, this result being very probably due to Italian and French influences.

Plate 352.

(After Moritz Heider, Louis XVI. und Empire.)

Fig. 1. Detail of part of a dwelling-house in Freising, Vienna.
  ,, 2. Entrance gate in the Gloriette in Schönbrunn.
  ,, 3. Panel from the same.
  ,, 4. Vase from Schönbrunn Park.
  ,, 5. Door of a house in the Freundgasse, Vienna.

Plate 353.

(After Moritz Heider, Louis XVI. und Empire.)

Fig. 1, 2, and 3. Pulpit in the Lichtental church Vienna, Rossau. In wood painted and partly gilt.
  ,, 4. Hanging lantern in Palace Schwarzenberg, Vienna.
  ,, 5. Lamp from the Wieden Freihaus, Schleifmühlengasse, Vienna.
  ,, 6. Lamp in the upper Augarten Strasse, Vienna.
  ,, 7. Stove in the Primate's Palace, Pressburg, of glazed terra-cotta, partly gilt.

Plate 352.   GERMAN 18TH CENTURY ORNAMENT.   561

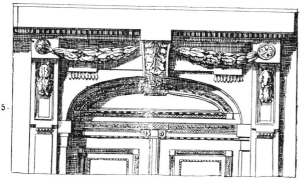

Plate 354.

Fig. 1. **Mantel piece in the castle at Mannheim** (Luthmer, Innenräume etc. im Louis XVI. und Empirestil).

„ 2. **Bracket candlestick of carved wood, from the Rein Monastery in Steiermark** (Heider).

„ 3—6. **Window grating and balconies in Vienna** (Heider).

Clock (Heider).

18th century Ornament in England.

(The Adam style.)

In accordance with the conservative character of the English people the Palladian style which was worked out and developed by many eminent architects in public buildings, was adhered to up to the third quarter of the 18th century, and the Louis XVI. style did not take any root in England. The principal founder of the classical revival was the architect Robert Adam (1723—1792) and his brother James. The former was a most prolific designer not only of architectural works but of furniture and decoration, so that he is virtually the creator of a new style known by his name, to which, after a Greek and a Gothic revival, there is now a tendency to return. Although as a rule, the work of Adam was inspired by Roman art and his designs for ceilings show how closely he had studied the stucco decoration in the tombs at Rome and in Hadrian's villa at Tivoli; there are occasions when he displays considerable acquaintance with Greek art as in Plate 357, representing work in Sion House, built 1761—64, which suggests that he must have had access to Stuart's drawings which were not published till 1769 by the Dilettanti Society.

After designs by R. and J. Adam.

Plate 355.

(Doric Order after Robert Adam.)

Fig. 1, and 2. **Entrance hall to Shelburne House in Berkeley Square.**
„ 3. **Door frame in same.**
„ 4. **Dado from same.**

Plate 356.

(Ionic Order after Robert Adam.)

Fig. 1, and 2. **From front of Shelburne House, Berkeley Square.**
„ 3. **Pilaster from Lord Mansfield's Villa at Kenwood.**

Plate 357.

(Ionic Order after Robert Adam.)

Fig. 1. **From the attic storey over the entrance hall of Sion House, residence of the Duke of Northumberland.**
„ 2, 3, and 6. **Column and entablature at Sion House.**
„ 4, and 5. **Door way of the same.**

Plate 358.

Fig. 1—3, 5, and 6. **Details from the entrance gateway at Sion House.**
„ 4. **Frieze from Luton House, country seat of the Earl of Bute.**

Plate 356.   ENGLISH 18TH CENTURY ORNAMENT.   567

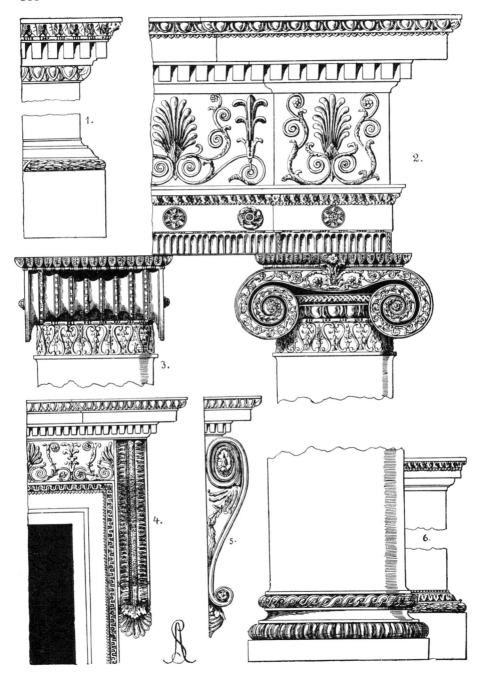

Plate 358.   ENGLISH 18TH CENTURY ORNAMENT.   569

Plate 360.   ENGLISH 18TH CENTURY ORNAMENT.   571

Plate 359.

Fig. 1. Capital from the first storey of the staircase in Luton House.
„ 2, and 3. Corinthian Order by Robert Adam.

Plate 360.

(After The Decorative Works of Robert and James Adam.)

Fig. 1. Moulding round the bas-reliefs in the hall of Sion House.
„ 2, 3, 8, and 9. Decoration of the attic window in the entrance Hall, Sion House.
„ 4, and 7. Greek Order in the dining-room of the house of Sir Watkins Williams Wynn, St. James's Square.
„ 5. Vase on the porter's lodge, Sion House.
„ 6. Decoration of the plinth of the large niche in the hall of Sion House.

Plate 361.

(After The Decorative Works of Robert and James Adam.)

Fig. 1, and 2. Design of the Order for Carlton House.
„ 3. Decorative vase in Sion House.
„ 4, and 5. Mantel piece at Sion House.

Plate 362.

(After The Decorative Works of Robert and James Adam.)

Fig. 1, and 4. Trophies in Sion House.
„ 2, 3, and 5. Frame work of window in the entrance-hall, Sion House.

Plate 363.

(After The Decorative Works of Robert and James Adam.)

Fig. 1. Mantel piece in St. James's Palace.
„ 2, and 3. Organ in the house of Sir Watkins Williams Wynn.

Plate 364.

(After The Decorative Works of Robert and James Adam.)

Fig. 1. Ceiling of the entrance-hall in Sion House.
„ 2. Ceiling of the dining-room of the house of Sir Watkins Williams Wynn.
„ 3. Ceiling in Sion House.
„ 4. Ceiling of the music-room in the house of Sir Watkins Williams Wynn.

Plate 363. ENGLISH 18TH CENTURY ORNAMENT. 575

Plate 365.

(After The Decorative Works of Robert and James Adam.)

Fig. 1, and 2. **Plan and elevation of design for table centre-piece.**
„ 3. **Design for frame and Royal coat of arms.**

Plate 366.

(After The Decorative Works of Robert and James Adam.)

Fig. 1. **Ceiling of a room, called the "Japanned Room" in the Queen's House, from a design by Adam.**
„ 2. **Bridge in the Park of Sion House.**

Plate 367.

(After The Decorative Works of Robert and James Adam.)

Fig. 1. **Sedan chair, from a design by Adam,** prepared for the King.
„ 2. **Console table with mirror over.**
„ 3. **Window mantle.**
„ 4. **Grate in brass and steel, in Library of Luton, 1764.**

Plate 368.

Fig. 1. **Tripod and vase for candles** (Adam).
„ 2. **Pier glass** (Adam).
„ 3. **Door knocker from the house of Sir Watkins Williams Wynn. St. James's Square** (Adam).
„ 4, and 5. **Sugar bowl and coffee-pot of the year 1770** (Champeaux).

Plate 369.

Fig. 1, and 2. **Piano in wood of various colours, made in London for the Empress of Russia** (Adam).
„ 3. **Design for a panel by Adam.**
„ 4. **Window mantle** (Adam).
„ 5. **Top of chest of drawers in the palace of the Countess of Derby** (Adam).

Furniture made from designs by Thomas Sheraton.

(After Sheraton, Cabinet maker and Upholsterer's Drawing Book, 1791—93.)

Plate 370.

Fig. 1. **Buffet or Sideboard.**
„ 2. **Toilet table.**
„ 3. **Fire-screen.**

1.

2.

3.

4.

Plate 368. ENGLISH 18TH CENTURY ORNAMENT. 581

Plate 370. ENGLISH 18TH CENTURY ORNAMENT. 583

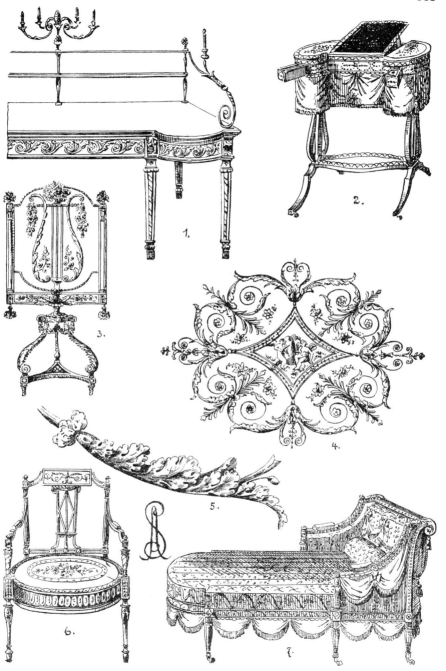

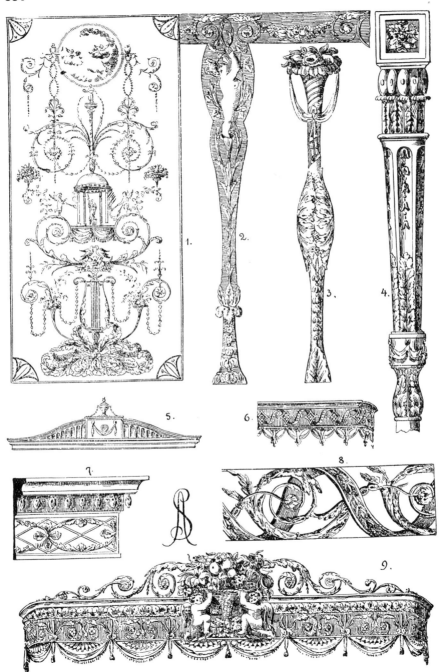

Fig. 4. Inlaid table top.
„ 5. Acanthus ornament.
„ 6. Arm chair.
„ 7. Sofa.

Plate 371.

Fig. 1. Panel decoration.
„ 2—5. Details of furniture.
„ 6, and 9. Window mantles.
„ 7. Head of doorway.
„ 8. Frieze in bas-relief.

Plate 372.

Fig. 1—3. Designs for Chair backs.
„ 4. Center for a Pier table to be painted or executed in Inlay.
„ 5. Design for a Secretarire and Bookcase.
„ 6. Design for a Cabinet.

Furniture made from designs by A. Hepplewhite.

(After Hepplewhite, The Cabinet maker and Upholsterer's Guide, 1789—94.)

Plate 373.

Fig. 1. Canopy bed.
„ 2. Writing table with cupboard over.
„ 3. Chair.
„ 4. Terminal vase.
„ 5—9, 11—17. Cornices for furniture.
„ 10. Glass door of cupboard.

Work prepared from various designs.

Plate 374.

Fig. 1. Design for ceiling by Pergolesi.
„ 2. Mantel piece by G. Richardson.
„ 3, and 6. Panels by Pergolesi.
„ 4. Mantel piece with mirror by William Thomas.
„ 5. Emblem by Pergolesi.
„ 7. Ceiling by G. Richardson.

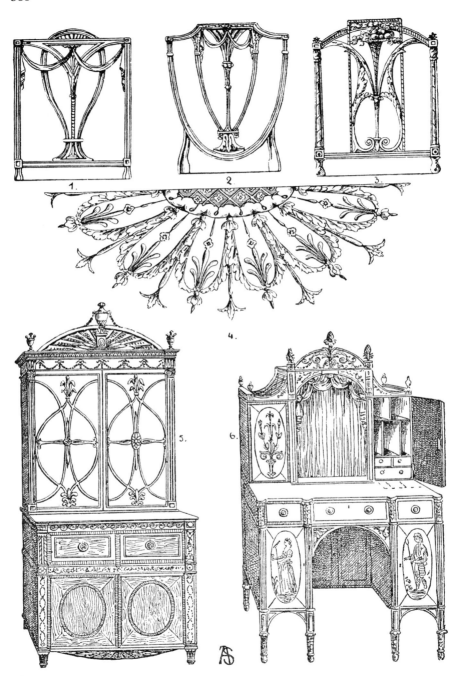

Plate 373.   ENGLISH 18TH CENTURY ORNAMENT.   587

Plate 375.   ENGLISH 18TH CENTURY ORNAMENT.   589

1.

2.

Plate 375.

(After Bailey Scott Murphy, English and Scottish Wrought Ironwork.)

Fig. 1. **Wrought-iron gate in screen to Dining Hall,** Queen's College, Cambridge, round which in the year 1734 the wood work in the prevailing Renaissance ·style was carried out.

„ 2. **Fan-light of a gateway in All Soul's College,** Oxford, the work of Hawksmoor.

English 18ᵗʰ Century Pottery.

Plate 376.

(After Examples of Early English Pottery by John Eliot Hodgkin and Edith Hodgkin.)

Fig. 1. **Plate.** Cock Pit Hill of the year 1734. Black enamel with bronze-coloured flowers.

„ 2. **Plate, of the same origin.** Brown glazing with yellow decorations, of the year 1749.

„ 3. **Drinking cup with handles, Sgraffito ware,** inscribed 1764.

„ 4. **Jug, Sgraffito,** inscribed 1779.

„ 5. **Drinking cup with handles** from Jackfield, 1760, with gold ornamentations.

„ 6, and 7. **Plates.** Delft porcelain, made in England, 1740.

„ 8. **Plate,** Staffordshire delft, about 1718.

„ 9. **Plate,** Lambeth delft, inscribed 1742.

Design for a bracket candlestick by Adam.

Frieze in mural painting (Percier et Fontaine).

Empire Ornament in France.

In the last quarter of the 18th century, Greek art commenced to exert its influence on architecture and the industrial arts, and its development by Percier and Fontaine in Paris for Napoleon I., resulted in that phase which is generally known as the style of the Empire. Although unable to supersede entirely the traditional crafts of the day, such as is found in the Louis XV. and XVI. Styles, it created a demand for decoration of a better character, and pure architectural forms were introduced in the place of the Rococo scroll-work thus the Greek Palmette and Acanthus, the egg and tongue, the guilloche and other decorative details came again into fashion and extended to furniture and other accessories, including also interior work and metal mounts.

Work made from designs by C. Percier and P. F. L. Fontaine.

Plate 377.

(After Percier et Fontaine, Recueil de Décorations intérieures.)

Fig. 1. **Capital and entablature.**
  ,, 2. **Soffit of cornice.**
  ,, 3. **Base of Pilaster.**
  ,, 4. **Wall decoration from the cabinet of King Joseph of Spain,** made in Paris from designs by Percier and Fontaine, and fixed in the Palace at Aranjuez.

Plate 377.   EMPIRE ORNAMENT IN FRANCE.   593

2

3

4

Plate 378.

Fig. 1. Ceiling painting in a studio at Paris.

Plate 379.

Fig. 1. Pier in the Venus Museum in the Louvre, Paris.
,, 2. Tribune from the hall of the Marshalls in the Tuileries, Paris.

Plate 380.

Fig. 1. Mantel piece in the Louvre, Paris.
,, 2, and 3. Mural paintings.
,. 4. Book cabinet, made in Paris for Amsterdam.

Plate 381.

Fig. 1. Branched candlestick, Paris.
,, 2. Soup tureen, made in Paris.
,, 3. Candelabrum, made in Paris.
,, 4. Bed stead and canopy, Paris.

Plate 382.

Fig. 1. Throne of Napoleon I. in the Tuileries, now destroyed.

Plate 383.

Fig. 1. Writing bureau, made in Paris.
,, 2, and 3. Table, made in Paris for St. Petersburg.
,, 4. Table, made in Paris for Count S. in St. Petersburg.
,, 5. Arm-chair, made in Paris for St. Petersburg.

Plate 384.

Fig. 1—6, 8—13. Furniture mountings (Recueil des Dessins d'ornements d'architecture de la Manufacture de Joseph Bennot à Sarrebourg et Paris).
,, 7. Furniture mounting (L'art pour tous).
,. 14. Upper part of a chest of drawers (L'art pour tous).

Plate 382. EMPIRE ORNAMENT IN FRANCE. 599

Plate 384.   EMPIRE ORNAMENT IN FRANCE.   601

Plate 385.

Fig. 1, 5, 8, 11—13. **Furniture mountings** (Bennot).
„ 2. **Mirror from a drawing by P. P. Prudhon,** in the Industrial Art Museum, Berlin.
„ 3. **Stand** (Beauvalet).
„ 4. **Sèvres Vase in Grand Trianon,** after a photograph.
„ 6, and 7. **Silver cradle of the Duke of Bordeaux** (L'art pour tous).
, 9, and 10. **Chairs of the Directory period** (L'art pour tous).

Bureau, made in Paris (Percier et Fontaine).

On the fall of the Empire, the same style continued but was much inferior both in character and execution. The nèogrec movement of 1840—60 led to more refinement in design, which after the Franco-German war tended towards a revival of the Louis XIV. and XV. Style.

Plate 386.

Fig. 1. **Work table,** of the year 1820 (Bajot).

„ 2. **Screen in Mahogany,** with gilt mountings (Bajot).

„ 3. **Arm-chair** of the year 1820 (Bajot).

„ 4. **Console table,** 1820 (Bajot).

„ 5. **Chair,** 1830 (Bajot).

„ 6. **Key-hole plate** (L'art pour tous).

„ 7. **Pilaster from the Café Gaulois, Rue Poissonière No. 46, Paris** (Thiollet et H. Roux).

Key-hole plate (L'art pour tous).

Empire Ornament in Italy.

Although the Empire Style was taken up in Italy later than in France, the country of its chief development on the other hand, it lasted much longer, being retained until the thirties, when Guiseppe Borsato became its chief exponent, his work being however, inferior to that of Percier and Fontaine.

Plate 387.

Fig. 1, and 5.   **Sofa and arm-chair in Directory Style by Guiseppe Soli** (Hirth).
  „   2.   **Sofa for the Milan cathedral, by Giocondo Albertolli** (Schoy).
  „   3.   **Stool in Directory Style, by Albertolli** (Hirth).
  „   4.   **Perfuming censer in Empire Style, by Albertolli,** Milan 1790 (Hirth).

Work done from designs by Borsato.

(After Percier et Fontaine, Recueil de Décorations intérieures avec des suppléments par Joseph Borsato.)

Plate 388.

Fig. 1.   **Internal decoration in the Imperial Palace in Venice.**
  „   2.   **Ceiling painting, carried out in the year 1817 for Count Albriggi in Venice.**
  „   3.   **Mantel piece in the Royal Imperial Palace in Venice.**

Plate 387. EMPIRE ORNAMENT IN ITALY. 607

Plate 389. EMPIRE ORNAMENT IN ITALY. 609

Plate 389.

Fig. 1. Internal decoration of reception room in the Royal Palace in Venice, of the year 1834.

Silver chandelier in the church of S. Giorgio de Greci, Venice
(Percier et Fontaine).

Empire Ornament in Germany.

Towards the close of the 18th century, at a time when the imitation of everything French grew to be a passion amongst the Germans, the German Rococo and Louis XVI. Styles which were imitations of the French gave way to imitations of the new French Empire Style. This change was furthermore favoured by the political conditions which ruled at the period.

Plate 390.

(After Moritz Heider, Louis XVI. und Empire.)

Fig. 1. **Parquetry floor in Schwarzenberg Palace, Vienna.**
„ 2. **Stove recess in the same palace.**
„ 3. **Stove from the Monastery of Rein in Steiermark.**
„ 4. **Ceiling decoration in Modena Palace, Herrengasse, Vienna.**

Plate 391.

Fig. 1. **Sofa in the collection of Duke Karl Theodor of Bavaria in Munich** (Luthmer, Bürgerliche Möbel).
„ 2, 4, and 6. **Sofa, stool, and small table in the appartments of the Grand Duchess of Modena, Munich** (Luthmer).
„ 3, and 7. **Bed and cupboard in possession of the art dealer Hugo Helbing, Munich** (Luthmer).
„ 5. **Piano in mahogany with gilt bronze, made by M. Seiffert in Vienna, 1790** (Bajot).

Plate 392.

Fig. 1. **Mirror and console table in the Bavarian National Museum, Munich** (Luthmer, Bürgerliche Möbel).
„ 2. **End of a sofa in the Royal Residence in Stuttgart** (Luthmer).
„ 3. **Toilet looking-glass from the collection of Duke Karl Theodor of Bavaria** (Luthmer, Bürgerliche Möbel).
„ 4. **Mantel piece in the Munich Museum** (Luthmer, Bürgerliche Möbel).

Plate 391.   EMPIRE ORNAMENT IN GERMANY.   613

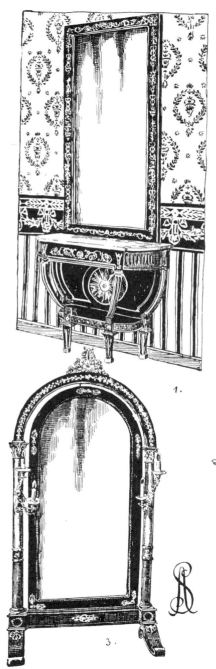

1.

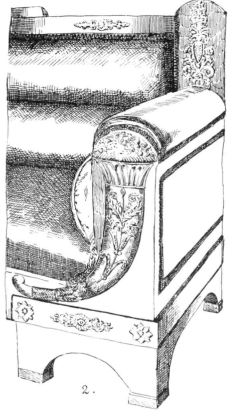

2.

3.

4.

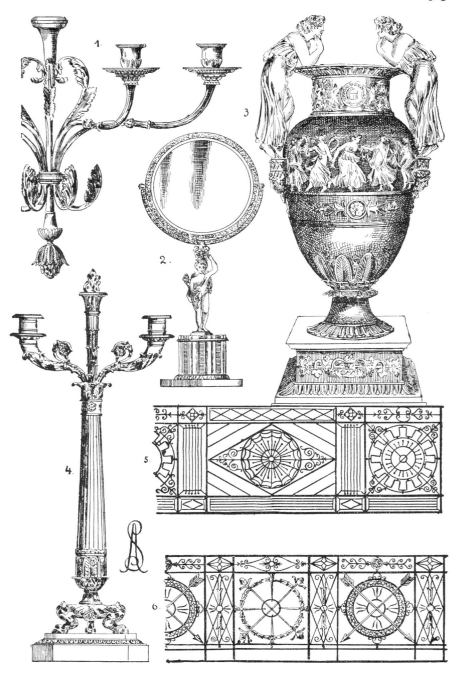

Plate 393.

Fig. 1. Branch bracket candlestick in bronze gilt (Heider).
„ 2. Toilet looking-glass with bronze frame (Heider).
„ 3. Bronze vase with the Dance of the Hours, in the Royal Residence in Stuttgart (Luthmer).
„ 4. Branch candlestick of bronze gilt (Heider).
„ 5, and 6. Balcony railings in Wickenburger Gasse, Vienna (Heider).

**Window of the Husar Inn in Garmisch,
Upper Bavaria**
(Zell, Bauernhäuser im bayerischen Hochland).

Biedermeier or old fashioned Style in Germany.

As a reaction from the elaborate ornament of the Louis XVI. and Empire styles, a new style arose in which work of the greatest simplicity and commonplace form the chief characteristics, this is known in Germany as the Biedermeier, or old fashioned style.

Plate 394.

Fig. 1. **Bed of Hungarian oak,** of the year 1830 (Joseph Folnesics, Innenräume und Hausrat der Empire- und Biedermeierzeit).

„ 2, and 3. **Chairs from Vienna,** 1820—30 (Folnesics).

„ 4. **Table from the castle of Obernzenn in Unterfranken** (Luthmer).

„ 5. **Sofa in possession of Baron von Pöllnitz, Bamberg** (Luthmer).

„ 6, and 7. **Sewing-tables from Vienna,** 1820 (Folnesics).

Silk stuff. After the original in the Industrial Museum, Berlin.

1.

2.

3.

4.

5.

6.

Plate 395.   BIEDERMEIER ORNAMENT IN GERMANY.   619

Plate 395.

Fig. 1, and 2. **Samples of cotton.** After the originals in the Industrial Art Museum in Berlin.
„ 3. **Cupboard from Unterammergau,** 1820 (Zell).
„ 4—7. **Sample of material for furniture covering.** After the original in the Industrial Art Museum, Berlin.

Neogrec Ornament in Germany.

n the period following the fall of the Empire, Art made fresh progress in Germany, in consequence of the revival of art and the exceptional genius of K. F. Schinkel (1781—1841) an architect whose works constitute the models in all the North German schools. Schinkel's chief work was the Museum in Berlin, he was followed by his pupil, A. Stüler (1800—1865) who built the additions to the Museum. In Munich, Leo von Klenze (1794—1864) led the way.

Plate 396.

(After Karl Friedrich Schinkel, Sammlung architektonischer Entwürfe.)

From the Ancient Museum in Berlin.

Fig. 1. **Wood ceiling in the Sculpture Hall.**
„ 2. **Principal entablature of one of the upper halls.**
„ 3. **Capital of column in the Sculpture Hall.**
„ 4. **Base of column in the portico.**
Fig. 5. **Capital of pier from Sculpture Hall.**
„ 6. **Cast-iron balustrade of the gallery in the Rotunda.**

Candlestick by Schinkel
(Vorbilder).

Plate 397.

(After Karl Friedrich Schinkel, Sammlung architektonischer Entwürfe.)

Fig. 1. **Window of the General Building School in Berlin.**
„ 2. **Principal entrance door of the same.**

Plate 398.

Fig. 1, 2, 6, and 7. **Grecian chairs and sofa** (L. Lohde, Sammlung von Möbelentwürfen, erfunden von Karl Friedrich Schinkel).
„ 3. **Marble tazza by Schinkel** (Vorbilder für Fabrikanten und Handwerker).
„ 4. **Grecian vase after Moses** (Vorbilder für Fabrikanten und Handwerker, auf Befehl des Ministers für Handel, Gewerbe und Bauwesen, 1821).

Plate 398.   NEOGREC ORNAMENT IN GERMANY.   623

Plate 400.   NEOGREC ORNAMENT IN GERMANY.   625

Plate 399.

Fig. 1. **Drawing-room table by Schinkel** (L. Lohde).
  „   2. **Mural painting from drawings by Stier** (Vorbilder).
  „   3. **Writing table by Schinkel** (L. Lohde).
  „   4. **Goblet-glass by Schinkel** (Vorbilder).
  „   5. **Wine cooler by Ruhl** (Vorbilder).
  „   6. **Sample of stuff from Bötticher** (Vorbilder).

Plate 400.

(From Examples for Manufacturers and Artisans, by order of the Minister for Trade, Industry and Building, 1821).

Fig. 1. **Chalice by Schinkel.**
  „   2. **Sample of stuff from Mauch.**
  „   3. **Sample of stuff by Schinkel.**
  „   4. **Vase from Mauch.**

Marble tazza by Schinkel
(Vorbilder für Fabrikanten und Handwerker).

REFERENCE BOOKS.

Adam (Robert and James), The decorative Work of.
Amelung, W. and Holtzinger, H., The Museums and Ruins of Rome.
Anderson, W. J., The Architecture of the Renaissance in Italy.
Anderson, W. J. and Spiers, R. Phené, The Architecture of Greece and Rome.
Architectural Association Sketch Book.
Arnott, J. A. and Wilson, J., The Petit Trianon, Versailles.
L'Art pour tous.
Audsley, G. A., Ornamental Arts of Japan.
Audsley, G. A. and Bowes, J. L., The Keramic Art of Japan.
Aufleger (Otto), Bauernhäuser aus Oberbayern.
Babelon, E., Archéologie.
Bajot, E., Collection de meubles anciens.
Bajot, Encyclopédie du meuble.
Bajot, Musées du Louvre et de Cluny.
Baumeister, A., Das klassische Altertum.
Baltzer, F., Das japanische Haus.
Bankart, Geo P., The Art of the Plasterer.
Barrière-Flavy, Les arts industriels des peuples barbares de la Gaule.
Belcher (John) and Macartney, M. E., Later Renaissance Architecture in England.
Beunat, (Josèphe), Recueil des dessins d'ornements d'architecture.
Bing, S., Japanischer Formenschatz.
Birch and Spiers Old House, Lime Street, City.
Birch, George H., London Churches of the XVIIth and XVIIIth Centuries.
Bird, Sir G., The Industrial Arts of India.
Blomfield, Reginald, A History of Renaissance Architecture in England.
Boito, Camillo, Architettura del medio evo in Italia.
Boito, Arte Italiana.
Bond, Francis, Gothic Architecture in England.
Borchardt, Die ägyptische Pflanzensäule.
Bourgoin, J., Les Arts Arabes.
Boetticher, A., Olympia.
Boettiger, Dr. John, Hedvig Eleonoras Drottingholm.
Brandon, R. and J. A., Analysis of Gothic Architecture.
Brandon, Open Timber Roofs of the Middle Ages.
Brinckmann, J. and Weimar, W., Das Hamburgische Museum für Kunst und Gewerbe.
Brinckmann, Justus, Kunst und Handwerk in Japan.
Brindley, Wm. and Weatherley, W. S., Ancient sepulchral monuments.
Brown, G. Baldwin, The arts in Early England.
Bühlmann, J., Die Bauformenlehre.
Burlington Fine Arts Club, Illustrated Catalogues of Loan Exhibitions.
Burton, Wm., English Porcelain.
Bury T. T., Remains of Ecclesiastical Woodwork.
Canina, L., Architettura antica.
Chambers (Sir W.), Designs of Chinese Buildings.
Champeaux, A. de, Portefeuille des Arts décoratifs.

Chancellor, A. E., Examples of Old Furniture.
Chippendale, T., Gentleman and Cabinet Makers Director.
Cicognara, L., Monumenti di Venezia.
Colling, J. K., Details of Gothik Architecture.
Crallan, F. A., Gothic Woodcarving.
Crane, E. A. and E. E. Soderholtz, Examples of Colonial Architecture in South Carolina and Georgia.
Czobor, Dr. Béla und Emmerich von Szaley, Die historischen Denkmäler Ungarns.
Dahlerup, Holm und Storck, Tegninger af ældre Nordisk Architectur.
Daly, César, Motifs historiques d'architecture et de sculpture d'ornament.
Day, Lewis F., Alphabets, Old and New.
Day, Enamelling.
Day, Lettering in Ornament.
Day, Ornament and its Application.
Day, Pattern Design.
Day, Windows, a Book about Stained and Painted Glass.
Dehio, G. und G. v. Bezold, Die kirchliche Baukunst des Abendlandes.
Dehli (A.), Norman Monuments of Palermo.
Dietrichson und Munthe, Die Holzbaukunst Nor wegens.
Dieulafoy, M., L'art antique de la Perse.
Dolmetsch, H., Ornamentenschatz.
Dolmetsch, H., The Historic Styles of Ornament.
Doerpfeld, Wilhelm, Das griechische Theater.
Drexler, Karl, Der Verduner Altar.
Dupont-Auberville, L'ornement des Tissus.
Ebe, G., Die Schmuckformen der Monumentalbauten.
Ebe, G., Die Spät-Renaissance.
Ellwood, G. M., English Furniture and Decoration, 1680—1800.
Errard, Ch. et Gayet, A., L'Art Byzantin.
D'Espouy, H., Fragments d'architecture de la Renaissance.
Evans, Sir John, The Ancient Stone Implements, Weapons, and Ornaments of Gt. Britain.
Evans, Ancient Bronze Implements.
Ewerbeck, F., und Neumeister, Die Renaissance in Belgien und Holland.
Falke, Mittelalterliches Holzmobiliar.
Falke und Frauberger, Deutsche Schmelzarbeiten des Mittelalters.
Fergusson, James, History of Architecture in all Countries.
Finsch, Otto, Erfahrungen und Belegstücke aus der Südsee.
Flandin et Coste, Perse ancienne.
Fletcher, B. and B. F., A history of Architecture.
Folnesics, (Joseph), Innenräume und Hausrat der Empire- und Biedermeierzeit.
Gailhabaud, J., L'architecture.
Gagarin, Prince G. G., Recueil d'ornaments et d'architecture byzantins, géorgiens et Russes.
Gardner, J. Starkie, Old English Ironwork.

Garner, T. and Stratton, A., The Domestic Architecture of England during the Tudor Period.
Gayet, A., L'art Arabe.
Gayet, A., L'art Persan.
Gélis-Didot, (P.) et Lafillée H., La peinture décorative en France du XI. au XVI. siècle.
Gerhard, E., Äußerliche Vasenbildung.
Gerhard, Etruskische Spiegel.
Gibbs, James, A Book of Architecture.
Gladbach, E., Der Schweizerholzstyl.
Glazier, R., A Manual of historic Ornament.
Goforth and McAuley, Old Colonial Architectural Details.
Gotch (J. A.), Architecture of the Renaissance in England.
Gotch, J. A., The Growth of the English House.
Gotch, Early Renaissance Architecture in England.
Gottlob, Fritz, Formenlehre der norddeutschen Backsteingotik.
Grandidiér, Erneste, La céramique Chinoise.
Graul, R., Dekoration und Mobiliar.
Gruner, L., Specimens of Ornamental Art.
Gruner, L., Fresco Decorations of the Churches and Palaces of Italy.
Gurlitt, Cornelius, Das Barock- und Rokokoornament.
Gurlitt, Geschichte des Barockstiles in Italien.
Gurlitt, Geschichte der Kunst.
Gusman, P., L'art decoratif à Rome.
Halm, P., Ornamente und Motive des Rokokostiles.
Haupt, Albrecht, Die Baukunst der Renaissance in Portugal.
Havard, H., Dictionnaire de l'ameublement et de la décoration.
Havard, Histoire et philosophie des styles.
Havard, Histoire de l'orfèvrerie Française.
Hefner-Alteneck, J. H. von, Ornamente der Holzskulptur.
Hefner-Alteneck, Trachten.
Heideloff, C., Ornamentik des Mittelalters.
Heider, Moritz, Louis XVI. und Empire.
Hepplewhite, A. & Co., The Cabinet Maker's Guide.
Hessling, E. und W., Englische Kunstmöbel.
Hessling, Vorbilder der Kunsttischlerei des 18. Jahrhunderts.
Hirth, G., Das deutsche Zimmer.
Hirth, G., Formenschatz.
Hittorff, J. J. et L. Zanth, Architecture moderne de la Sicile.
Hittorff et Zanth, Architecture Antique de la Sicile.
Hodgkin, Eliot and Edith Hodgkin, Examples of Early English Pottery.
Hoffmann, J. und Klopfer, I. P., Baukunst und dekorative Skulptur der Renaissance in Deutschland.
Holtzinger, H., Geschichte der Renaissance in Italien.
Hörner, Urgeschichte.
Hottenroth, F., Trachten.
Hurrell, J. W., Old Oak English Furniture.
Ilg, Dr. Albert, Sammlung kunsthistorischer Gegenstände des Allerhöchsten Kaiserhauses.
Ilg, Dr. A. und Dr. Heinrich Kábdebo, Wiener Schmiedewerke des 17. und 18. Jahrhunderts.
Jaennicke, F., Handbuch der Glasmalerei.
Jones, Owen, Grammar of Ornament.
Joseph, D., Geschichte der Architektur Italiens.
Joseph, D., Geschichte der Baukunst.
Junghändel, M., Die Baukunst Spaniens.
Köppen und Breuer, Geschichte des Möbels.
Krauth, T. und Meyer, F. S., Das Schreinerbuch.
Kutschmann, Th., Meisterwerke sarazenisch-normannischer Baukunst in Sizilien und Unteritalien.
Labarte, Jules, Histoire des Arts Industriels au moyen-age et de la Renaissance.

Lacroix, P., Les arts au moyen-age et de la Renaissance.
Lambert, A. und Stahl, E., Motive der deutschen Architektur.
Lamprecht, Dr. Karl, Initialornamentik.
Layard, Sir A. H., Monuments of Niniveh.
Lebon, Dr. Gustav, Les civilisations de l'Inde.
Lebon, Gustave, Les monuments de l'Inde.
Lepsius, C. R., Denkmäler aus Aegypten u. Aethiopien.
Lessing, Julius, Ancient Oriental Carpet Patterns.
Lessing, Möbel des 17. Jahrhunderts.
Lessing, Italienische Möbel des 16. Jahrhunderts.
Lessing, J., Vorbilderhefte aus dem Kgl. Kunstgewerbemuseum.
Leybold, L., Das Rathaus von Augsburg.
Libonis, L., Les Styles.
Lindenschmit, L., Handbuch der deutschen Altertumskunst.
Lindenschmitt, Aus der heidnischen Vorzeit.
Lohde, L., Sammlung von Möbel-Entwürfen, erfunden von Karl Friedrich Schinkel.
Luthmer, F., Innenräume im Louis XVI.- und Empirestil.
Luthmer, Bürgerliche Möbel aus dem ersten Drittel des 19. Jahrhunderts.
Lübke, Dr. W., Die Kunst des Altertums.
Macquoid, Percy, History of English Furniture.
Martha, I., L'art Etrusque.
Martha, I., Manuel d'archéologie Etrusque et Romaine.
Martin, C., L'art Romane en France.
Mau, A., Pompei, its life and art.
Mauch, J. M., Architektonische Ordnungen.
Meurer, M., Vergleichende Formenlehre des Ornaments.
Meyer, F. S., A Handbook of Ornament.
Middleton, J. H., Illuminated Manuscripts in Classical and Mediaeval times.
Migeon, S., Manuel d'art Musulman; arts plastiques et industriels.
Millingen, J. V., Peinture des vases Grecs.
Mohrmann, Prof. Karl und Dr. Eugen Ferd. Eichwede, Germanische Frühkunst.
Monumentos arquitetonicos de España.
Müller, H. A. und Mothes, O., Archäologisches Lexikon.
Murphy, Bailey Scott, English and Scottish Wrought Ironwork.
Nash, J., Old English mansions.
Nicolai, H. G., Ornament der italienischen Kunst des 15. Jahrhunderts.
Nye, Alvan C., Colonial Furniture.
Oakeshott, G. J., Detail and Ornament of the Italian Renaissance.
Oberhänsli, Aufnahmen alter schweizerischer Kunstschmiedearbeiten.
Odrzywolski, S., Die Renaissance in Polen.
Ohmann, Barock.
Opderbecke, Bauformen des Mittelalters.
Ortwein, (A.), Die deutsche Renaissance.
Ongania, F., Basilica di San Marco, Venezia.
Pannewitz, von, Formenlehre der romanischen Baukunst.
Parker, J. H., Glossary of Terms used in Architecture.
Paukert, F., Tiroler Zimmergotik.
Percier et Fontaine, Recueil de décorations intérieures.
Pergolesi, M. A., Ornamental Designs.
Perrot and Chipiez, History of art in ancient times.
Petrie (Dr. Hinders), Tel el Amarna.
Pfnor, R., Ornamention de toutes les Epoques.
Pfnor, Palais de Fontainebleau.
Piranesi, G. B., Antiquità Romane.
Prentice, A. N., Renaissance Architecture and Ornament in Spain.
Prisse d'Avennes, Histoire de l'art Égyptien.
Prisse d'Avennes, La décoration Arabe.
Pugin, A., Specimens of Gothic architecture.

Pugin, A., Examples of Gothic Architecture.
Pugin (Welby), Glossary of ecclesiastical ornament and costume.
Racinet, A., Le costume historique.
Racinet, A., L'ornement polychrome.
Raguenet, A., Matériaux et documents.
Rajendralalá, Mitra, The antiquities of Orissa.
Reichhold, K., Griechische Vasenmalerei.
Reichhold, Kunst und Zeichnen.
Revoil (Henri), Architecture romane du midi de la France.
Revue générale de l'architecture.
Rhead, G. W., Principles of Design.
Richardson, C. J., Studies from old English Mansions.
Richardson, C. J., Architectural Remains of the Reigns of Elizabeth and James.
Richardson, C. J., Observations on the Architecture of the Reigns of Queen Elizabeth and King James I.
Roger-Milès, L., La Bijouterie.
Roger-Milès (L.), Beaux-Arts.
Roger-Milès (L.), Comment discerner les styles.
Rohault de Fleury (G.), La Toscane au Moyen-Age.
Rouyer (Eugène), L'art architectural en France.
Roux, H., Herculanum et Pompéi.
Ruprich-Robert (N.), L'architecture Normande.
Saladin, H., Manuel d'art Musulman: Architecture.
Salin, S., Die altgermanische Tierornamentik.
Salzenberg (W.), Altchristliche Baudenkmäler von Konstantinopel.
Sanders, W. B., Carved Oak Woodwork.
Sanders, W. B., Half Timbered Houses and Carved Oak Furniture of the 16th and 17th centuries.
Sarre (Friedrich), Denkmäler der persischen Baukunst.
Schinkel (Karl Friedrich), Sammlung architektonischer Entwürfe.
Schliemann, H., Tiryns and Mycenæ.
Schmidt, Karl und Schildbach, Der königliche Zwinger in Dresden.
Schoy, A., Die architektonisch-dekorative Kunst der Zeit Ludwigs XVI.
Schütte, Ornamentale und architektonische Studienblätter aus Italien.
Scott, W. B., Antiquarian Gleanings in the North of England.
Sebah, P., L'architecture Ottoman.
Seesselberg, F., Helm und Mitra.
Semper, G., Der Stil.
Shaw, Henry, Handbook of mediaeval alphabets and devices.
Shaw, H. and Madden F., Illuminated Ornaments from Manuscripts 6th to 17th Century.
Shaw, H., Details of Elizabethan Architecture.
Sheraton, T., Cabinet Maker and Upholsterer's Drawing Book.
Smith, George, Assyrian Discoveries.
Speltz, Alex, Säulenformen der ägyptischen, griechischen und römischen Baukunst.
Spiers, R. Phené, The Orders of Architecture.
Spiers, Architecture, East and West.
Stiehl, O., Das deutsche Rathaus im Mittelalter.
Stiehl, Backsteinbau romanischer Zeit.
Stokes, Margaret, Early Christian Art in Ireland.
Strange, T. A., English Furniture, Decoration, Woodwork and Allied arts.
Stothard, C. A., The monumental effigies of Great Britain.

Stueckelberg, E. A., Longobardische Plastik.
Suireischchikov, N. P., et Trener, D. K., Ornements sur les monuments de l'ancien art Russe.
Suslov, V. V., Monuments de l'ancienne architecture Russe.
Tanner, Henry Jr., English Interior Woodwork of the XVI, XVII and XVIII centuries.
Tatham, C. H., Etchings of Ancient Ornamental Architecture.
Teirich, V., Ornamente aus der Blütezeit italienischer Renaissance.
Teirich, V., Intarsien.
The Builder.
The Building News.
Thierry, C., Klassische Ornamente.
Thiollet, F. et H. Roux, Nouveau recueil de menuiserie.
Triggs, H. I. and Tanner, H., Some Architectural Works of Inigo Jones.
Uhde, Constantin and Spiers, R. Phené, The Architectural Forms of the Classic Ages.
Uhde, Die Konstruktionen und die Kunstformen der Architektur.
Ungewitter, G. C., Land- und Stadtkirchen.
Van Ysendyk, Documents classés de l'art dans les Pays-Bas.
Vacher, S., Fifteenth Century Italian Ornament.
Victoria and Albert-Museum, Handbooks on Art.
Viollet-le-Duc, Dictionnaire raisonné de l'architecture française du XI. au XII. siècle.
Viollet-le-Duc, Dictionnaire raisonné du mobilier français.
Vogüe, Comte de, La Syrie centrale.
Vulliamy, L., and Spiers, R. Phené, Examples of Classic Ornament from Greece and Rome.
Ware (W. Rotch), The Georgian Period. Colonial or XVIII-Century Architecture in the United States.
Waring, J. B., Stone Monuments, tumuli, and ornament of remote ages.
Waring, J. B., Illustrations of Architecture and Ornament.
Warner, G. F., Illuminated Manuscripts in the British Museum.
Wasmuth, E., Alte und neue Kirchenmöbel.
Watt, J. Cromar, Greek and Pompeian Decorative Work.
Weaver, Lawrence, English Leadwork, its Art and History.
Weimar, W., Ein Führer durch die Sammlungen.
Weimar, Monumentalschriften.
Wessely, J. E., Das Ornament und die Kunstindustrie.
Westlake, N. H. J., A History of Design in Painted Glass.
Westwood, J. O., Paleographia Sacra Pictoria.
Westwood, Facsimiles of Anglo Saxon and Irish Manuscripts.
Wornum, R. N., Analysis of Ornament.
Zahn, W., Ornamente aller klassischen Kunstepochen.
Zahn, W., Die schönsten Ornamente aus Pompeji, Herkulanum und Stabiae.
Zeller, Adolf, Die romanischen Baudenkmäler von Hildesheim.
Zell, Franz, Bauerntrachten aus dem bayrischen Hochland.

INDEX OF ILLUSTRATIONS

ACCORDING TO
SUBJECT AND MATERIAL.